Accelerating Possession

Critical Theory Institute Books

Critical Theory Institute Books

The Aims of Representation: Subject/Text/History
edited by Murray Krieger

The States of "Theory": History, Art, and Critical Discourse
edited by David Carroll

Politics, Theory, and Contemporary Culture
edited by Mark Poster

"Culture" and the Problem of the Disciplines
edited by John Carlos Rowe

Accelerating Possession

Global Futures of Property and Personhood

Edited by Bill Maurer and
Gabriele Schwab

COLUMBIA UNIVERSITY PRESS NEW YORK

COLUMBIA UNIVERSITY PRESS
Publishers Since 1893
New York Chichester, West Sussex

Library of Congress Cataloging-in-Publication Data

Accelerating possession : global futures of property and personhood / edited by Bill Maurer and Gabriele Schwab.
p. cm. — (Critical Theory Institute Books)
Includes bibliographical references and index.
ISBN 0-231-13784-2 (cloth : alk. paper)
1. Property. 2. Privatization. 3. Persons. 4. Humanism. 5. Postmodernism. I. Maurer, Bill, 1968– II. Schwab, Gabriele. III. Critical Theory Institute Books at the University of California, Irvine.

HB701.A26 2006
306.3'2—dc22

2005054751

Columbia University Press books are printed on permanent and durable acid-free paper
Printed in the United States of America

c 10 9 8 7 6 5 4 3 2 1

Contents

Part II. Posthuman Futures: Literature, Art, and the Politics of Personhood

Acknowledgments

The editors would like to thank Lisa Ness, administrative coordinator of the Critical Theory Institute at the University of California, Irvine, for her assistance in the coordination of the series of lectures and conversations that led to this volume, as well as in the preparation of the manuscript itself. We also thank Bruce Barnhart and Erin Ferris. We extend deep appreciation to each of the contributors for their work and their patience, and to our fellow members of the Critical Theory Institute at UC Irvine. Finally, we would like to thank Jennifer Crewe and Juree Sondker at Columbia University Press for their support of the project and their assistance, as well as the numerous anonymous reviewers whose criticisms and suggestions helped give the volume its present shape and force.

We also extend thanks for permission to reprint the following:

Chapter 3 is a revised and edited version of James G. Ferguson, "Power Topographies," in *Companion to the Anthropology of Politics*, ed. David Nugent and Joan Vincent, Blackwell Publishers, 2004, 383–399. Reprinted with permission of Blackwell Publishers.

Chapter 5 is an earlier version of Marilyn Strathern, *Kinship, Law, and the Unexpected: Relatives Are Always a Surprise*, Cambridge University Press, 135–161. Reprinted with the permission of Cambridge University Press. Copyright © 2005 Marilyn Strathern. The tale of this chapter is itself a complicated temporal tangle of property relations: readers will note that the Cambridge book acknowledges *Accelerating Possession* as the original source of this work, yet a special memorandum of understanding needed to be drawn up for this chapter, as the Cambridge book preempted the present volume.

Chapter 9 appears in N. Katherine Hayles, "(Un)Masking the Agent: Stanislaw Lem's 'The Mask,'" in *My Mother Was A Computer: Digital Subjects and Literary Texts*, University of Chicago Press, 2005.

Accelerating Possession

Introduction
The Political and Psychic Economies of Accelerating Possession

Bill Maurer and Gabriele Schwab

In the early months of its rule, and in the aftermath of the war of 2003, the Coalition Provisional Authority administering the occupation of Iraq "promulgated"—its term—two new freedoms. The first, announced in June 2003, granted Iraqis the freedom to establish direct trade relationships with international companies.[1] The second, announced in September 2003, protected foreigners' property rights in Iraq.[2] While the promotion of these freedoms was a relatively transparent attempt to create deregulated markets and promote foreign investment, the details were a bit more complicated than simple neoliberalism or the laissez-faire promoted by a conquering power to serve the economic interests of its patrons. In fact, they indicate a crucial shift in the notion of liberal personhood's traditional association with property rights. Symptomatic of this shift is the fact that while guaranteeing property and trade, the CPA at the same time disassembled precisely those constituent elements of property rights linked to personal ownership. Hence they could stand without the buttressing historically provided them in the form of political recognition and liberal personhood. The move secured property without the warrant of the proprietarian conception of the human from which Euro-American understandings of property emerged, with Descartes and Locke, in the European Enlightenment. And it guaranteed property rights in the absence of—indeed, through the negation of—the overarching public sphere within which property rights are negotiated and claims to property, and thus to personhood, are recognized. The CPA also reserved to itself the power to determine the ultimate disposition of Iraq's national properties, specifically, its natural resources. It thus managed to keep in place, albeit under a different name, the Baath Party's highly centralized Soviet-style system for the management of oil and other mineral deposits in the country. While other national enterprises were privatized, the oil and resource extraction industries were governed according to the principles of usufruct or use rights granted to an occupying power by the 1907 Hague Regulations Concerning the Laws and Customs of War on Land.[3]

The new rule of property for Iraq was thus a rather peculiar beast, not quite the same unfolding of liberal property that has been documented in classic studies of other colonial ventures like Ranajit Guha's *A Rule of Property for Bengal* (1982). There, establishing a rule of property meant providing individuals with a title to land, so that the value of the land could be assessed for taxation purposes and the populace could be "registered," monitored, and governed by the persuasive power of property rather than through force of arms. In consequence, the East India Company's rapaciousness could be tempered, if only a little, and if only to secure colonial political legitimacy. In Iraq, establishing title to property was set behind the immediate push to allow Iraqis the freedom to contract with foreign trading companies and to grant foreign trading companies the right to Iraqi property—even before the latter could be appropriately registered and assessed. The CPA's public notice regarding foreign trading companies removed *all* administrative procedures—and protections—from the process of setting up a trade relationship. The contractual situation was not just freedom from force and fraud but freedom from everything that would hinder or help an Iraqi negotiating an agreement with another party. In a sense, it was freedom from, not freedom to, contract.

In addition, the CPA's Order No. 39 on foreign investment claims to safeguard the Iraqi people by protecting the property rights of *foreign* investors: "This Order promotes and safeguards the general welfare and interests of the Iraqi people by promoting foreign investment through the protection of the rights and property of foreign investors in Iraq" (CPA/ORD/19 September 2003/39, section 2).

Foreign participation in the business affairs of Iraq was to be unlimited as well, except in the areas of natural resources, banking, and insurance. Foreign participation in retail sales was prohibited unless the foreign entity maintained a deposit of at least $100,000 in a non-interest-bearing account in an Iraqi bank for the duration of its business activity in the country (CPA/ORD/19 September 2003/39, sections 4 and 6). As for oil, land, and natural resources, the CPA maintained the right to issue leases of no more than forty years in duration to foreign investors or businesses.

As several commentators pointed out at the time, the CPA's rule of property for Iraq was not necessarily within the bounds of international law. The

Hague Regulations prohibit "pillage" and demand that the laws of the occupied country be respected. The CPA's public notices and orders "promulgated" some administrative procedures and abrogated others, certainly altering if not disintegrating the administrative law of Iraq, while remaining just this side of transforming the constitutional and judicial legal forms that empower administrative regulation. The CPA's treatment of oil and natural resources was particularly suspect, since the Hague Regulations grant "usufruct" to the occupying power, and usufruct generally entails the enjoyment "without altering the substance of the thing" of a property (Mate 2003). Extracting any natural resource necessarily entails alteration. Hence, the charge of pillage.

The CPA, however, saw a double historic inevitability to its privatization of Iraqi industries outside of oil: private property *must* be ascendant, because for the CPA there simply are no alternatives; and it must be ascendant even though private property *will*, according to the CPA, inevitably create great hardship for the Iraqi people. The lessons of the post–Cold War era in Eastern Europe were clearly on the minds of the American promoters of the new rule of property. In selling off state-owned enterprises, L. Paul Bremer III, the United States administrator in Iraq, admitted that "Iraq will no doubt find that opening its borders to trade and investment will increase competitive pressure on its domestic firms." This, he maintained, will "thereby raise productivity" (Andrews 2003).

Libertarian and free-market commentators cast a skeptical eye on the CPA's plans for Iraqi oil, if only because those plans did not include a massive titling and property registration program. The Peruvian economist Hernando de Soto was frequently invoked or quoted in these accounts (e.g., Ponnuru 2003). For de Soto (2000), title to property means access to the equity contained in that property. In de Soto's neoliberal vision, the link between title and tax emphasized by Guha is not nearly as important as the link between title and collateral for loans, which link renders liquid all real assets and facilitates their dissolution into that most magical of substances, capital. "No property rights, no modern Iraq," according to de Soto (Ponnuru 2003).

With the Iraqi elections in 2005 and the subsequent distraction of much of the American public from the conflict, few at the time of our writing (February 2005) may appreciate the relevance of the new rule of property for Iraq. But if it is true that we live in the era of the passing of socialist and capitalist mass utopia, as Susan Buck-Morss (2000) has argued, then this new rule of property seems an appropriate place to begin an inquiry into the transformations of the individual and collective proprietary logics animating those utopian visions. The CPA's "promulgations," after all, created curious hybrids, and it remains to be seen whether and how those hybrids will grow: there is to be complete freedom to trade, yet no clear title to the properties being traded except for foreign investors; there is to be neoliberal privatization, a rolling back of the state, and an elimination of the revenues that provide the state its lifeblood (taxes were set at a flat 15%, and customs and tariffs were suspended), yet oil and natural resources remain in the tightly centralized system of control that existed under the Baath regime. Leases have been granted to corporations like Bechtel and Halliburton, whose connections with U.S. government officials and authority with U.S. policy makers are so strong as to render them quasi-state-run enterprises. Property—of a sort—has been protected, but publicity—the public sphere of political participation and recognition—has been abrogated. Guarantees of some property exist without their corresponding guarantees of personhood, a profoundly illiberal formation that either perverts its Enlightenment model or merely reveals the latter's own perverse potentialities. The CPA in Baghdad created property with no institutional supports: in effect, with no law, just "rights," which are presumed to be a natural thing inhering in individual persons or corporations, but with no administrative regulation of trade and therefore no administrative warrants for either individual persons or corporations. It replicated the centrally planned structures of the Baath regime for natural resources, but it did so under a doctrine of usufruct. It privatized everything else with the full knowledge that doing so would further the immiseration of the people.

In short, the CPA tinkered with spare parts of the wreckage of both capitalist and socialist utopias, implicitly recognizing that both utopias have passed and failed to live up to their promises (hence Bremer's acknowledgment of the inevitability of suffering in the wake of privatization: we know what the effect will be, yet we will do it anyway). Nonetheless, the CPA, and the "sovereign" Iraq that followed, continued in the fantasy-space of those utopias; indeed, they *accelerated* the foundational traditions of each utopia. Descartes argued that putting our faculties to their full use and arriving at the knowledge only perceptible by a sovereign human mind would render us "lords and possessors of nature" (*maîtres et possesseurs de la Nature*).[4] It is unclear whether that sovereign mind can be sustained when (1) the relations of mastery and possession are in acceleration while all other terms are entangled with their opposites, and (2) there is no universal cover of law for property, the proper, or the relations of recognition and publicity they supposedly warrant.

We borrow the concept of acceleration from Baudrillard. In his essays on science fiction, Baudrillard queried the genre's traditional reliance on "other" worlds, and reflected on the manner in which certain authors (Philip K. Dick, J. G. Ballard) redirect the science fictional imaginary. Dick, Baudrillard writes,

> does not create an alternate cosmos ... the reader is, from the outset, in a total simulation without origin, past, or future—in a kind of flux of all coordinates (mental, spatio-temporal, semiotic). It is not a question of parallel universes, or double universes, or even of possible universes: not possible nor impossible, nor real nor unreal. It is *hyperreal*.... One is already in the other world, an another world which is not another.
>
> (Baudrillard 1991, 2)

In Ballard's *Crash*, Baudrillard continues,

> Nothing is really "invented" therein, everything is hyper-functional.... Everything is ... an acceleration of our own models, of all the models which surround us, all mixed together and hyper-operationalized in the void.... [*Crash*] projects into the future along the same lines of force and the same finalities as those of the "normal" universe.... SF of this sort is no longer an elsewhere, it is an everywhere: in the circulation of models here and now, in the very axiomatic nature of our simulated environment.
>
> (ibid., 3)

We suggest that the futures of property and personhood examined in this volume and made explicit in the new rule of property for Iraq are on the order of an acceleration of the model, a ramping-up of the liberal proprietarian modalities of the Enlightenment, which are rebuilding the world on the ruins of its failed utopias.

These futures are, of course, deeply familiar to our own social practice as academics, even if we rarely reflect on them directly. Contemporary debates over genetically modified organisms, intellectual property, new reproductive technologies, computer file sharing over the Internet, and the like all make for compelling pedagogical examples in the classroom when exploring the limits and expirations of liberalism. The more mundane practicalities of scholarship in an era of the simultaneous ramping-up and apparent expiration of proprietarian logics present themselves to us more directly in our everyday professional activities: in negotiating the intellectual property agreements we sign as a condition of our university employment or the publication of our articles, in figuring out the ethical and political conundrums involved in using other people's knowledge productions as the basis for our own (a perennial problem in anthropological research), and in securing (or failing to secure!) permissions to reprint chapters or works of art in our scholarship.[5] Property is seemingly everywhere, and everywhere outpacing us, yet also everywhere coming undone.

In the 1999–2000 academic year, the Critical Theory Institute (CTI) at the University of California, Irvine began a three-year research project, The Futures of Property and Personhood. In its focus on property, the topic explored the challenges to social and cultural theory posed by privatization and its broader political, cultural, and institutional effects. It also considered the manifold changes in the status of personhood brought about by the forces of privatization and globalization, as well as the new technologies that facilitate the remaking of human bodies and determine the politics of reproduction. The most pervasive effects of privatization include a general weakening of liberalism's hold on the social imaginary, a trend that profoundly affects state practices, sociocultural reproduction, and the institutional production of knowledge. By exploring the synergy and dissonance between conceptions of the private as marketable and the private as inalienable, the CTI posed the question of how critical theory can productively engage with the contemporary transformations and futures of notions such as property, personhood, and related concepts of citizenship, state, culture, and knowledge.

At least since the Enlightenment, if not before, definitions of property have entailed corresponding configurations of the person who owned and/or was subjected to property. We open our volume with a reading of John Locke's *Essay on Human Understanding* by Etienne Balibar. Balibar shows that the vexed relationship between the *self* and the *own* structures not only the classical theory of "personal identity," but continues to haunt Western theories of the self and the subject. He concludes that "there is nothing natural in the identification of self and own, which is really a norm rather than a necessity, and reigns by virtue of a postulate." Being oneself, in other words, is not identical with having or possessing oneself, because identity includes the disturbing presence of otherness within every consciousness and must be defined in relation to its other. If, following a Hegelian tradition, one defines the subject as an infinite process of identification through appropriation, then selfhood or personhood evolves within the problematic and uneasy relationship between the individual and the community. According to Balibar, this internal dialectic opens the ground for the multiple divisions of self into personalities, each of which pertains to specific networks of social communication. Placing Locke at a crucial moment in Western history that allows one to think a direct line from ancient speculations on the transmigration of souls to typically modern considerations of multiple personalities, Balibar also emphasizes the crucial role that linguistic and rhetorical choices play in the definition and indeed formation of personhood and self-ownership.

Lindon Barrett's "Mercantilism, U.S. Federalism, and the Market Within Reason" provides a succinct counterpoint to Balibar's essay. Barrett contrasts Balibar's perspective, developed from within Western philosophies of the subject, with a perspective anchored in the histories of people excluded from Western definitions of the human. Racial blackness, he argues, constitutes a conceptual impossibility that exposes the limits of both the economic fundament and the psychic formation of the subject in the modern West. The peculiar subjectivity typical of capitalist social formations is so inextricably bound to a logic of commodity fetishism that the economic can no longer be extracted from the psychic. Concepts such as the nation and "the people" are generated in a confluence of economics, race, and imagination. The cultural imagination of concepts such as *the nation*, *the people*, or *the subject* has rhetorical and linguistic as well as philosophical and epistemological implications that profoundly mark Western definitions and indeed productions of subjectivity and personhood. As the conscription of African slaves lies at the heart of mercantile capitalism and concomitant national formations, racial blackness marks their unnamed violence, challenging the conceptual and rhetorical links between modern definitions of personhood and property.

It is both the linguistic-rhetorical and the philosophical-epistemological emphasis that provides the methodological links between the essays selected for our volume. Many of the essays ground their reflections on property and personhood in literary, textual, or artistic objects, specifically exploring the challenges they pose to current debates in critical theory. If the essays in part 1, "Histories, Nations, Institutions," look at the political economies of proprietarian acceleration and transformation in national and postnational contexts, the essays in part 2, "Posthuman Futures," look at alternative literary and artistic models of personhood that serve both as historical allegories and as futuristic projections of current changes that challenge the boundaries of how Western theories have conventionally defined personhood in relation to property. Multiple resonances between the essays in part 1 and part 2—particularly between Balibar and Lippit, Barrett and Schwab, and Gelley and Strathern—are designed to create a network of dialogical reflections and rhetorical readings that span the volume and, indeed, that span disciplinary divisions in the academy, helping to map new models of personhood as they have evolved in recent theoretical debates in the humanities and social sciences.

In the past three decades, critical theories have devised and debated new models that respond to historical changes in the relation between property and personhood. Most of these theories challenge the classical paradigms of liberalism, Marxism, and psychoanalysis, expanding their focus to include issues such as symbolic economies, regimes of power and knowledge, or the superimposition of commodity and sexual fetishism. Many of these theories rethink the legacy of Nietzsche, Marx, and Freud from the vantage point of the new economies of a global corporate media culture and its continually changing effects on relations between property and personhood. Today, new forms of privatization demand that we rethink the range of available models of subjectivity in relation to late capitalist, global, imperial, and corporate economies and their effects on personhood. We need to ask whether contemporary critiques of the subject are adequate to challenge narratives of the triumph of the market and the privatization of knowledges, persons, and life itself. We also need to reflect on the very model of knowledge as the discovery of adequate critiques, on whether the old formula *adequatio intellectus et res*, itself intimately bound to commodity and monetary logics (Shell 1982), is adequate to the task. Finally, we need to explore the extent to which today's global media system determines the formation and interpellation of subjects, thereby profoundly challenging philosophical concepts of personhood and property we continue to carry as theoretical baggage. Inversely, we may ask whether those very traditional concepts may be used critically to illuminate and critique the profound challenges posed by today's global and corporate media culture to the boundaries of personhood, property, and the human. In his essay on Jenny Holzer's art, for example, Alexander Gelley argues that the most provocative American art of the present is situated at a crossing of institutions of art and political economy, and addresses the social, cultural, and sexual formation of subjects at the sites of their daily interpellation by media and commercial "environments" of global corporate capitalism. Appropriating the tools of commercial interpellation subversively, Holzer exposes that, since it is formed at the intersection of public and private spheres, personhood has become haunted and indeed "expropriated" by the mandates of corporate and media privatization.

Privatization, as we understand it, refers to a complex array of interconnected processes and relationships through which political rights, social membership, knowledge production, and the related spheres that constitute personhood are increasingly brought within the ambit of the capitalist marketplace. We are currently living through a profound acceleration of such processes of privatization, and witnessing their far-reaching effects on the social and cultural imaginary and the very fabric of social life, as demonstrated in both Ferguson's and Cheah's essays on postnational futures and topographies of power. Acceleration here has two senses: increases in both the speed and scale of these processes, and also the sense that we are living in the hyperreality of the models of the Enlightenment and its alters, a world where the pieces are mixed up in impossible configurations (free trade with Soviet-style centralization? Property without proprietors? Fetishism of genes and body parts without an overarching conception of the human?). Critique exhausts itself: its answers to the array of problems occasioned by "privatization" come from the stock toolkit of the philosophies that animated proprietary logics and the Cartesian confidence in the infinite apprehension of human mental faculties—even as the uniqueness of those mental faculties disappears in the distributed networks of the cognitive and computer sciences. In borrowing *acceleration* from Baudrillard, we must acknowledge that we also borrow it from the world around us—the CPA in Baghdad, the "rights and permissions" apparatus of academic publishing and artistic reproduction—but accelerate it in turn, setting it in motion to other tasks and articulating it to other tools, mixing up the models of the everywhere, the here and now, laterally extending the assemblages of the current moment.

More conventionally, we note the effects of privatization and the lateral extension of the property form. Among such effects we may count the economic, political, and epistemological reworking of notions of citizenship, the redefinition of the nation-state in relation to a transnational economy and its global markets, and the privatization of services formerly under state management. Similarly, privatization deeply affects social and cultural identities, subjectivities, and cosmologies of personhood. Niche marketing and demographic "indicators" of consumer preference, for example, are rendered as self-identity. Moreover, identity itself is increasingly framed through acquisitive individualism. Self-identity becomes a product to be worked on, invested in, medicated, and competitively performed and deployed as a social currency. In a similar vein, identitarian forms of social protest are increasingly recoded as consumptive and private. We witness a pervasive expansion and transformation of property, accompanied by concomitant changes in the self-as-proprietor and the self-as-investor. Newly expanded property constructs and laws extend from rights in potential and future ideas to rights in cells, organs, and genetic material.

These complicated economic, legal, and social changes are also transforming the very category of culture. As the concept itself comes under scrutiny in the anthropological and literary circles that for the greater part of the century made it their hallmark, culture is now increasingly recoded in proprietary terms. Collectivities and corporations battle over knowledges and practices that have been newly configured as potentially alienable and commodifiable cultural properties. Individuals protect cultural works through the apparatus of patent and copyright. Opponents of a neoliberal stance often frame their project in terms of claiming collective properties, reimagining the commons, and reinvigorating the community. But what is the status of commonality and community when culture itself—in Marilyn Strathern's phrase—has been "enterprized up?" What happens if culture can be both chosen and selected from a seemingly infinite array of patented goods for consumption? What are the consequences when culture is deemed intrinsic to identity and becomes the object of collective property rights?

These processes are transforming not only the world "at large" but also the immediate environment of our intellectual activity, making explicit the fact that this distinction was never as neat as many had claimed. Everyday practices of privatization in the academy include the university's use of market models to guide curricular changes and the privatization of knowledge—from information technologies and copyright restrictions affecting the classroom to modes of knowing and new categories of the known. These practices are radically transforming the most fundamental relations concerning the conceptions of person, knowledge, and property on which intellectual production has long rested. The consequences of such transformations have yet to be fully anticipated and explored.

The project identified three rubrics within which to focus its analysis of how privatization and the related reconfiguration of the social imaginary pose a challenge for contemporary debates in critical theory: property, citizenship and personhood, and the posthuman. These are variously taken up in the essays collected in this volume.

Liberal nation-states in the postwar era claimed to serve the public good through social services and economic redistribution, with the promise of full "social" as well as political citizenship for all. Today, deregulated markets and international trade and finance, together with the increasing importance of international organizations, have produced a world in which such promises are explicitly disavowed, even as an ideal. But if the welfare state is dying, the interventionist ways of the nation-state are alive and well. States today subsidize and enforce markets through tax policies, enterprise zones, interest rates, and central banking, as well as through property regimes and the promise of violence should they be breached. At the intergovernmental level, states attempt to harmonize their protocols both for the use of force to guarantee property and for the construction of proprietary entities. Labor emerges as the only commodity that does not enjoy freedom of movement.

We are thus witnessing less the decline of state regulation than the expansion and acceleration of the domain of property itself. The state gives over some of its traditional functions to private enterprise and to the voluntary sector, resulting in increased competition, which also means increased risk. New property regimes demand new forms of securitization, resulting in the creation of fungible, negotiable proprietary interests in any thing or entity. Financial entities tie property so closely to risk that it threatens to collapse into risk itself. We witness the emergence of actuarial properties, persons rendered as risk-profiles, and contracts specifying corporate relationships to "potential" properties. What are the implications for critical theory of a change in the very meaning of property? What new theories of capitalism, labor, and value are called for in response to such reconfigurations? How can critical theory recognize and provide insight into both the new forms of oppression or exploitation as well as the new possibilities for liberation and resistance that such transformations may open up?

Critical theorists have successfully demonstrated the bankruptcy of narratives of linear development and progress. But we have not yet thought through the consequences of this bankruptcy for the production of knowledge and for the logic and justification of our own knowledge practices. Critical theory traditionally saw itself in opposition to nationalism and liberalism alike. But how can critical theory remain "critical" at a time when the fundamental principles of liberalism are themselves being called into question, less by theoretical critique than by socioeconomic transformation? Furthermore, in the absence of an overarching state commitment to social citizenship, as Ferguson, Cheah, and other contributors to this volume indicate, and in a property regime that restricts dissemination and use of knowledge, what becomes of the traditional function of the university and its project of imparting "universal" knowledge to the citizens of the nation? If we reject both the liberal assertion of knowledge as universal enlightenment and the "privatized" notion of knowledge as a commodity for sale in the market, then how do we understand the place and efficacy of our own knowledge production? And how can we reimagine the university in a way that enables a critique of the logic of privatization without reaffirming notions of liberal enlightenment or an unsituated, universal knowledge?

In classical liberalism, the private sphere entailed the domain of home, religion, family, personal relationships, and affiliations through which individuals created and realized themselves. It was also the domain where individuals came to know their interests—personal and economic—and to go about fulfilling them. The public existed above and between various "private spheres," providing a space in which everyone was supposedly allowed to pursue his or her private interests and affiliations without threat of force or fraud. How are private and public being rerouted and redefined in the present? How are new proprietarian logics challenging the vision of personhood at the heart of liberal conceptions of the public (the world of the citizen, equal to all others) and the private (the world of the individual, unique among all others)?

In much of the world today, social citizenship is no longer a central goal of the state. In rolling back the contract between state, capital, and labor, abandoning social welfare policies to private and voluntary enterprises, and replacing social citizenship with consumer citizenship, the state seems uninterested in its traditional civic obligations. Who "belongs" in a world of consumer citizenship where one participates in the nation by virtue of one's investment in the national productive-consumptive product? What are the boundaries of rights and obligations, given the extensive commodification of citizen identity? And what are the limits of protest, given the commodification of dissent and the sale of a politics of lifestyle choice or gut-level preference?

In addition to a change in relation between citizen and state, the expansion of privatization brings in its wake new exclusions within and between states. Suprastate organizations like the WTO, MAI, and GATT reconfigure sovereignty and political liberalism even as strong states dictate foreign policy through the language and mechanisms of the "market." Working less in terms of "national interests" than in terms of free market principles, states have not so much abandoned their powers as transformed the field in which they operate. Privatization thus has a direct effect on concepts and practices of "security" both within and between states. In much of the world, public police are increasingly supplanted by private security corporations, public prisons by corrections management facilities, and state armies by private mercenary forces. The privatization of security means both new forms of "war" and new forms of "peace." It thus gives new meaning to the "rule of law," dismembering liberalism's promise of rules of law over rules of men, of public over private interest. How can critical theory address these challenges to citizenship without falling into nostalgia for the citizen-subject of liberalism, the rule of law as guarantor of rights and freedoms, and modern notions of belonging and identity that continue to animate conflict and community?

What futures hold for the category of the human when the self-as-proprietor explodes into a dispersed network of corporate interests? Whither social protest when the privatization of identity recodes interests as fungible preferences? How can critical theory map this posthumanist—or as some prefer to call it, posthuman—landscape? How can we provide a theoretical grip on the new subjects and objects of a hypercommodified world? Can we find theoretical means or grounds for a critique of the privatized human body that does not fall back into a humanist nostalgia?

Across disciplines and theoretical orientations, the very boundaries of the human are in the process of being redefined. The challenges to personhood have vast implications and ramifications beyond the material, political, economic, social, and cultural spheres. They affect the social and cultural imaginary, the psychosocial formation of persons or subjects, as well as possible philosophical, ethical, and epistemological conceptions of the subject, personhood, and agency more generally. A wide range of recent theories on the posthuman and the posthuman body (inspired by Deleuze and others) as well as the inhuman (beginning with Lyotard) have been engaged in theorizing, analyzing, and conceptualizing these profound changes in the status of personhood. An array of current theoretical work on the politics of reproduction is equally concerned with issues of privatization and related challenges to property and personhood.

Many current debates, ranging from genetic engineering and the Human Genome Project to the "sustainability" of our planet, focus on the relationship between property, privatization, and reproduction. Current changes in the politics of reproduction challenge fundamental theoretical concepts across disciplines and force us to rethink the relationships among, and the erosion of boundaries of, traditional categories such as nature and culture, the subject, the human, civil rights, property, and the body. Moreover, economic reproduction is itself linked to the "politics of reproduction" more generally, particularly in light of the reconfiguration of the human body to serve industrial production and of its submission to a regime of discipline and punishment. As Susan Squier argues in *Reproducing the Posthuman Body*, discourses about reproduction and reproductive representations "help to consolidate the global power of multinational late capitalism," defining and distributing difference "within and across a variety of temporally and geographically overlapping power grids," including civil society, institutional science, medicine, and industrial capitalism (1995, 115).

These profound challenges force us to rethink the boundaries of the human while we already witness their tangible material, psychological, ideological, and rhetorical redefinitions. It is therefore no coincidence that several of the authors we invited to contribute to this volume—Cheah, Schwab, Hayles, and Strathern—directly address the global *futures* of property and personhood. Schwab and Hayles use readings of science fiction in order to explore visions of a futuristic politics of reproduction as well as alternative modes of cognition and alternative relationships between body and mind inspired by the new sciences and new technologies. The protagonists in the science fiction stories under consideration display futuristic subjectivities that challenge not only familiar notions of property and personhood but also the available theoretical models within which we have come to think of those terms. They also explore challenges, limitations, and dangers posed to human subjects and communities by the new scientific discoveries and technologies that have inspired their visions. As Akira Lippit suggests in his essay, we need a new "psychic economy" attuned to the new corporate and political economies, with their multiplicity of global technologies and topographies of power and interpellation.

Finally, the changing relationship between the public and the private, and the challenges posed by privatization and new property constructs, similarly determine the politics of cultural reproduction, pertaining to the renegotiation—if not obliteration—of the boundaries between nature and culture, human and nonhuman, inhuman or posthuman. According to Halberstam and Livingston, "the posthuman does not necessitate the obsolescence of the human; it does not represent an evolution or devolution of the human. Rather it participates in re-distributions of difference and identity" (1995, 10). Such profound redefinitions of personhood, and of the boundaries of the human more generally, pertain to global culture and global flows of capital, information, discourses, and bodies. In the social imaginary, they engender a particular "postmodern gothic," a "gothicization of the body" (Halberstam and Livingston) afloat with phantasms of the "body without organs" (Deleuze and Guattari; Beckett) or even of the "grotesque clone" (Baudrillard). If this posthuman body is, as Halberstam and Livingston argue, only the "seismograph and epicenter" of epistemic changes, the concomitant revaluation of cultural values affects all politics, transcoding the spheres of economy, technology, law, biology, culture, and psychology. Theories that trace the effects of globalization in the cultural imaginary—such as those of Appadurai, Jameson, Deleuze and Guattari, and Haraway, among others—prepare the futures of theoretical models that make such transcodings part of their basic presuppositions.

Such transformations are, of course, often partial and even contradictory. Even while the very categories of the human, the subject, and personhood are under revision, the "human" is enjoying a remarkable renaissance in global discursive fields centered on "human rights." Human rights are precisely not a universal standard applied irrespective of place; neither are they a bulwark against the processes of privatization or the reconfiguration of personhood. On the contrary, the very notion of human rights circulates within the circuits of governmentality structuring and structured by a privatized, neoliberal, and global economy. For example, the World Bank and IMF attach "human rights conditionality" to countries receiving "assistance" in "structural adjustment." Human rights become a device of governmentality and commodification when deployed as an index of "liberalization" (of markets) and "democratization" (of non-Western political orders). Thus, discourses of the human, human rights, and humanitarianism need to be critically explored under these changed conditions.

The trends and developments outlined herein should make it clear that the anticipated futures of property and personhood fundamentally affect the most central parameters of the debates in critical theory as they have developed in the past decades. They, in fact, reach far beyond the now familiar critique of the categories and values of the tradition of humanism and enlightenment. The gradual refashioning of fundamental theoretical concepts and binaries such as nature/culture, body/mind, self/other, human/inhuman, life/death, man/woman, and subject/object has begun to converge in a pervasive epistemological change. At stake is nothing less than the sustainability of theoretical concepts in a global ecology in which transcoded social, cultural, economic, political, somatic, and psychic energies and flows have transcended even the familiar signatures of the postmodern.

The reader will note that some of the more literary essays (Gelley, Lippitt, and Hayles) do not operate analytically on the same timescale or intellectual horizon as some of the others. The volume as a whole simultaneously speaks to different audiences in different registers about both the rapidly accelerating changes in property and personhood as well as their enduring, *longue durée* legacies.

The intellectual project of the volume, however, is not simply to suggest analytical strategies for approaching emergent forms of property and person that both exemplify and unseat the logics of globalization, the postmodern, or whatever spatiotemporal configuration we might analytically specify to name the incomprehensibility of the present. The volume's purpose is also to bring into dialogue the intellectual concerns of bodies of scholarship and criticism that rarely engage one another, to let them sit beside one another in order to generate a critical effect. That critical effect is just as much a comment on the production of knowledge in the postglobalization university as it is about the rapidly changing conditions in the university's broader sociopolitical context.

We find the juxtaposition between the rapidly accelerating (and just as rapidly receding) configurations of property/person described in some essays and the longstanding aesthetic and philosophical debates engaged by other essays to speak centrally to the enduring legacies of liberalism in various domains of inquiry. It is rare in academic criticism to find "social scientific" pieces together with "literary critical" pieces, where each retain their distinctive voices and styles even as they butt against one another. We would like to suggest that the juxtaposition points to a densely lateralized and networked, not synthetic, knowledge formation that opens up new possibilities for critical inquiry because it replicates (and accelerates) at another level of scale the very phenomena it would describe.

Notes

1. Office of the Administrator of the Coalition Provisional Authority, Baghdad, Iraq. Public Notice Regarding Administrative Procedures for Establishing Trading Agencies, 9 June 2003.

2. Coalition Provisional Authority Order Number 39: Foreign Investment (CPA/ORD/19 September 2003/39).

3. Convention (IV) Respecting the Laws and Customs of War on Land and its Annex: Regulations Concerning the Laws and Customs of War on Land ("Hague Regulations"), The Hague, 18 October 1907, article 55.

4. René Descartes, *Discourse on Method,* chapter 6 (London: J. M. Dent and Sons, 1934).

5. Indeed, in the course of producing this volume, the editors and a network of curatorial professionals ran into difficulties not simply securing permission to reproduce certain artworks, but figuring out in whom or what the ownership rights to these works resided.

References

Andrews, Edmund L. 2003. "Overseer in Iraq Vows to Sell Off Government-Owned Companies." *New York Times*, June 23.

Baudrillard, Jean. 1991. "Two Essays: Simulacra and Science Fiction, and Ballard's *Crash.*" *Science Fiction Studies* 55, 18(3) (November). Available at http://www.depauw.edu/sfs/backissues/55/baudrillard55art.htm.

Buck-Morss, Susan. 2000. *Dreamworld and Catastrophe: The Passing of Mass Utopia East and West*. Cambridge, Mass.: MIT Press.

De Soto, Hernando. 2000. *The Mystery of Capital: Why Capitalism Triumphs in the West and Fails Everywhere Else*. New York: Basic Books.

Guha, Ranajit. 1982. A *Rule of Property for Bengal: An Essay on the Idea of Permanent Settlement*. New Delhi: Orient Longman.

Halberstam, Judith, and Ira Livingston, eds. 1995. *Posthuman Bodies*. Bloomington: Indiana University Press.

Mate, Aaron. 2003. "Pillage is Forbidden: Why the Privatization of Iraq is Illegal." *Guardian*, November 7. Available at http://www.guardian.co.uk/Iraq/Story/0,2763,1079563,00.html.

Ponnuru, Ramesh. 2003. "Who Should Own Iraq?" *National Review*, May 5. Available at http://www.nationalreview.com/ponnuru/ponnuru050503.asp.

Shell, Marc. 1982. *Money, Language, and Thought: Literary and Philosophical Economies from the Medieval to the Modern*. Berkeley: University of California Press.

Squier, Susan. 1995. "Reproducing the Posthuman Body: Ectogenetic Fetus, Surrogate Mother, Pregnant Man." In *Posthuman Bodies*, ed. Judith Halberstam and Ira Livingstone, 113–132. Bloomington: Indiana University Press.

Part I
Histories, Nations, Institutions

1 My *Self* and My *Own*

One and the Same?

Etienne Balibar

In this lecture, I want to tell two stories concerning words. One is a public story, or better said and more reasonably, it is a fragment of a grand story concerning words that I think we would all agree lie at the heart of the so-called occidental philosophical culture, the so-called personal pronouns "I" and "Me" (therefore also the others), and the names *self* and *own*. The other is a private one, although it owes everything to the public institutions who have invited me to this country; it is the story of my journey into the English language, or a nice moment in it. And the point where these two stories interfere is a mistake, actually a rather big and naïve mistake. I made it because I was as presumptuous as to imagine that I was advanced enough in my understanding of some idiomatic properties of English to be able to solve a riddle concerning the reasons why it was precisely in English, in the work of one of the greatest English-writing philosophers of the seventeenth century, that the relationship of the *self* and the *own* that structures the classical theory of "personal identity" was invented. I made a mistake: I wrote and published (fortunately, in French) something that is clearly wrong. But you learn from your mistakes, and I will be trying now to give to the presentation of this mistake and what I hope is its correction a form that could be of general interest—which is probably again very presumptuous.

But I should be more specific. Some years ago I had embarked on a project of translation and commentary of the chapter of Locke's *Essay on Human Understanding* called "Of Identity and Diversity" (2.27), which is often regarded as the chapter on "personal identity," and constantly referred to in philosophical and anthropological discussions as the standard exposition of the "classical" theory that makes the continuity or the "stream" of consciousness (therefore the intrinsic relationship, or the reciprocity, of consciousness and memory) the "criterion" of personal identity, and carries this idea to its extreme consequences, metaphysical, psychological, and social. This is justified by the fact that the presentation of this criterion and the discussion of its implications is really the heart of the chapter, and by the fact that it forms something like an autonomous essay within the *Essay*. Rather than deriving from previous developments in the book, it provides a new foundation or formulates a posteriori a principle that clarifies the intentions of the whole book. This cannot be separated indeed from the fact that this chapter was written separately. It was added in the second edition (1694) to respond to violent critiques from the theologians who claimed that Locke's conception of the mind, by substituting the "empirical," or we would say today, phenomenological, description of the operations of reflection and the association of ideas for the metaphysical assumptions concerning the substance of the soul, would destroy the moral and religious notion of personal responsibility. And we know that Locke's reply to these critiques, the so-called consciousness theory of personal identity (and therefore also responsibility), immediately raised new objections, from Butler and Leibniz to Hume and onwards, some more radically empiricist, others trying to resume the substantialist point of view, which until today have kept the philosophers extremely busy.[1]

The reason, however, why I wanted to translate anew and comment on the text of Locke's chapter was not directly associated with the argument concerning personal identity but with an encounter of three orders of interests and concerns that I still have. One has to do, precisely, with translations and limits to translations or, as we say in French *intraduisibles*, in this case the change from the French "*moi*," which was used by Descartes and Pascal, to the English "self," which became through the translation of Locke into French (made under his own guidance) "*soi*" or "*soi-même*." I was working on this for my contribution to the *Vocabulaire européen des philosophies*.[2] My second interest has to do with a classical issue in philosophical anthropology, one with obvious political implications: the definition or identification of the "individual" as a "*Proprietor of his own Person*," which, again in Locke, but this time in the *Second Treatise of Government* (§§ 27, 44, etc.), replaces the traditional notion of being master of oneself (*dominium sui*) or living on one's own right (*sui iuris esse*) to become the foundation of a contractual or equalitarian political order—in other terms, the key notion of what MacPherson has called "the political theory of possessive individualism."[3] Finally, my third interest has to do with the genealogy of the modern concept of subjectivity and the concept of the *subject* itself. I was particularly focusing on the fact that, contrary to what many discussions for and against the primacy of the subject in the last fifty years have assumed, *the issues of subjectivity and consciousness are not identical*. This is true not only today, because of the influence of psychoanalysis and other theories that insist that the subject is essentially unconscious, but already and perhaps more radically in the classical age, the very moment of the constitution of the metaphysics of subjectivity, as can be demonstrated by the fact that Descartes' philosophy of the thinking subject has nothing to do either with the term or the notion of consciousness.[4] And again, it was Locke who appeared to have inaugurated and actually invented a conception of individual subjectivity that places it within the realm of consciousness and practically identifies it, as later in Kant, with the possibility of self-consciousness. It happened, then, that all my interests were converging toward the study of Locke, a philosopher whose importance I was not disputing but of whom I must say I had a very academic and general knowledge.

But there was another reason that pushed me to become interested in the linguistic aspects of Locke's philosophy or, better said, to the importance of Locke's working with and within language, perhaps with several languages, in the elaboration of his own philosophy, which in turn led me to the endeavor of partially remaking the existing translation myself.[5] It was the fact that the original seventeenth-century French translator (Pierre Coste) had himself discussed in a fascinating way the *impossible equivalence* of certain English and French vocabularies, in particular three key terms: (1) the English *self*, which he proposed translating as the neologism "*soi*" or "*soi-même*" in order to mark the difference with the meaning of "*moi*" or "*le moi*" in French metaphysics; (2) the English *consciousness*, a quasi-neologism in Locke's text,[6] which he suggested translating as "*con-science*" at the price of a possible confusion with conscience (which confusion he tried to avoid through a trick, the use of a hyphen in the French spelling of the word); and (3) the English *uneasiness*, which he proposed translating as "*inquiétude*" (instead of "*malaise*" or "*malêtre*"), thus basing it linguistically in the great theme of "*inquiétude*" and "*Unruhe*" of eighteenth- and nineteenth-century literature and philosophy.[7] This gave me the impression that the critical and philological work that I was trying to do was in fact not a secondary work of commentary on the classical texts but a continuation of the very translinguistic process, or the process of impossible translation that coincided with the history of philosophy itself.

Let me now try and explain to you as simply as possible how I understood the question of the intrinsic association of *self* and *own* in Locke's text, and how I was lead to my mistake. I think that the best thing to do here is to literally quote from three crucial passages in the development of Locke's argument where you will see, so I hope, that the two words *self* and *own* are closely associated, so that indeed the meaning that Locke wants to communicate, and in reality progressively creates or elaborates himself, directly depends on this close association. I should ask you also to bear in mind that the problem is presented to you by a French speaker who does his best to directly read and understand in English but also wants and needs to find French "equivalents" for the phrases he is reading. And maybe, I wish I could convince that this passage through equivalents in a neighboring language (the one, for example, in which Locke would have read the texts of his closest interlocutors, such as Descartes and Malebranche) is useful—perhaps indispensable—in properly understanding and discussing the meaning of these English phrases. But in reality there is no equivalent, or no exact equivalent. Most of these phrases are literally untranslatable, *intraduisibles*, and this is due in particular to the semantic and syntactic properties of the terms *self* and *own* in English, as compared with their nearest counterparts in French, such as *moi* or *soi* in the first case, and *propre* and *le propre* in the second. And I will have to draw your attention to the spellings that are used by Locke, conforming to seventeenth-century habits that today look a little archaic but are still understandable, in particular the habit of spelling such expressions as *myself, itself, himself,* or *oneself* as two separate words—a spelling that allows Locke to consciously play on the double understanding of the expressions as pronouns or possessive expressions, literally or implicitly, such as *my self* (the self that is mine, that is my own self, or simply that is my own), but also by analogy, *it self* (*its self,* the self that belongs to it, that is its own self, or that is its own). I will return to these grammatical subtleties, which I think are anything but external to the semantic and theoretical effects of Locke's writing. And now let me give you some examples:

> [In the course of the discussion of the question whether different consciousnesses or memories in the same individual would make different persons or identities, and conversely, whether one single consciousness or a continuity of memory from one to the other would make one single identical person of two men or individuals]: Let any one reflect upon himself, and conclude that he has in himself an immaterial spirit, which is that which thinks in him, and, in the constant change of his body keeps him the same: and is that which he calls himself: let him also suppose it to be the same soul that was in Nestor or Thersites, at the siege of Troy... which it may have been, as well as it is now the soul of any other man: but he now having no consciousness of any

of the actions either of Nestor or Thersites, does or can he conceive himself the same person with either of them? Can he be concerned in either of their actions? attribute them to himself, or think them his own, more than the actions of any other men that ever existed?

(*Essay on Human Understanding*, book 2, chapter 27, § 14)

(17) *Self* is that conscious thinking thing ... which is sensible or conscious of pleasure and pain, capable of happiness or misery, and so is concerned for itself, as far as that consciousness extends. Thus every one finds that, whilst comprehended under that consciousness, the little finger is as much a part of himself as what is most so. Upon separation of this little finger, should this consciousness go along with the little finger, and leave the rest of the body, it is evident the little finger would be the person, the same person; and *self* then would have nothing to do with the rest of the body.... That with which the consciousness of this present thinking thing can join itself, makes the same person, and is one self with it, and with nothing else; and so attributes to itself, and owns all the actions of that thing, as its own, as far as that consciousness reaches, and no further; as every one who reflects will perceive. (18) In this personal identity is founded all the right and justice of reward and punishment; happiness and misery being that for which every one is concerned for himself, and not mattering what becomes of any substance, not joined to, or affected with that consciousness. For, as it is evident in the instance I gave but now, if the consciousness went along with the little finger when it was cut off, that would be the same *self* which was concerned for the whole body yesterday, as making part of itself, whose actions then it cannot but admit as its own now. Though, if the same body should still live, and immediately from the separation of the little finger have its own peculiar consciousness, whereof the little finger knew nothing, it would not at all be concerned for it, as a part of itself, or could own any of its actions, or have any of them imputed to him.

(§ 17–18)

So that self is not determined by identity or diversity of substance, which it cannot be sure of, but only by identity of consciousness. (24) Indeed it may conceive the substance whereof it is now made up to have existed formerly, united in the same conscious being: but, con-

> sciousness removed, that substance is no more it self, or makes no more a part of it, than any other substance; as is evident in the instance we have already given of a limb cut off.... In like manner it will be in reference to any immaterial substance, which is void of that consciousness whereby I am my *self* to my *self*: if there be any part of its existence which I cannot upon recollection join with that present consciousness whereby I am now my *self*, it is, in that part of its existence, no more my *self* than any other immaterial being. For, whatsoever any substance has thought or done, which I cannot recollect, and by my consciousness make my own thought and action, it will no more belong to me, whether a part of me thought or did it, than if it had been thought or done by any other immaterial being anywhere existing.
>
> (§ 23–24)

> Person, as I take it, is the name for this *self*. Wherever a man finds what he calls himself, there, I think, another may say is the same person. It is a forensic term, appropriating actions and their merit; and so belongs only to intelligent agents, capable of a law, and happiness, and misery. This personality extends it self beyond present existence to what is past, only by consciousness,—whereby it becomes concerned and accountable; owns and imputes to it self past actions, just upon the same ground and for the same reason as it does the present. All which is founded in a concern for happiness, the unavoidable concomitant of consciousness; that which is conscious of pleasure and pain, desiring that that *self* that is conscious should be happy. And therefore whatever past actions it cannot reconcile or appropriate to that present *self* by consciousness, it can be no more concerned in than if they had never been done.
>
> (§ 26)

I apologize for these long quotations, but there is something material here that has to be heard and shown. I think that you would agree with the following two suggestions. One, an essential part of the argument rests upon the idea that consciousness (or consciousness and memory) is the operator or system of mental operations that appropriates the self (or simply *self*, as a proper name) to itself, where to "appropriate" at the same time means to identify with and to make a property, a separated or private ownership of, and where also itself should be heard as it(s) *self*, in a mirror construction, which becomes more evident when the idea is transposed at the first person (but the corresponding experience is by definition an experience in the first person): consciousness appropriates *my* self to my *self*. Second, an equally essential part of the meaning of the argument rests upon the use of the whole spectrum of uses and significations of the word *own*, which is both adjective (as in "my own thought and action") and verb, and as a verb, used equivocally as signifying either to acknowledge or confess (in French, "*avouer*"), or to possess or be the owner of (in French, "*posséder*" or "*avoir*")—or indeed both, because you cannot own something that is not your own, or the fact that you own something, that is, recognize that you are accountable for it ipso facto makes it your own, particularly in the case of *actions*, which we will see is the crux of the problem. As a consequence of these remarkable linguistic and theoretical operations depending on pure words, I was led, and I am led, to suggest that the fundamental logic of this argument is a circularity, where the ideas of identity and identification on one side and of appropriation and the property or the *propre* on the other side continuously exchange their functions and become virtually equivalent. So that what I can consider as me, myself, is *my self*, and "my" *self* is some "thing" that I *own*, or that I must own (confess) is mine, was done or thought by me, has become my own because I appropriated it to me by doing it or thinking it consciously. But to appropriate it to me is to appropriate/identify it to my *self*, to what is already properly mine and indiscernible from me because I appropriated it to me, etc. What is my own in the strong sense is myself/my self, and what is myself (or identical with me: you find in the text the compound adjective *self-same*, which Latin speakers would say combines the objective meaning of *idem* and the reflective meaning of *ipse*, bringing together the notions of *sameness* and *selfhood*) is my self, that is, anything that is my own (possession) that I can own (confess), and only that.

I thought that this was not only a linguistic curiosity or a nice rhetorical use of remarkable properties of the English language on the part of Locke, but also a metaphysical fact or event, or better, say a *metaphysical linguistic game*, that had just the same importance as other well-known cases, such as in particular the syntactic properties of the Greek verbs *einai, eimi, esti, on, ousia*, etc. for the constitution of the metaphysics of "being," or the latent play on words in any use of the term "subject," because of its double Latin etymology, which combines a reference to the impersonal *subiectum*, the bearer or substratum of certain properties, with a reference to the personal *subiectus*, the individual who is subjected to the rule, authority, or domination of another person.[8] And I thought that I could ground on the discovery of this linguistic game if not an explanation then at least an interpretation and a better understanding of the close relationship that exists in Locke and others between a problematic of the subject where consciousness becomes the criterion of personal identity and a political theory where the notion of citizenship becomes generalized, or better said universalized, because any individual ought to be considered a "proprietor of his/her own person" or a self-owning personality, to the extent that he or she is such a proprietor (it seems, I must say, that "she" has more difficulties than "he," but I leave this aside for the moment). And the reason for this close relationship, which indeed is an equivalence, would be precisely this metaphysics of *appropriation* or, as Derrida would say, *propriation*, whose linguistic expression but also linguistic anticipation is provided by the circularity of meanings between *my self* and *my own*, or the fact that you can explain *self* only by referring to *own*, and *own* only by referring to *self*. This, I thought, was the heart of, if not Western ontology, as MacPherson has written, then at least of Western or more precisely European psychological, moral, juridical, and political individualism.[9]

But I was tempted to assert more, and once again this temptation was associated with a reading of an English text—a presumptuous reading, I must say. I was tempted to assert that *self* and *own*, or, if you prefer, *my self* and *my own, the self* and *the own*, were indeed *one and the same*. This would be both a *speculative* identity and a very trivial, material identity, inscribed in the materiality of language, or rather in the language of a specific idiom. In historicist terms, this amounted to explaining that Locke could give European individualism its metaphysical foundations because he was English and spoke English, because there was in English a "speculative" element represented by the synonymy of *my self* and *my own*, at least in some uses. It is always nice to discover or imagine that any language has its speculative elements, in each case different, but in each case with huge consequences, and that the existence of these elements is not the privilege of Greek or German. How was I led to this illusion or simplification? I ask you to remember the formulations that I extracted from the *Essay*: they sometimes indeed come very close to this equivalence, but they never purely and simply exchange the expressions "my self" and "my own," or they identify their meaning only implicitly and with the help of such mediations as "appropriation" or "concern" or "attribute" or "impute." The evidence had to come from outside.

It happened that at the time I was working on this I was also rereading the diary of André Gide, don't ask me why.[10] You may know that Gide was very fond of English literature, had a good mastery of the English language, and played an important role in the introduction and translation of contemporary English writers in France (such as Joseph Conrad). In his diary you find quotations from poems in the original language, and I fell upon the following strophe from the poem by Robert Browning called “By the Fire Side,” which has become part of the collection “Men and Women”:

My own, confirm me! If I tread
This path back, is it not in pride
To think how little I dreamed it led
To an age so blest that, by its side,
Youth seems the waste instead?

I must say that I was deeply moved by these verses, probably because I erroneously thought that the “age” of which it is a question here was old age, the age into which I felt that I was entering now, or would soon be (and I was probably fooled to understand it that way by the context in which André Gide quoted it, which had to do with the problem of seeking an assurance against the uncertainty of one’s own identity or self in the recollection of memory). But above all, I took it that the interpellation, represented here by the beginning of the strophe “My own, confirm me,” was a self-interpellation, a classical rhetorical move in which the poet lyrically addresses himself or calls himself as a witness of his own life. And somehow, identifying with him, I would repeat: “My own, confirm me,” believing that I was speaking to myself. But above all, and I recognize that this was not very serious, that it was much too fragile a basis for a scholarly interpretation, I thought (and wrote) that I had found an example where “my self” and “my own” in English are, that is, mean, one and the same.[11] But actually, as you all understand because English is your mother tongue, this is not the case. As for myself, apart from some embarrassed reactions that I received from friends, which should have acted as warnings, I had to wait until I found the whole poem on the shelves of UCI’s main library, in Robert Browning’s *Collected Works*. Allow me to take the time to read not only the following strophe, where the apostrophe “My own …” returns, but two or three others, not only because they are so beautiful, but because, while lifting any ambiguity even for a French reader, they introduce a speculative dimension, the dimension of the tension between unity and duality, or the fusion of the lovers into a mystic unity and the perhaps more disturbing emergence of the double who owns the identity of the subject:

My own, confirm me! If I tread
This path back, is it not in pride
To think how little I dreamed it led

To an age so blest that, by its side,
Youth seems the waste instead?

My own, see where the years conduct!
At first, 'twas something our two souls
Should mix as mists do; each is sucked
In each now: on, the new stream rolls,
Whatever rock obstruct.

Think, when our one soul understands
The great Word which makes all things new.
When earth breaks up and heaven expands,
How will the change strike me and you
In the house not made with hands?

Oh I must feel your brain prompt mine,
Your heart anticipate my heart,
You must be just before, in fine,
See and make me see, for your part,
New depths of the divine!

But who could have expected this
When we two drew together first
Just for the obvious human bliss,
To satisfy life's daily thirst
With a thing men seldom miss?[12]

Now quickly to remind you some facts about theses verses. First, of course, "my own" does not designate the poet himself, it designates his beloved wife. This is a love poem, a poem of bliss, dedicated by the young husband to his wife, recalling their first encounter and their night of love under the Italian sky near an old chapel, etc., etc. And the allusion to the old age, if it is there, is only an anticipation, as shown by a previous strophe which adds interesting variations on the theme of own and owning:

My perfect wife, my Leonor,
Oh heart, my own, oh eyes, mine too,
Whom else could I dare look backward for,
With whom beside should I dare pursue
The path grey heads abhor?

(We may remember also that this love story was soon interrupted by the premature death of his wife, but let's not add pathos.) Now playing the role of the French student a little longer, let me remark that, although the expression "my own" in such circumstances and relations is very common in English, only a presumptuous apprentice could ignore it; it remains very idiomatic. In French or German or Italian (which perhaps comes closest), you have similar expressions, but they never have quite the same simplicity—I am tempted to say the same brutality, the same brutal tenderness and closeness. "*Mon trésor*" and "*mon chéri*" are deemed vulgar, "*mon âme*" and "*mon Coeur*" are elevated and old fashioned, as are "*Mein Schatz*" and "*mio bene*" and "*caro mio bene*," as in Gluck's *Orfeo ed Euridice*. I will not embark on discussing whether English lovers are more possessive than others, and so curb the language to express this possessive character of their feelings—which is also a way to make love the only true form of possession—but I will return to the construction of "personal identity" or "identity through consciousness" in Locke, and show that there can be a benefit in the detour provoked by my mistake. I mean that a benefit can be found in reading together Robert Browning's poem and John Locke's essay. This benefit has to do with a better understanding of the extremely subtle and in a sense confusing modality in which the question of *duality* is involved in this construction of the *concept of identity*.

Why is it subtle and perhaps confusing? This is because in a sense it is simultaneously asserted at one level and denied at another, asserted at the level of enunciation and denied at the level of the enunciated, or asserted at the level of the *signifier* and denied at the level of the *signified*. More precisely, language continuously works with dualities that theory immediately blurs or nullifies. Language continuously duplicates a self, or a self who is owning and a self who is owned, and has to do it in order to *name* the poles, the moments of the process of identification described, whereas theory explains that the self is one and the same, "the same to itself," because it "owns itself" or is its "own self." Let us not hasten to declare that this tension falls under the accusation of "performative contradiction," or if this is the case, let me suggest that the text really makes a productive use of the contradiction, that is, it can be associated with several important aspects of the problem of personal identity that are *practically taken into account by Locke himself*, or he would not have produced such a complicated, lengthy, rhetorical, and poetical argument in order to explain that we ought to judge of a person's identity and therefore responsibility (be it before human tribunals or before the tribunal of God on the Day of the Last Judgment) after the only criterion the person herself can accept and verify, namely her own consciousness of having thought and acted in a certain manner. And if the text makes a productive use of the contradiction, that is, of the fact that the unity of the self is divided or duplicated by the simple fact of *naming* it (and here the use of *self* as *proper name* becomes particularly interesting) while the theory demonstrates its identity, this is because the text of course is acutely aware of the fact that the whole meaning of the argument can be captured only if it is meant and reproduced in the *first person* (this is the only "Cartesian" element in this text, perhaps, but it is a powerful one). *I* speak about myself, therefore about my "self," and therefore put it or him at a distance, nearly to become able to *address* or *interpellate* it (or him), but the content of this interpellation is self-identification, not a disowning but an owning of oneself, a discovery of what is not separable, not alienable from me, because it is me indeed—that is: my consciousness. The first person is a shifter (Roman Jacobson): it enacts the performative contradiction continuously, or it bridges the gap between enunciation and enunciated while displaying their difference.

This could be said in *Lockeian* terms, and this is probably one of the most fascinating interpretive possibilities that are opened by the conceptual fabric of the *Essay*. We could say that by purely and simply posing the identity of *my self* and *my own*, and above all, by confirming this identity as an essential identity on the basis of a wrong linguistic argument, I actually blurred the element of *uneasiness* that characterizes or affects this unity. The developments on *uneasiness* arise in another fantastic chapter of book 2 of the *Essay*, chapter 21, "Of Power," where, in a manner that is not so different from what we find in Spinoza, for example, Locke explains that there is no *consciousness* that is not associated with *desire* and at the same time troubled and pushed by it toward ever new contents or ideas, so that the notion of a fixed or stable consciousness is a contradiction in terms. Consciousness is by its very nature *restless*, it must *escape itself* toward new contents; its identity is associated with a perpetual flow, change, or "train of ideas," and the category that names this intrinsic association of consciousness and desire being precisely *uneasiness*.[13] So I would suggest by recurring to Locke himself, although from another place, that what I tended to blur and in the end ignore, by progressively identifying *self* and *own* and by posing that the self is exactly the same thing as the own—what is owned by me inasmuch as I own it (speaking of thoughts, and actions)—was the *uneasiness* of this relation, the fact that the identity or sameness of *self* and *own* does indeed exist, but only as an *uneasy* one. And it is all the more remarkable that Locke, so to speak, expressed this uneasiness not mainly in the form of an explicit thesis or theorem, but above all in the materiality and linguistic subtlety of his writing, which so to speak *mimics* the uneasy process of the differentiation of the unity in order to produce identity, or the process of differed *appropriation or ownership of the self*, or the dialectical process of the production of a difference within self-consciousness that exists only in order to become suppressed and negated, the production of a *vanishing difference*.

But allow me to return for a second to Robert Browning's poem. There is an element in this poem that indeed made all the difference with a pure and simple appropriation of identity or one's own identity, which I have apparently made no use of, although it was precisely the absent cause of my mistake: this is the element of sexual difference. My own is my wife, perhaps it could be also my husband, or more generally, we would say today it is my partner. It is the *other* with whom I make one and the same precisely because we can never become identified, indiscernible, in other terms, with whom I experience the uneasy relationship of identity and difference, not only because it is conflictual, but because the identification of what is shared or what is the same and of what is separated or divorced can never be established in a clear-cut and stable manner. The name of this uneasy experience conventionally is "love," but we know that love is anything but a simple thing, perhaps because in love there is precisely so much consciousness associated with so much desire. In short, *duality* is *neither unity nor multiplicity* (remember again a linguistic hint: the Greeks had a grammatical category of the dual). Let us see, to conclude, if we can draw something for the understanding of the relation of *self* and *own* in Locke, from the fact that their "uneasy" relationship might refer, at least in an oblique way, to the sexual difference, or to the general fact that a unity haunted by its own scission or reduplication, or the idea of a self striving at its appropriation of itself (himself, herself) or at *becoming its own* through the projection of doubles, however vanishing they will prove, must bear at least a metaphoric relationship with the sexual difference. Not so much perhaps the difference among "sexes" or even "sexualities," as if they were fixed terms already existing before the process, but rather again a differentiation whose definition would have a necessary relation to the experiences of sexuality. This will lead me to suggest another range of textual comparisons.

If I had time, I would start here a discussion centered on the adventures of the idea of the "vanishing duality" of the phenomenon of consciousness after Locke, and as a consequence, of Locke's formulations. But this would be much too long, and in a sense you would not be very surprised, even if the details of the various philosophical figures of the analysis of consciousness or personal identity or both, in terms of a unity of opposite aspects of the self that allow it to become its own and the rhetorical or linguistic instruments that have to be implemented or invented in order to describe such a dialectic, are incredibly complex and diverse. There would be Hegel of course, and it is not by chance that I have been playing at times with a Hegelian terminology to suggest that already in Locke there is a passage from a point of view of appropriation as a fact, or a result, to the point of view of appropriation as process. What is particularly interesting in Hegel, in the way in which he describes the experience of consciousness as an experience of successive scissions and unifications or syntheses, where the self appears to itself alternatively in the form of "certainty" and "truth," which are at the same time inseparable and incompatible, is indeed the fact that Hegel displays with an extraordinary force the ambivalence of the process of "appropriation," which produces at the same time identification and de-identification, or dis-owning (in the *Phenomenology of Mind*). This can be explained by the fact that in Hegel, the "subject" of the process is no longer the individual self and neither is it a collective substantial self, but it is the problematic, precisely uneasy relationship between the individual and the community or the general substance that can be viewed and that can view itself as a "self," an infinite process of identification through appropriation. There are other formulations equally remarkable: Adam Smith's construction of the "supposed impartial Spectator" as the *internal* or *interiorised* figure of the generic other produced by the effect of sympathy within the self: "I divide myself as it were, into two persons";[14] or George Herbert Mead's internal dialectic of the "self" as a tendential opposition of "I" and "Me," where I become divided among personalities, each of which represent a sharing or participation in a specific network of social communication,[15] for example. What is remarkable in Locke is the fact that precisely in his case the duality or dualism (if only the duality of the past self and the present self, or the owned and the owning, or the identified and the identifying self), without which the idea of appropriation could not be sustained, is *essentially vanishing*: it is not theorized—one might say fetishized—in the form of "instances" or "agencies" or "moments" in a dialectic of consciousness. It is rather simply indicated in its elusive and vanishing nature, in its nature of pure temporal or memorial flow, through the rhetoric of the discourse and its play on words.

Now this characteristic, which I call the subtlety of Locke, is compensated, so to speak, or it has a counterpart, which is the emergence of duality in another form, which is fantastic indeed, and which I would suggest—at least through comparisons—ultimately has a "sexual" content, in the general sense. I am thinking here of the extraordinary developments in the division or fusion of personalities as a consequence of actual or imaginary divisions or fusions of consciousnesses (it is a remarkable stylistic trait of Locke that he allows himself to use the term consciousness in the plural), which historically place Locke somewhere on the path that leads from ancient speculations on the transmigration of souls and reincarnation to typically modern experimental considerations (which for all that are perhaps no less speculative) on "multiple personalities" and the so-called multiple personality syndrome.[16] In fact, I think that the whole problem of multiple personalities is a pure Lockeian problem, whether or not authors admit that such a thing exists in the strong sense as a horizontal division of memory and time, whereby one and the same physical individual becomes split into two, three, or more (up to eighteen) "personalities," each of them "owning" her own experiences, memories, and behavior toward others and calling herself by her own name, in short living her own life, with discontinuous transitions from one to another. Now let's read the following passage in the *Essay*, from which I have already extracted one phrase:

> Nothing but consciousness can unite remote existences into the same person: the identity of substance will not do it; for whatever substance there is, however framed, without consciousness there is no person: and a carcass may be a person, as well as any sort of substance be so, without consciousness. Could we suppose two distinct incommunicable consciousnesses acting the same body, the one constantly by day, the other by night; and, on the other side, the same consciousness, acting by intervals, two distinct bodies: I ask, in the first case, whether the day and the night-man would not be two as distinct persons as Socrates and Plato? And whether, in the second case, there would not be one person in two distinct bodies, as much as one man is the same in two distinct clothings? Nor is it at all material to say, that this same, and this distinct consciousness, in the cases above mentioned, is owing to the same and distinct immaterial substances, bringing it with them to those bodies; which, whether true or no, alters not the case: since it is evident the personal identity would equally be determined by the consciousness, whether that consciousness were annexed to some individual immaterial substance or no. For, granting that the thinking substance in man must be necessarily supposed immaterial, it is evident that immaterial thinking thing may sometimes part with its past consciousness, and be restored to it again: as appears in the forgetfulness men often have of their past actions; and the mind many times recovers the memory of a past consciousness, which it had lost for twenty years together. Make these intervals of memory and forgetfulness to take their turns regularly by day and night, and you have two persons with the same

> immaterial spirit, as much as in the former instance two persons with the same body. So that self is not determined by identity or diversity of substance, which it cannot be sure of, but only by identity of consciousness.
>
> (2.27 § 23)

In this passage, we see clearly how the Lockeian rejection of the old dualisms of body and soul or mind, through the radical use of the criterion of identical consciousness, with its internal uneasy or vanishing process of differentiation, directly conduces to the admission of another duality, which I called fantastic, or which becomes easily projected into the fantastic realm, where the distinction of "personalities" or "identities" or "selves" coincides with a cosmic conflict between day and night, or the forces of the good and the forces of evil, whose origin and consequences are beyond human reach and perhaps beyond human understanding.

This will become clearer if we recognize that Locke's passage cannot be isolated; it forms a link in a chain or belongs to a tradition where the same question of the division of the self expressed in the form of a duality of consciousness or consciousnesses has received a full treatment. In my earlier commentary,[17] I suggested that this passage be compared, on the one hand, with a passage in Augustine's *Confessions*, and on the other hand, with the novel or short story by Robert-Louis Stevenson, *The Strange Case of Dr. Jekyll and Mister Hyde* (published in 1886). Locke is halfway between these two texts, somehow, but he is also at a distance. These are three stories of the conflict and the separation, possible or impossible, of the Day-man and the Night-man, who are acting along opposite moral values and impersonating opposite principles, and, together with others that we might add, they cannot be unrelated.

Here is Augustine's passage:

> iubes certe ut contineam a concupiscentia carnis et concupiscentia oculorum et ambitione saeculi. iussisti a concubitu et de ipso coniugio melius aliquid quam concessisti monuisti. et quoniam dedisti, factum est, et antequam dispensator sacramenti tui fierem. sed adhuc vivunt in memoria mea, de qua multa locutus sum, talium rerum imagines, quas ibi consuetudo mea fixit, et occursantur mihi vigilanti quidem carentes viribus, in somnis autem non solum usque ad delectationem sed etiam usque ad consensionem factumque simillimum. et tantum valet imaginis inlusio in anima mea in carne mea, ut dormienti falsa visa persuadeant quod vigilanti vera non possunt. numquid tunc ego

> non sum, domine deus meus? et tamen tantum interest inter me ipsum et me ipsum intra momentum quo hinc ad soporem transeo vel huc inde retranseo! ubi est tunc ratio qua talibus suggestionibus resistit vigilans et, si res ipsae ingerantur, inconcussus manet? numquid clauditur cum oculis? numquid sopitur cum sensibus corporis? et unde saepe etiam in somnis resistimus nostrique propositi memores atque in eo castissime permanentes nullum talibus inlecebris adhibemus adsensum? et tamen tantum interest ut, cum aliter accidit, evigilantes ad conscientiae requiem redeamus ipsaque distantia reperiamus nos non fecisse quod tamen in nobis quoquo modo factum esse doleamus.[18]

What seems to be important in the case of Augustine's description of the involuntary emissions of seminal liquor provoked during the night by the visit of feminine figures returning from the luxurious past of the saint (*incubae*) is its contribution to the discussion of the extent to which a *conversion*, that is, a turn from the love of one-self or self-love to the exclusive love of God, and therefore also the abandonment (*subiectio*) to the absolute power of God, determines a radical change of identity, the emergence of a *new man*. We know that book 10 of the *Confessions* is entirely devoted to a complex discussion of the relationship between memory (*memoria*, which practically subsumes all the intellectual operations of the mind as well) and desire (*concupiscentia*) in the constitution of the moral personality, or the relationship of one with oneself.

What I find particularly interesting is the fact that Augustine, while he compares different modalities of desire from his own experience by telling the story of his own life, would make a difference between sexual desire and other forms of desires associated with pleasures that we have more difficulties forgetting. While he asserts that sexual desire, at least in the form of the physical desire for the beauty and sensuality of other bodies, can be completely overcome or suppressed—and this is what he claims he has been successful in achieving—the pleasure of eating and drinking, the pleasure of seeing beautiful landscapes and works of art, the pleasure of learning and discovering through the exercise of intellectual capacities, and the pleasure of being morally right and so appreciated by others are much more difficult to forget: they give rise to an *infinite* conflict, a struggle that is coextensive with life, where the "two men," who are associated with "two loves" (human and divine) and belong to "two Cities" or two worlds, this one and the Other, exist simultaneously and confront each other. Now this situation can be read in the other direction, as a consequence of the symptomatic accident that takes place during the night. Augustine is lead to ask the question: *who is the sub-*

ject of this involuntary pleasure for whom the traces of memory are in a sense more real than the real? Is that me, or is it not me? The two hypotheses are equally disturbing, and the uneasiness that they provoke should be related to the reflections of Augustine on the involuntary element that resides within the will itself and testifies to the presence of evil as a "sleeping" element that disturbs the inclination toward the good itself. But there is worse than that, since the only possible explanation for the persistence of a desire, and with the desire, a personality or "man" who has been entirely suppressed, is that this desire or relationship with pleasure is preserved by God: it resides in the very same *intimate place* of the self as God and the truth itself, *interior intimo meo*, which appears to be the place of Otherness, or the place of the worrying ambivalence of love. The Night-man is the remainder of ambivalence that prevents the love of God from reaching certainty, and keeps throwing a doubt or a shadow over the intentions of God concerning His servant.

How about Stevenson now? The text is very complex and there is certainly not one way to read it. First of all, it seems to me more than likely that Stevenson is permeated with Augustinian themes and literal reminiscences, not only of course the designation of the last chapter as a "confession" of Jekyll's. Second, I have no precise idea concerning a possible reading of Locke by Stevenson, but it strikes me that, in a sense, the full story of Jekyll and Hyde is a passage from the second hypothesis proposed by Locke (one single mind or consciousness in two different bodies) to the first one (two different consciousnesses within one single body). This is also the reason why the story told by Stevenson is not exactly a "multiple personality" story; it is rather a play with this scientific imaginary and a critical questioning about its meaning.

The crucial passage takes place when, in the course of his "confession," Jekyll explains how he discovered that the second personality (he writes "the second self") that he has created through the use of "transcendental" medicine, in order to *exteriorize the "dual nature"* of man, or to carry an experience of effective dissociation of the good man and the evil man, the Day-man and the Night-man, is no longer his "own." That is, it emerges in an unpredictable manner *as if* by his own (evil) will, but in reality as a consequence of the blind forces of degeneracy or "bestiality" that have been unleashed. This is truly the moment in which the "thing" created by Jekyll and in which he has projected or concentrated all his desires to be "himself," free from the constraints of society (from what is called "the very pink of the proprieties") becomes a "person," because it becomes a monster, the master's master (as the butler explicitly declares in the novel). And this is the moment when in his confession Jekyll declares himself unable to identify with Hyde, or to say

"I" when describing Hyde's actions. But in reality, or "in the real," not to say "in the thing" (except that this real is the real of a fiction, created by writing), this is the moment when the two identities have become so inseparable that they cannot even be separated by death. Jekyll has to kill himself in order to kill Hyde (of course the play on words has been remarked on by, among others, Masao Miyoshi, and it is a French-English play on words: the name says "I kill," or better, "I kill the '*Je*,'" the I, or the otherness of the I).[19] But this killing is so ambiguous that we cannot even know if it means absolute dissociation or ultimate identification, or *who*, exactly, will be "judged" after that. Unless we purely and simply take it as a perfect allegory of the death drive, Jekyll being clearly a melancholic figure. Witness the following passage:

> My reason wavered, but it did not fail me utterly. I have more than once observed that in my second character, my faculties seemed sharpened to a point and my spirits more tensely elastic; thus it came about that, where Jekyll perhaps might have succumbed, Hyde rose to the importance of the moment. My drugs were in one of the presses of my cabinet; how was I to reach them? That was the problem that (crushing my temples in my hands) I set myself to solve. The laboratory door I had closed. If I sought to enter by the house, my own servants would consign me to the gallows. I saw I must employ another hand, and thought of Lanyon. How was he to be reached? how persuaded? Supposing that I escaped capture in the streets, how was I to make my way into his presence? and how should I, an unknown and displeasing visitor, prevail on the famous physician to rifle the study of his colleague, Dr. Jekyll? Then I remembered that of my original character, one part remained to me: I could write my own hand; and once I had conceived that kindling spark, the way that I must follow became lighted up from end to end.... Thenceforward, he sat all day over the fire in the private room, gnawing his nails; there he dined, sitting alone with his fears, the waiter visibly quailing before his eye; and thence, when the night was fully come, he set forth in the corner of a closed cab, and was driven to and fro about the streets of the city. He, I say—I cannot say, I. That child of Hell had nothing human; nothing lived in him but fear and hatred. And when at last, thinking the driver had begun to grow suspicious, he discharged the cab and ventured on foot, attired in his misfitting clothes, an object marked out for observation, into the midst of the nocturnal passengers, these two base passions raged within him like a tempest. He walked fast, hunted by his fears, chattering to himself, skulking through the less frequented thoroughfares, count-

ing the minutes that still divided him from midnight. Once a woman spoke to him, offering, I think, a box of lights. He smote her in the face, and she fled.

At all hours of the day and night, I would be taken with the premonitory shudder; above all, if I slept, or even dozed for a moment in my chair, it was always as Hyde that I awakened. Under the strain of this continually impending doom and by the sleeplessness to which I now condemned myself, ay, even beyond what I had thought possible to man, I became, in my own person, a creature eaten up and emptied by fever, languidly weak both in body and mind, and solely occupied by one thought: the horror of my other self. But when I slept, or when the virtue of the medicine wore off, I would leap almost without transition (for the pangs of transformation grew daily less marked) into the possession of a fancy brimming with images of terror, a soul boiling with causeless hatreds, and a body that seemed not strong enough to contain the raging energies of life. The powers of Hyde seemed to have grown with the sickliness of Jekyll. And certainly the hate that now divided them was equal on each side. With Jekyll, it was a thing of vital instinct. He had now seen the full deformity of that creature that shared with him some of the phenomena of consciousness, and was co-heir with him to death: and beyond these links of community, which in themselves made the most poignant part of his distress, he thought of Hyde, for all his energy of life, as of something not only hellish but inorganic. This was the shocking thing; that the slime of the pit seemed to utter cries and voices; that the amorphous dust gesticulated and sinned; that what was dead, and had no shape, should usurp the offices of life. And this again, that that insurgent horror was knit to him closer than a wife, closer than an eye; lay caged in his flesh, where he heard it mutter and felt it struggle to be born; and at every hour of weakness, and in the confidence of slumber, prevailed against him, and deposed him out of life. The hatred of Hyde for Jekyll was of a different order. His terror of the gallows drove him continually to commit temporary suicide, and return to his subordinate station of a part instead of a person; but he loathed the necessity, he loathed the despondency into which Jekyll was now fallen, and he resented the dislike with which he was himself regarded. Hence the ape-like tricks that he would play me, scrawling in my own hand blasphemies on the pages of my books, burning the letters and destroying the portrait of my father; and indeed, had it not been for his fear of death, he would

> long ago have ruined himself in order to involve me in the ruin. But his love of me is wonderful; I go further: I, who sicken and freeze at the mere thought of him, when I recall the abjection and passion of this attachment, and when I know how he fears my power to cut him off by suicide, I find it in my heart to pity him.[20]

To conclude briefly: how shall we understand these variations? We can remark that both Augustine and Stevenson clearly describe a duality that has a sexual connotation, or more generally concerns the disturbing presence of otherness within every consciousness that seeks to identify itself with a "self," or reach self-identity, as a radical conflict that cannot be solved in ordinary life. One of them describes it in moral-theological terms and the other in physiological-fantastic terms. In both cases the "end" is *absolute disowning of the self*, either in God, in the form of God's love who installs himself *in interiore homine* to reveal a truth and embody an authority that is the condition for man's salvation, or in the form of Death, the master's master, which becomes also projected in the form of a being that is at the same time interior and exterior, myself and my monstrous desire to escape all identity, therefore also all accountability. Now we might say that what distinguishes Locke from these two extremes is the fact that the supreme principle in his case is neither God nor the Death, but something like *life* (and consciousness is clearly associated with life, or better, it is the instrument of the elevation of life to the status of principle or value). But Locke is a really great philosopher, therefore also a writer: while carrying to the last consequences the project of defining the "self" not in terms of internal conflict or as *divided self*, but in terms of progressive *appropriation* and tendential identity of *self* and *own*, being oneself and having or possessing oneself, he cannot purely and simply ignore the fact that any identity includes otherness or has to be defined in terms of an intrinsic relationship to its other. But he separates two figures: one is the figure of *uneasiness*, the tension between self and own that keeps life and consciousness in a condition of perpetual motion: we might say that this is the *normal* form of life, but we might also say that *the normality of life is uneasy*. The other figure is a *limit form*, or a form (and also a state) of exception, which takes place when normality is not only uneasy but mentally or morally impossible: it is the radical dissociation of personality and individuality or the cleavage of the bodily and mental life. In a sense it is the truth of the first, because it shows that there is nothing natural in the identification of self and own, which is really a norm rather than a necessity, and reigns by virtue of a postulate.

Notes

1. John Locke, *An Essay Concerning Human Understanding*, ed. Peter H. Nidditch (Oxford: Oxford University Press, 1975). Among the commentaries, see in particular: Henry E. Allison, "Locke's Theory of Personal Identity: A Re-Examination," in *Locke on Human Understanding*, ed. I. C. Tipton (Oxford: Oxford University Press, 1977); Michael Ayers, "The Arguments of the Philosophers," in *Locke, Epistemology, and Ontology* (London: Routledge, 1991); Cathy Caruth, *Empirical Truths and Critical Fictions: Locke, Wordsworth, Kant, Freud* (Baltimore: Johns Hopkins University Press, 1991); K. Olivecrona, "Locke's Theory of Appropriation," *Philosophical Quarterly* 24/96 (1974); Udo Thiel, "Locke's Concept of Person," in *John Locke. Symposium Wolfenbüttel 1979*, ed. R. Brandt (Berlin: Walter de Gruyter, 1981); Udo Thiel, *John Locke. Essay über den menschlichen Verstand*, Klassiker Auslegen 6 (Berlin: Akademie Verlag, 1997).

2. Barbara Cassin, ed., *Vocabulaire européen des philosophies* (Paris: Editions du Seuil-Le Robert, 2004).

3. John Locke, *Two Treatises of Government*, ed. Peter Laslett, rev. ed. (Cambridge: Cambridge University Press, 1963); Crawford Brough MacPherson, *The Political Theory of Possessive Individualism: Hobbes to Locke* (Oxford: Oxford University Press, 1962).

4. In what is arguably his most extraordinary and decisive philosophical essay, Jean-Paul Sartre demonstrates this point from a phenomenological point of view. See Jean-Paul Sartre, "La transcendance de l'Ego," in *La transcendance de l'Ego et autres textes phénoménologiques*, ed. V. de Coorebyter (Paris: Vrin éditeur, 2003).

5. John Locke, *Identité et différence. Le chapitre II, xxvii de l'*Essay Concerning Human Understanding *de Locke. L'invention de la conscience*, ed., trans., and commentary by Etienne Balibar (Paris: Editions du Seuil, 1998).

6. Invented by the Cambridge Neoplatonist Ralph Cudworth, in his monumental work *The True Intellectual System of the Universe, The First Part; Wherein All the Reason and Philosophy of Atheism is Confuted; and Its Impossibility Demonstrated* (London, 1678; repr. Bristol: Thoemmes Press, 1995).

7. See Jean Deprun, *La philosophie de l'inquiétude en France au XVIIIe siècle* (Paris: Librairie J. Vrin, 1979).

8. On the metaphysical "consequences" of the properties of the Greek verb, see the classical essay by Emile Benveniste, "Catégories de pensée et catégories de langue," in *Problèmes de linguistique générale*, 63–74 (Paris: Gallimard, 1966); and the critique by Jacques Derrida, "Le supplément de copule," in *Marges de la philosophie*, 209–246 (Paris: Les éditions de Minuit, 1972). More recently, Barbara Cassin has proposed a new understanding of the issue in Parmenides, *Sur la nature ou sur l'étant: La langue de l'être?*, ed., trans., and commentary by Barbara Cassin (Paris: Editions du Seuil, 1998). On the double genealogy of the subject as *subjectus* and *subjectum*, see Etienne Balibar, "The Subject," *UMBR(A), a Journal of the Unconscious* 1 (2003): 9–24.

9. See in particular Jacques Derrida, *Spurs: Nietzsche's Styles*, trans. Barbara Harlow (Chicago: University of Chicago Press, 1979), 109–111 and 121–123; C. B. MacPherson, *Democratic Theory: Essays in Retrieval* (Oxford: Oxford University Press, 1973), 24ff.

10. André Gide, *Journal*, Bibliothèque de la Pléiade (Paris: Gallimard, 1997), 659.

11. Locke, *Identité et différence*, 252.

12. Robert Browning, "By the Fire Side," in *The Complete Works of Robert Browning, with Variant Readings and Annotations*, ed. Roma A. King, Jr., 5: 205–206 (Athens: Ohio University Press, 1981).

13. Locke, *Essay Concerning Human Understanding*, 233–287. The discussion of "uneasiness" begins on 251.

14. Adam Smith, *The Theory of Moral Sentiments*, intro. E. G. West (Indianapolis: Liberty Classics, 1969), 247, 352, 371, etc. Adam Smith calls the Impartial Spectator "the Man within the breast" of every man.

15. George H. Mead, *Mind, Self, and Society from the Standpoint of a Social Behaviorist*, ed. Charles W. Morris (Chicago: University of Chicago Press, 1934), 135–226.

16. Mikkel Borch-Jacobsen, "Who's Who? Introducing Multiple Personality," in *Supposing the Subject*, ed. Joan Copjec (London: Verso, 1994).

17. Locke, *Identité et différence*. See note 5 of this chapter.

18. *The Confessions of Augustine: An Electronic Edition*, text and commentary by James J. O'Donnell (1992), book 10, § 30.41. The translation by Edward B. Pusey (New York: Collier & Son, 1909–1914) reads: "Verily Thou enjoinest me continency from the lust of the flesh, the lust of the eyes, and the ambition of the world. Thou enjoinest continency from concubinage; and for wedlock itself, Thou hast counselled something better than what Thou hast permitted. And since Thou gavest it, it was done, even before I became a dispenser of Thy Sacrament. But there yet live in my memory (whereof I have much spoken) the images of such things as my ill custom there fixed; which haunt me, strengthless when I am awake: but in sleep, not only so as to give pleasure, but even to obtain assent, and what is very like reality. Yea, so far prevails the illusion of the image, in my soul and in my flesh, that, when asleep, false visions persuade to that which when waking, the true cannot. Am I not then myself, O Lord my God? And yet there is so much difference betwixt myself and myself, within that moment wherein I pass from waking to sleeping, or return from sleeping to waking! Where is reason then, which, awake, resisteth such suggestions? And should the things themselves be urged on it, it remaineth unshaken. Is it clasped up with the eyes? Is it lulled asleep with the senses of the body? And whence is it that often even in sleep we resist, and mindful of our purpose, and abiding most chastely in it, yield no assent to such enticements? And yet so much difference there is, that when it happeneth otherwise, upon waking we return to peace of conscience: and by this very difference discover that we did not, what yet we be sorry that in some way it was done in us."

19. "The Divided Self," in *The Definitive* Dr. Jekyll and Mr. Hyde *Companion*, ed. Harry M. Geduld (New York: Garland, 1983), 104–105.

20. Robert Louis Stevenson, *The Strange Case of Dr. Jekyll and Mr. Hyde*, ed. Martin A. Danahay (Peterborough, Ont.: Broadview Literary Texts, 1999), 75–91. The chapter is entitled "Henry Jekyll's Full Statement of the Case."

2 The Future of Nationalist Appropriation

Pheng Cheah

In a set of reflections published in 1948 as *Notes on Dialectics: Hegel, Marx, Lenin*, C. L. R. James outlines what can be called the dialectic of property and appropriation in Marxist thought. Commenting on Trotsky's equation of socialism with nationalized property, James turned back to Hegel's philosophical logic (the teleology of the concept) to argue that Trotsky had mistakenly substituted the concrete experience of socialism particular to *his* Russia for the self-determining socialist universal as such. In this manner, the socialist project had been truncated. It had been reduced to statist bureaucratic planning, which was nothing else but "state-capitalist barbarism."[1] James reminded his readers that Marx had shifted the terms of analysis from property to production, from ownership of things to labor as a socializing human process.

> The Universal of socialism is not nationalized property and plan. The marxist movement did not say this until about 1929. That is the theory of both stalinism and trotskyism. The Universal of socialism is the free proletariat.... Marx established this in Volume I of *Capital* as his grand conclusion, excluding the market, and purposely confining himself to production.... The bourgeois thinkers have perpetually concerned themselves with *property* (and for very good reasons): it is the appearance, the very real appearance of bourgeois society. The marxist has always concentrated upon production and workers in production. The great transformation that is to take place in bourgeois society is the negation of capital by the proletariat, the primary position in the opposition is

> to be taken by the proletariat, with capital sublated, the proletariat made richer, with the achievements of capital stored up in it. Marxists have not spent these long decades analysing property. An economic order, production, is a relation between people and people. Property is a relation between people and things.[2]

The primacy accorded to production over property as a category for the analysis of economic, social, and political relations captures in shorthand the philosophical basis for Marx's exhortation to abolish the property form. The abolition of property (*Eigentum*) is the necessary concrete outcome of Marx's analysis of alienated labor. Paradoxically, property is what is radically and fundamentally improper to human beings despite its etymological relationship to the proper (*eigentlich*), what is of one's own (*eigen*) or co-belongs with oneself. Property is a form of expropriation (*Enteignung*). As a privative relationship of possession between *particular* individuals and things, it violates and profanes creative labor as a purposive process properly unique to human beings, a process through which we create our universal humanity.[3]

Marx argued that society is the rational essence of universal *human* existence and the substrate for actualizing our humanity.[4] Economic activity (production, distribution, consumption) transforms us into *social* beings because it requires social cooperation between human individuals. Private property, on the other hand, is a function and expression of alienated social relations. The alienable nature of property presupposes the worker's alienation (*Entfremdung*) from the products of his living activity, a condition exacerbated by the modern commodification of labor. As the autonomized property of an other, these products constitute an alien and hostile second nature that dominates their producer like a monstrous power (*OPM*, 1.2: 365; 324). But more importantly, wage labor depletes the worker's subjectivity. Instead of augmenting and adding greater meaning to his life, labor is a heteronomous activity that miscultivates and deforms his inner being: "the more values he creates, the more worthless he becomes; the more his product is shaped [*geformter*], the more misshapen [*mißförmiger*] the worker; the more civilized his object, the more barbarous the worker" (*OPM*, 1.2: 366; 325). The worker is eventually dispossessed of his humanity. His life activity has been reduced to a mere means of subsistence and he can no longer recognize his species-being in it or in his relations with others.

The proper philosophical meaning behind the abolition of property is thus not only to take back what has been alienated from this or that producer but to put an end to alienation and alienability in general. The word

Marx chooses to designate this total *Aufhebung* of alienation is appropriation (*Aneignung*).

> Thus things have now come to such a pass that the individuals must appropriate [*aneignen*] the existing totality of productive forces, not only to achieve self-activity, but also, merely to safeguard their very existence.... With the appropriation of the total productive forces by the united individuals [the universal union of the proletariat as universal class and overthrow of all previous social, political, and economic forms], private property will come to an end.[5]

Whereas property is improper, revolutionary proletarian appropriation recalls the link to the proper, especially as instantiated by creative labor's original appropriative character. As objectification, labor is also the appropriation of external nature. In the later Marx's less metaphysical language, "the labour process ... is purposive [*zweckmäßige*] activity aimed at the production of use-values. It is an appropriation of what exists in nature for the needs of man" (*K1*, 2.10: 167; 290). The proletarian revolution is living labor's return to itself, where the alienated totality of productive forces is restored to individuals as social beings. Appropriation in the sociopolitical sense is the reincarnation and magnification of appropriative labor into a world-historical movement against capital. It accomplishes the actualization of humanity by restoring the individual's social being and self-activity. In the process, it destroys the property form as a defective, inadequate, and improper expression of humanity. Henceforth, what is appropriated will be universally owned and, hence, will no longer be the property of any owner in the privative sense these terms imply. To return to C. L. R. James's point, the mistake of Russian socialism is that it did not abolish property as such. By merely transforming private property into state property, Soviet socialism maintained alienation by interposing the state between the people and what they produce.

The self-recursive structure of the proletarian revolution *qua* appropriation, with its promise of the abolition of private property, clearly indicates that Marx's understanding of the exploitative institutions of wage labor and private property is derived from and underwritten by a theory of the human being as a laboring subject, where creative labor, as a mode of self-activity, is regarded as the process by which the human subject achieves self-propriety and self-presence. Creative labor is the process in which the subject is able to recognize his humanity in the objective products of his activity, thereby affirming the dignity that is proper to every human personality. This thematic link between the abolition of property and the achievement of human personality is even more pertinent and poignant in the historical scene of decolonization, where what needs to be reappropriated through revolutionary struggle is not only the material economic wealth and political integrity of a people, but also the nation's spiritual or cultural personality. Colonialism and neocolonialism is the alienation of a people's autonomous personality. Territorial imperialism subjugates this personality, and it continues to be expropriated by neocolonial forces. Hence, in Amilcar Cabral's exemplary reformulation, national liberation is a mode of reappropriation at the level of culture: "the phenomenon in which a socio-economic whole rejects the denial of its historical process.... The national liberation of a people is the regaining of the historical personality of that people, it is their return to history through the destruction of the imperialist domination."[6]

The idea of nationalist appropriation guiding historical movements of decolonization thus introduces a crucial qualification into the Marxist dialectic of property, appropriation, and personality. It emphasizes the importance of the reaffirmation of cultural personality as a primary goal of revolutionary struggle in the colonized world. As such, revolutionary decolonization movements were an important correction to the largely Eurocentric debate concerning communism and nationalism.[7] The intellectuals who wrote about these movements such as Cabral and Frantz Fanon argued that because of imperialist capitalist exploitation, the shape of struggles for the colonized peoples constituting the mass of the world's population was necessarily nationalist. Revolutionary appropriation must remove the *nation* from the global circuit of property and commodification so that its people *as a people* can have access to the products of their labor. However, for this to happen, the people must first achieve or regain their rightful cultural *personality*, which imperialism has violently usurped. Hence, Cabral notes that cultural autonomy is a corollary of "the inalienable right of every people to have their own history."[8] But more importantly, culture is the fundamental precondition of revolutionary appropriation. It is the original source of resistance to colonial domination and precedes and lays the ground for political, economic, and social liberation. In Cabral's words, "if imperialist domination has the vital need to practise cultural oppression, national liberation is necessarily an *act of culture*."[9]

It is important to rigorously distinguish the national personality that cultural appropriation attempts to restore from national chauvinism. National chauvinism, which Lenin called the bourgeois nationalism of oppressor nations, is a form of property at the level of culture, the nation as a commodified and privative cultural *identity* that is defined by excluding other peoples, often on the grounds of race or ethnicity. Precisely because property is a form of alienation, the cultural personality formed through the revolutionary struggle of cultural appropriation necessarily involves the dissolution of cultural identity *qua* exclusive property of a chauvinistic, xenophobic people. The historical personality of which Cabral speaks is not a primordial or archaic essence but an evolving product of a people's actions in their ongoing interaction with the external world and other peoples. This is why every radical-progressive decolonizing nationalism is in principle also internationalist and universalistic.

The purpose of this chapter is to examine the continuing feasibility of the Marxist dialectic of property, appropriation, and personality by focusing on the modality of postcolonial cultural appropriation. This dialectic is clearly now in crisis. We have witnessed the failure of state socialism in the former Eastern bloc and the management of the crisis of capitalism in the West through social welfare, consumerism, and an international division of labor. The popular-radical postcolonial nationalist project is possibly the last remaining theater where the idea of revolutionary appropriation maintains a certain efficacy. But how exactly is postcolonial cultural appropriation able to transcend the global capitalist circuit of commodification and consumption? I have chosen to explore this question via a study of the Kenyan novelist Ngugi Wa Th'iongo's project of revolutionary nationalist culture for two reasons. First, the concrete situation Ngugi depicts—the devastation of peoples of the African Fourth World in an uneven global capitalist economy—is even more dire than the utter immiseration of the urban proletariat in nineteenth-century industrial Europe that Marx thought would catalyze the process of restoring the worker's full personality through revolutionary appropriation. Second, insofar as it takes the form of literary culture, Ngugi's project is an exemplary instantiation and test case for the general claim of revolutionary nationalist appropriation implied by Cabral's aphorism that national liberation is an act of culture, namely, that culture is the paradigmatic activity by which a people can return to itself, become proper to itself, and regain its rightful personality.

The key characteristics of the "African tragedy," which Ngugi's Kenya exemplifies, have been amply documented in the social-scientific literature. It begins with the failure of formal decolonization to constitute a decisive break with colonial administrative institutions and economic infrastructures despite the desire to Africanize each country's economy and political life.[10] Within the framework of the uneven development of global capital, the initial momentum of popular-nationalist social, political, and economic reform has been actively retarded and suppressed by the establishment of neocolonial states run by a comprador elite in collaboration with multinational capital. The economies of these countries, which are crippled by the heinous crony or theft capitalism of the native elite, are also repeatedly subject to internationally imposed structural adjustment policies. Their political life is plagued by ethnic and tribal conflict and varieties of undemocratic authoritarian rule. The failure of constitutionalism and the poor human rights records of many African states routinely decried by the Northern media are only the most extreme symptoms of a profounder crisis that cannot be solved by formal legality and the protection of abstract human rights on a case-by-case basis. Ngugi attempts to offer a solution to this misery, but as I will argue, the irresolvable aporias his project encounters radically disturb the dialectic of the people's self-propriety/appropriation that his project exemplifies, to the point where the idea of appropriation must be rethought from the ground up.

National Culture as Self-Recursive Mediation

The fundamental premises of Ngugi's project are as follows: global capital reproduces neocolonial relations within postcolonial space by attaching various prostheses onto the popular-national organism. A prosthesis is a secondary, artificial object that is added onto a more substantial original body.[11] Although it is *prima facie* a foreign body that intrudes upon the proper human body's organic wholeness, a prosthesis can supplement a deficiency and provide essential support if it is properly attached and utilized. For instance, as long as they receive life from or are animated by the organic body, artificial teeth and limbs augment and restore the body's original integrity. The organic body remains self-supporting precisely because the prosthesis has been organicized, made an integral part of its proper self. In contradistinction, a bad prosthesis acts as a conduit that makes the body vulnerable to hostile foreign elements. Instead of becoming an organic member of the body, it opens the body up to external forces and even makes it dependent on them. Thus, an export-oriented comprador economy and neocolonial cultural images are malignant prostheses that alienate the nation from its proper self so that it can be remade in the image of dead capital. The neocolonial state is the deadly prosthesis *par excellence*.

In Ngugi's view, national culture is of paramount importance in the overcoming of the Kenyan people's economic and political alienation because it is crucial to securing neocolonial political and economic control in the contemporary American-dominated world order. Accordingly, he directly addresses the effects of a neocolonial global cultural economy on revolutionary national culture's power of self-recursive mediation. Most of his fiction has a contemporary setting, where the rise of a global "culture industry" (the Frankfurt School) through the rapid development of global communications and technomediation threatens to erode and deform national culture. Ngugi likens the nation's evolution to an organic body's development according to its inner biological processes and its interactions with external surroundings:

> The air and food the body takes from its contact with the external environment are digested and become an integral part of the body. This is normal and healthy. But it may happen that the impact of the external factor is too strong; it is not taken in organically, in which case the body may even die. Floods, earthquakes, the wind, too much or too little air, poisoned or healthy food ... are all external factors or activities that can affect the body adversely. The same with society. All societies develop under conditions of external contact with other societies at the economic, political and cultural levels. Under "normal" circumstances, a given society is able to absorb whatever it borrows from other contacts, digest it and make it its own. But under conditions of external domination ... the changes are not as a result of the working out of the conflicts and tensions within, and do not arise out of the organic development of that society but are forced upon it externally. This may result in the society becoming deformed, changing course altogether or even dying out. Conditions of external domination and control, as much as those of internal domination and oppression, do not create the necessary climate for the cultural health of any society.... Hence, [I insist] ... on the suffocating and ultimately destructive character of both colonial and neo-colonial structures.[12]

This distinction between "good" organic development, typified by the inner-directed ingestion of external elements and unhealthy, externally dictated modes of force-feeding, necessarily pertains to all finite beings. Finite beings are constitutively vulnerable to the outside because living is a perpetual struggle with externality. Echoing Marx's metaphor of the human metabolism with nature, Ngugi points out:

> Our external life is an integral part of ourselves. None of us can live without breathing in air.... Yet at the same time, air is out there, external to us. It's give and take or die. By emphasizing the ideal of organic development, I mean that whatever comes from outside ... must

> not deform internal development. Taking in air supports our internal organs, yet if there is too much, like a blast of air, it can hurt one as much as a lack of air. This is a kind of healthy struggle and a system which must not be deformed by either external circumstances or by such internal imbalance so as to completely deform the possibilities of development.[13]

The same logic applies to the use of prostheses. The colonial state exposed the national body to the capitalist world-system and linked it up to an entire series of prosthetic processes such as commodification, financial circulation, and so on. With the transformation of the nation's useful labor into abstract labor-power, the people's products become alienated and no longer augment its own life. Instead, they reflect and further impoverish the nation's already depleted and fragmented body, which is now reduced to spare parts for the global capitalist machine. Decolonization was supposed to restore the nation's integrity by removing the colonial state. But in fact, a similar foreign prosthesis has been reattached onto the nation, which continues to harness and bend it toward multinational capital's inhuman interests. This is the neocolonial state with its oppressive military apparatus and foreign gadgets.

> [The indigenous elite], pampered with military gadgets of all kinds with which to rein in a restive population, has often turned an entire country into a vast prison-house. Africa is a continent alienated from itself by years of alien conquests and internal despots.... *The Man Died*; *Things Fall Apart*; *No Longer at Ease*; *The Beautyful Ones Are Not Yet Born*; *From a Crooked Rib*; the titles of many novels in Africa speak clearly of this alienation, or this dismemberment of parts that could have been made whole.
>
> (*MC*, 107–108)

For Ngugi, the national organism's liberation from neocolonial domination is a matter of rationally regulating its opening out onto the external other, which fundamentally affects its self-creative or productive capacity. Hence, the unfinished nationalist project must remove the neocolonial state. Culture, a *psychical* prosthesis, has a paramount but fundamentally ambivalent role in this ongoing project. Following Marx's definition of creative labor as the actualization of ideal forms, Ngugi characterizes the national body's productive capacity as its ability to form externality in its own image so that it can develop itself. This autonomized image is a good prosthesis because it can be fully integrated, absorbed until it becomes part of the national body. *Popular-national culture* is the paradigmatic example of a good prosthesis for two mutually reinforcing reasons. It originates from the people. But more importantly, through collective psychical incorporation, it also plays a crucial role in the nation's continuing self-formation. In Ngugi's words, "culture gives ... [a] society its self-image as it sorts itself out in the economic and political fields" (*MC*, xv). As long as these cultural images are self-prescribed and their ingestion inner-directed or self-determined, as long as culture is genuinely national, it will be self-recursive. Through this movement of reflection from the outside back to itself, the nation gets to know and position itself within the world so that it can better appropriate it for the purposes of its development. A people's culture is thus the formative attachment and ingestion of a self-prescribed rational image, the interiorization of an other that the national organism posits for itself. It is an ideational form that is externalized and given objective shape so that it can be reappropriated by the national body. Like a pilot in a machine, genuine culture directs the national body's interaction with economic and political forces so that it can finally return home to itself from externality. The nation recognizes itself in the world, which thereby becomes a world *for* it.

It is important to emphasize that culture's power of self-recursive mediation is also central to social-scientific debates about contemporary Kenyan politics. According to the Marxist view, the neocolonial state is a mechanism of the ruling class, "an organization for the protection of the possessing class against the non-possessing classes."[14] In liberal accounts of Moi's one-party state, the party is no longer a forum for articulating the interests of different economic groups or for mobilizing support for the regime through interest aggregation. It has degenerated into "an adjunct of the executive or office of the president," which "has assumed the role of transmitter and enforcer of policy decisions, with executive police powers."[15] In both cases, the oppressive party or state is essentially an alienating prosthesis that is inappropriate to the people and fails to respond to their needs. Conversely, accountability to the people, the essence of multiparty democracy, is the reappropriation of a defective prosthesis by the national organism.[16] The problem with many postcolonial African regimes, Ngugi notes, is that "they never see their inspiration as coming from the people, because they know very well that their being in power is not dependent on Somalian people, on Kenyan people, on Zairian people.... They don't feel accountable to the people."[17]

But national culture's self-recursivity does not make it a static natural entity. Ngugi emphatically rejects a simple return to traditional structures.

> Culture, in its broadest sense, is a way of life fashioned by a people in their collective endeavour to live and come to terms with their total environment.... In the course of their creative struggle and progress through history, there evolves a body of material and spiritual values which endow that society with a unique ethos.... No living culture is ever static.
>
> It is surely not possible to lift traditional structures and cultures intact into modern Africa. A meaningful culture is the one born out of the present hopes and especially the hopes of an impoverished peasantry, and that of the growing body of urban workers.[18]

Hence, culture is the basis of a people's resistance to domination and their political and economic freedom. Indeed, Ngugi suggests that a people are born anew in the very act of resistance:

> It is when people are involved in the active work of destroying an inhibitive social structure and building a new one that they begin to see themselves. They are born again.... If we are to achieve true national cultures we must recognize our situation. That means we must thoroughly examine our social and economic structures and see if they are geared to meeting the needs and releasing the energy of the masses. We must in fact wholly Africanize and socialize our political and economic life.[19]

Indeed, genuine (popular-national) culture is in a relation of symbiotic feedback with revolutionary struggle to the point that they are synonymous. Because it adequately expresses the masses' needs, such culture is a source of sustenance for organized anti-imperialist politics, which necessarily involves "the patriotic defence of the peasant/worker roots of national cultures."[20] By the same token, true national culture is itself "a people's fighting culture," "the fighting culture of the African peasantry and working class... [that is] a product and reflection of real life struggles going on in Africa today" (*MC*, 45).

Ngugi's account of national culture connects the Marxist topos of appropriation in the political and economic spheres to the recognitive structure of national *Bildung*. The project of appropriation is therefore also a cultural repatriation or "homecoming," the task of building "a true communal home for all Africans" (*H*, xix). Whether or not other African writers agree with Ngugi's socialist inclinations, his definitions of national culture as a mediating prosthesis that enables a people's self-return through self-incarnation and recognition in the external world, and education as giving "people the confidence that they can in fact create a new heaven on earth," are central to most theories of African literature.[21] Chinua Achebe similarly points to the prosthetic function of culture in his characterization of art as "man's constant effort to create for himself a different order of reality from that which is given to him; an aspiration to provide himself with a second handle on existence through his imagination." The cultural ideals of African socialism, negritude, etc., he suggests, are "all props we have fashioned at different times to help us get on our feet again."[22]

But like any prosthesis, culture can also be malignant. As a product of capitalism, it is an "anti-human culture," "a culture that is only an expression of sectional warring interests" (*H*, 12). Ngugi argues that the global circulation of neocolonial cultural images generated by intellectual centers in the North and the Northern-controlled international media maintains alienation and undermines nationalist *Bildung* through ideological brainwashing. Whereas economic globalization reshapes the material world in the image of the North, cultural globalization molds the spiritual world to perpetuate Northern hegemony.

> *The entire economic and political control is effectively facilitated by the cultural factor*.... The maintenance, management, manipulation, and mobilisation of the entire system of education, language and language use, literature, religion, the media have always ensured for the oppressor nation power over the transmission of a certain ideology, set of values, outlook, attitudes, feelings, etc. and hence *power over the whole area of consciousness*. This in turn leads to the control of the individual and collective self-image of the dominated nation and classes as well as their image of the dominating nations and classes. By thus controlling the cultural and psychological domain, the oppressor nation and classes try to ensure the situation of a slave who takes it that to be a slave is the normal human condition.
>
> (*MC*, 51, emphasis added)

Neocolonial cultural control retards the formation of a collective subject of national resistance by blunting the perceptions of mass consciousness about modern imperialism and planting doubts in the minds of the African people about the moral rightness of their struggle.

In the cultural sphere, therefore, unhealthy ingestion is an unhealthy form of *identification*. It is not only the introduction of a foreign toxin into the bloodstream but the mistaking of an alien personality for the nation's real self. Worse than ingesting poison, it is the internalization of forces within one's personality that will produce the means and desire to kill oneself. Cultural alienation is more dangerous than economic or political alienation because it makes the enemy indistinguishable from the self. It makes death the vocation of a neocolonized people. Neocolonial culture "makes [the oppressed] want to identify with that which is furthest removed from themselves.... It makes them identify with that which is decadent and reactionary, all those forces which would stop their own springs of life.... The intended results are despair, despondency and a collective deathwish" (*DM*, 3).

Echoing Fanon and Cabral, Ngugi argues that the national organism can only restore its original integrity and dynamism by transcending these oppressive conditions. The people need to recognize that neocolonial capital and its prostheses are their alienated products, which they can reappropriate. But because neocolonial cultural control obstructs this recognition, *cultural* reappropriation—the reversal of cultural alienation—is the first step to "a liberated people's consciousness and creativity" (*MC*, 57). But Ngugi's argument is riven by a fundamental ambivalence. On the one hand, since the masses are mystified by the neocolonial culture industry, cultural reappropriation will only take place if the masses are educated by the Third World writer or intellectual worker to see the truth of neocolonialism. The latter's task is to create pictures that harmonize with revolutionary forces and to be a conduit that introduces these sanguine, patriotic images into popular consciousness. When they identify with these cultural images, the oppressed masses will be instilled with hope, clarity, and strength. They will be organized and transformed into a collective subject of resistance capable of realizing their vision of a new future. In other words, the postcolonial intellectual should be the catalyst and facilitator of nationalist appropriation, which will lead to the sublation of the neocolonial system.

But the intellectual's socioeconomic position makes him or her a fundamentally ambivalent mediator, one that can either facilitate the national body's self-return or exacerbate cultural alienation and lead to deeper self-loss. First, the postcolonial intellectual can also willingly serve neocolonial interests. He or she can be "trained and cultured into drawing pictures of the world in harmony with the needs of U.S. imperialism" (*MC*, 53). Second, even benevolent intellectuals who act on behalf of the masses—and here, Ngugi includes first-generation postcolonial African leaders like Kenyatta and Nkrumah—inevitably fail to achieve a true homecoming if their thought and action remain imprisoned within European languages. The nation sends these individuals abroad to learn, but they "will never bring home their share of knowledge."[23] These intellectuals literally personify nonrecursive *techne*, instruments that refuse to be part of the organic whole.

> For Africa the thinking part of the population, the one with the pool of skills and know-how in economics, agriculture, science, engineering, is divorced from the agency of social change: the working majority. At the level of economics, science, and technology, Africa will keep on talking about transfer of technology from the West. . . . Yet the African intellectual élite, with their *episteme* and *techne*, refuse to transfer even the little they have already acquired into the language of the majority below. . . . There can be no real economic growth and development where a whole people are denied access to the latest developments in science, technology, health, medicine, business, finance, and other skills of survival because all these are stored in foreign languages.
>
> (*Penpoints*, 90)

Ngugi's well-known decision, first elaborated in *Decolonising the Mind*, to write criticism and literature in Gikuyu, is not a dogmatic nativism but a component of this larger project of nationalist appropriation.[24] Its basic premise is that a language organic to a people is the necessary precondition of a nation's spiritual and material integrity, its ability to recognize itself in and return to itself from the world. This argument inventively combines the Fichtean idea that language is the sensuous expression of a people's spiritual values with Marx's idea of "the language of actual life [*wirklichen Lebens*]," where "language *is* practical, actual consciousness."[25] An organic language is fundamental to national culture's organic development because language is the bearer and transmitter of the cultural values through which a people view themselves as a self-identical unity, an organismic whole with a particular place in the external world *and* the ability to persist, develop, and grow through historical time. "Language as culture is the collective memory bank of a people's experience in history" (*DM*, 15). But more importantly, although language is a product of history, it does not merely reflect material life. It can be an effective, actual historical cause because it is crucial to the formation of human agents. Ngugi writes:

> Language as culture is an image-forming agent in the mind of a child. Our whole conception of ourselves as a people, individually and collectively, is based on those pictures and images which may or may not correctly correspond to the actual reality of the struggles with nature

> and nurture which produced them in the first place. But our capacity to confront them creatively is dependent on how those images . . . distort or clarify the reality of our struggles. Language as culture is thus mediating between me and my own self; between my own self and other selves; between me and nature. Language is mediating in my very being.
> (*DM*, 15)

Marx's idea of language as practical consciousness only referred to its practical origins as a communicational instrument integral to the social process of creative labor. The practicality of language consists in the fact that the ideas and images it expresses are "immediately [*unmittelbar*] interwoven with the material activity and intercourse of men."[26] The agency Ngugi accords to language as culture, however, is a type of mediation that actually forms consciousness. Optimally, it should approximate or recover the immediacy of the language of actual life by drawing truthful images that enable a subject to recognize the true nature of external reality. It would then be a self-recursive mediation that facilitates the subject's self-proximity or presence to itself, thereby maintaining at the collective level the national organism's integrity. In Ngugi's words, "language is what most helps in the movement of a community from the state of being in itself to a state of being for itself and this self-awareness is what gives the community its spiritual strength to keep on reproducing its being as it continually renews itself in culture, in its power relations, and in its negotiations with its entire environment."[27] But by the same token, language can also be an agent of *constitutive* ideological alienation. Historically, the language policies of colonial regimes imposed a foreign tongue on some African peoples, which facilitated the inculcation of negative self-images through education and religious doctrine that justified colonialism as a civilizing mission. Ngugi suggests that a child educated in the colonizer's language conceptualizes in a manner utterly alien to his everyday life experiences. He is no longer at home in the immediate world of his family and community because they are seen through the culture of the imposed language. Whereas genuine *Bildung* generates living bodies, linguistic alienation produces phantasmic monstrosities. It involves

> an active (or passive) distancing of oneself from the reality around; and an active (or passive) identification with that which is most external to one's environment. It starts with a deliberate dissociation of the language of conceptualisation, of thinking, of formal education, of mental development, from the language of daily interaction in the home and in the community. It is like separating the mind from the body so

> that they are occupying two unrelated linguistic spheres in the same person. *On a larger social scale it is like producing a society of bodiless heads and headless bodies.*
>
> (*DM*, 28, emphasis added)

The postcolonial intellectual undertaking the task of radical nationalist *Bildung* must therefore contend with the historical legacy of his own formation. The intellectual must first undergo a process of counter-*Bildung* or unlearning that will return him to the masses who have not been linguistically alienated. Before the intellectual can teach the masses, he must first communicate with and learn from them, because they continue "to breathe life into our languages" and "help to keep alive the histories and cultures they carried" (*MC*, 35). But the task is problematic for Ngugi not only because it confronts the existence of a neocolonial global culture industry, but also due to the fact that most African literature is written in a colonial language. In Kenya, there is no spoken or written lingua franca that can easily be used to replace English. A critical public sphere of vernacular print needs to be created almost from scratch. But in which vernacular? Gikuyu, Swahili, Kalenjin, Somali, or one of the country's other languages?

The Onus of Narrative Fiction

Because Ngugi intends his literature to be a practical exemplar of his theoretical writings, his literary works seek to fulfill two tasks. First, they must depict the cruel reality of neocolonial Kenya in a stylistically cogent manner that will shock their implied reader, the Kenyan people. This exposure of the neocolonial state's nonsubstantial and fictional nature continues Marx's depiction of the distorted, upside-down world haunted by Monsieur le Capital and Madame la Terre. Postcolonial national *Bildung* is more challenging. Paradoxically, the neocolony's hyperbolic excesses are so normalized in daily existence that the depravity is difficult to represent fictionally. Ngugi asks:

> How does a novelist capture and hold the interest of the reader when the reality confronting the reader is stranger and more captivating than fiction? ... How do you shock your readers by pointing out that these [African leaders] are mass murderers, looters, robbers, thieves, when they, the perpetrators of these anti-people crimes, are not even attempting to hide the fact?
>
> (*DM*, 78, 80)

The same quandary also gave rise to magical realism, which in Salman Rushdie's estimation "expresses a genuinely 'Third World' consciousness" and "deals with what Naipaul has called 'half-made' societies, in which the impossibly old struggles against the appallingly new, in which public corruptions and private anguishes are somehow more garish and extreme than they ever get in the so-called 'North' where centuries of wealth and power have formed thick layers over the surface of what's really going on."[28] Ngugi's project is more affirmative. He represents degraded reality in order to sublate it. His fiction not only aims to thematically portray the national spirit's genesis from colonial resistance and its survival and promise of full actualization beyond the profane neocolonial present, but also to be an active part of its unfolding. It is intended to create a collective subject of resistance through its structure of address.

The success of Ngugi's project of cultural repatriation depends on the ability to make a rigorous distinction between good and bad prostheses, the inside and the outside. The nation can only transcend neocolonial reality if it recognizes and reappropriates its original cultural self, which has been alienated from it. If it fails to distinguish between a cultural device that is its own and one that originates from the other, it will be heteronomously determined and deprived of its bodily integrity. It is important to stress that cultural repatriation does not seal off the national body from the outside world. From *Petals of Blood* (1978) onwards, Ngugi's fiction welds the revived Christian topos of incarnation to a Marxist discourse of transcendence, on the basis that revolutionary nationalism expresses the true content or rational kernel of historical-positive forms of Christian doctrine because it locates the true God in the people, even though both Marxism and the Bible are foreign imports, and Christian education, which preaches quietism, is complicit with British colonialism and contemporary neocolonialism. These appropriations indicate again that Ngugi's revolutionary nationalism is not a nativism but a process of *Bildung*, in which the nation can digest foreign elements and make them part of its organic body. The problem lies rather with foreign prostheses that are mistaken as part of oneself and expose the nation to the perpetual risk of losing itself without the possibility of return. We have already broached the possibility of irretrievable self-loss in terms of the ambivalent sociological figure of the postcolonial intellectual, who is simultaneously the exemplary agent of cultural repatriation and also the most likely channel for neocolonial cultural influences. But in its thematization of national incarnation, does Ngugi's own fiction convincingly demarcate good prostheses from bad, the living body from death?

Monstrous Bodies and Non-Functional Organs

Ngugi's novels evoke the nation's birth and imminent resurrection through recurring images of pregnancy. But because the nation cannot be fully incarnated within a neocolonial order, the portrayal of decolonization is not marked by the unqualified euphoria that greets an infant's accomplished delivery but by anxious expectation. In Ngugi's earlier novels, this sense of foreboding always gives way to a redemptive hope that the degraded present will be transcended. In stark contradistinction, the figure of pregnancy in *Devil on the Cross* is marked by a radical ambivalence. Muturi, a former freedom fighter and the personification of the urban proletariat, observes, "This country, our country, is pregnant. What it will give birth to, God only knows.... Our country should have given birth to its offspring long ago.... What it lacks now is a midwife.... The question is this: who is responsible for the pregnancy?"[29] This rich allegorical question could be soliciting the identity of the midwife who can facilitate the birth of a new national existence without exploitation and suffering. But it could also be pointing to the indeterminate parentage of the fetus. For under a neocolonial regime, it is unclear whether what is awaiting birth is the child of God or the child of the Devil, the living people or dead capital.

For the most part, the novel seems to support the first interpretation. Its plot charts the *Bildung* of its two main protagonists, Wariinga, a village girl forced to become a secretary in Nairobi after being seduced and abandoned by a rich old man (the archetypal tale of "traditional" patriarchal oppression of women), and Gatuiria, a research fellow in the music department at the University of Nairobi, who plans to compose "a truly national piece of music," an oratorio for an orchestra made up of the instruments of all the Kenyan nationalities (*DC*, 60). They embark on a journey from Nairobi to Ilmorog in a shared cab where they meet Muturi, Wangari, a representative of the peasantry, and other sociological types. Along the way, they attend a Devil's Feast, the novel's set-piece, where various indigenous capitalists compete for the title of the King of Theft and Robbery, and witness a failed uprising against neocolonial forces. Wariinga also meets the Devil on a golf course and resists his temptations. Wariinga's and Gatuiria's romantic relationship is an icon of the alliance between the organic intellectual and the masses that will engender a corporeally self-proximate nation. The organic intellectual who creates a patriotic culture that displaces the ideological myths of neocolonial culture is both father and midwife who guides the nation into healthy life.

Accordingly, the novel repeatedly juxtaposes two different forms of corporeal augmentation. On the one hand, augmentation through human labor and social cooperation is salutary. It forms a collective human heart, a humanity that transcends the circuit of exchange.[30] Communal endeavors are figured as the mutual cooperation and interdependence of corporeal organs. On the other hand, the novel is filled with images of the national body's profanation by neocolonial forces that oppress creative labor and suppress humanity. As Muturi puts it, "there are two hearts: the heart built by the clan of parasites, the evil heart; and the heart built by the clan of producers, the good heart" (*DC*, 53–54). At the Devil's Feast, one competitor dreams of becoming the personification of capital's prosthetic powers. He wishes to set up a factory that can manufacture spare parts for the human body so that the rich man can be the prosthetic body *par excellence*: "every rich man could have two mouths, two bellies, two cocks, two hearts—and hence two lives! Our money would buy us immortality! We would leave death to the poor!" (*DC*, 181). In a grotesque reinscription of the Marxian topos of man's enslavement by the machine, another competitor wants to set up a farm where electrical machines are attached to the bodies of workers to milk their sweat, blood, and brains for commodification and export to feed foreign industry (*DC*, 188–89).

In an earlier speech, Gatuiria had attempted to locate the origin of exploitation definitively in a foreign source. "Kenya, our country," he asserts, "has no killers or eaters of men, people who drink blood and kidnap the shadows of other men" (*DC*, 67). However, the grotesque images of the Devil's Feast depict the form of alienation Ngugi fears most. The postindependence state, originally intended as an instrument of popular interests, has become a prosthesis serving the indigenous bourgeoisie, the agents of global capital, and has so completely possessed the nation-people that they are not aware of their own exploitation. This is, in other words, an alienation that originates from within the nation itself, where the foreign prosthetic body becomes indistinguishable from the real body and death emerges from within life itself.

Ngugi attempts to maintain the boundary between life and death by counterposing the living nation to these images of living death. As the novel draws to a close, two years after the initial journey, Wariinga has earned the right to assume the authority of the national voice. Politically educated about the structural-systemic causes of her past sufferings, she now earns a living as a mechanic. In a blazonlike sequence, the narrator celebrates Wariinga as the personification of the self-reliant, organically united popular-national body:

> The Wariinga of today has decided to be self-reliant all the time, to plunge into the middle of the arena of life's struggles in order to discover her real strength and to realize her true humanity.... Today, Wariinga strides along with energy and purpose, her dark eyes radiating the light of an inner courage ... the courage and faith of someone who has achieved something through self-reliance. What's the use of shuffling along timidly in one's own country? ... Wariinga of the mind and hands and body and heart, walking in the rhythmic harmony of life's journey! Wariinga, the worker!
>
> (*DC*, 216–18)

The novel's final chapter is set on the day of her wedding to Gatuiria. This consummation would be an apposite figure of the nation's teleological promise, since it symbolizes the union of the intellectual with the worker necessary to cultural repatriation. But this consummation does not take place. The nation's resurrection is indefinitely deferred. As it turns out, Gatuiria's father is the rich old capitalist who had seduced and abandoned Wariinga. Transfigured into "a people's judge," Wariinga shoots him and departs, miraculously unrestrained, into a utopian horizon (*DC*, 253). But Gatuiria cannot follow her because he is unable to renounce his class and family ties: "Gatuiria did not know what to do: to deal with his father's body, to comfort his mother or to follow Wariinga. So he just stood in the courtyard, hearing in his mind music that led him nowhere" (*DC*, 254). Here is how the novel ends: "Wariinga walked on, without once looking back. But she knew with all her heart that the hardest struggles of her life's journey lay ahead" (*DC*, 254).

The ending is simultaneously a step forward and a moment of paralysis. The utopian moment of poetic justice and Wariinga's flight is the projection of the nation's future coming-to-be, the promise of the negation and transcendence of the neocolonial system in the form of a deferred hope. But this figuration of teleological time is also arrested and interrupted. In Ngugi's theory of national *Bildung*, the postcolonial intellectual is an important agent in the freeing of the national body from possession by death-dealing prostheses it mistakes for its real self. Yet in the ending, the agent of corporeal self-proximity becomes a nonrecursive, inorganic prosthesis that blocks the teleological time of national incarnation. Frozen into corpselike inaction, Gatuiria "stood there in the yard, as if he had lost the use of his tongue, his arms, his legs" (*DC*, 254).

Devil on the Cross thus dramatizes the issue of how the postcolonial intellectual's socioeconomic status on the margins of the same class as the comprador elite makes him a chameleon with a vacillating social and psychological make-up, able to collaborate with reactionary forces or to serve the masses. Earlier, the problem is phrased as a repeated question lodged within Wariinga's and Gatuiria's streams of consciousness:

> We the intellectuals among the workers, which side are we on? . . . Are we like the hyena which tried to walk along two different roads at the same time? Wariinga . . . was pursuing similar thoughts: We who work as clerks, copy typists and secretaries, which side are we on? . . . Who are *we*? Who are *we*? Who are *we*? Wariinga's heart beat in time to her question, raising problems to which nobody could provide her with solutions because they concerned the decision she would have to make herself about the side she would choose in life's struggle.
>
> (*DC*, 205–6)

The novel aims to induce the same self-questioning in its Kenyan reader.

Now, this rich Marxist theme of the intellectual's social-political responsibility has only ever been posed as a *sociological* question, in terms of the individual moral-existential choices of the privileged life form we call *human*. In fact, it raises the more profound question of culture's *formative* role in nationalist appropriation. For the intellectual only has this effect on postcolonial national *Bildung* because Ngugi views nationalist culture as an exemplary prosthetic process that maximizes the nation's capacity for life. This means that the impossibility of definitively distinguishing between good and bad prostheses is logically implied in the idea of *Bildung*. One has to remember that the culture-concept refers to a self-directed process of cultivation according to a rational-ideal image. *Bildung* presupposes an inner susceptibility to the prosthetic use of images. The danger of (dis)possession by alien prostheses thus arises from the initial possibility of supplementing/completing one's personality or proper self with an image. The postcolonial intellectual's Januslike oscillation is merely a case of this deadly expropriation that shadows and complicates postcolonial nationalist appropriation.

The Surviving of Surviving

The nation is subject to a similar dispossession even in *Matigari*, which assumes that the popular nation has been incarnated and actively challenges the neocolonial state. *Matigari*'s primary concern is not the intellectual's equivocation about the rightness of nationalist appropriation. The struggle's universal imperativity is asserted and the reader is drawn into the nation's teleological time by a contract that must be accepted before stepping across the book's threshold: "Reader/listener: may you allocate the duration of any actions according to your choice! ... So say yes, and I'll tell you a story! Once upon a time, in a country with no name ..."[31] The nation's incarnation is embodied in the book's title character, Matigari ma Njiruungi, a messianic Christlike figure, whose name, a footnote in the translation tells us, means "'the patriots who survived the bullets'—the patriots who survived the liberation war, and their political offspring" (*M*, 20).[32] He has buried his weapons, put on the belt of peace, and seeks to return home. As a common noun, then, "Matigari" refers to the patriot, an exemplary member of the nation. It is the mark of *survival*, the nation's survival after colonialism, and the promise of its survival beyond neocolonialism, "in a future time when," as Simon Gikandi puts it, "the 'Matigaris' would return from the forest to reverse the betrayal of independence."[33] When Guthera, the main female character, hears Matigari's name, she says, "a patriot? Are you one of those left behind in the forest to keep the fire of freedom alive?" (*M*, 37)

An allegory for the unfinished nationalist project, Matigari's homecoming is an attempt to find habitation in one's land when it has become so alien that it is no longer a home, a place to which one belongs. His repatriation thus involves at least two tasks. First, there is no returning home until the home belongs to one, that is, until political and economic alienation have been overcome. Ngugi figures the people's reappropriation of the country's economic infrastructure and political superstructures as Matigari's attempt to repossess and rebuild his house. But this is not enough, for the home is not an empty edifice but the seat of organic familial generation. As Matigari keeps repeating, he will not go home until he has found his people: "he reminded himself that he had not yet found his people. He could not go home alone" (*M*, 12). The children are a synecdoche for the people. They can inherit and defend the home in the future by assuming the nationalist vocation. "A child belongs to all," Matigari observes, "a nation's beauty was borne in a child, a future patriot" (*M*, 48). Colonial education is a sin because it steals the nation's future by corrupting the children of the indigenous elite. But the neocolonial state commits an even more heinous crime. When Matigari attempts to tell the children that "the years of roaming and wandering are over," that they "shall all go home together," he discovers that the children of the masses have been dispossessed (*M*, 10).[34] They have become street urchins who live in a scrapyard, in the shells of discarded foreign cars, so dehumanized that they fight amongst themselves like scavenging animals.

As he wanders throughout the country seeking truth and justice, Matigari is absolutely confident in the nation's second coming. Thrown into prison, he tells his fellow prisoners that "truth never dies, therefore, truth will reign in the end, even if it does not reign today. My house is my house. I am only after what I have built with my own hands. Tomorrow belongs to me. I invite you all to my house the day after tomorrow. Come to a feast and celebrate our homecoming!" (*M*, 64). As word of his deeds spreads after his miraculous escape from prison, he becomes a mythical figure who threatens the state by challenging its official views of reality. He is likened to Christ and Marx. Commentators have been critical of Ngugi's mystical portrayal of Matigari, arguing that his supernatural powers undermine the historical-realist aspects of the novel that are more appropriate to the portrayal of Kenyan politics.[35] But this misses the point that Matigari is not a realistic character but the personification of the national spirit. Matigari himself points out that he embodies the entire history of nationalist struggle: "I did not begin yesterday. I have seen many things over the years. Just consider, I was there at the time of the Portuguese, at the time of the Arabs, and at the time of the British" (*M*, 45).

Hence, although the rumors about Matigari are not empirically true (we find out that he escapes from the prison not because he made the prison walls open but because Guthera gave herself to a policeman and stole his keys), and although he displays all the attributes of a finite person, for instance, the political naïveté of someone out of touch with the contemporary world, his intentions and actions still represent a higher truth. This truth is neither the reflection of empirical reality governed by immutable mechanical causal laws nor the official interpretation of reality disseminated by the Ministry of Truth and Justice through its radio program, the Voice of Truth, to justify neocolonial exploitation as an unchangeable reality. It is a projected future reality that is reconciled with human ideals and has greater actuality than the neocolonial state. Matigari's truth is ontological and performative. It concerns a transfigured reality that will arise from united human labor: "The children would come out of this graveyard into which their lives had been condemned. They would build their lives anew in the unity of their common sweat. A new house. A paradise on earth. Why not? There is nothing that a people united cannot do" (*M*, 16).

Indeed, what is of primary importance about Matigari's appearance in the narrative present is his amorphousness and nondeterminability, the impossibility of locating him in a physiological individual. Even as a proper name, "Matigari" refers to a shape that seems to mutate endlessly by feeding off the energy of the people who talk about him, so much so that the soldiers who try to capture him cannot determine who or what he is: "Who is Matigari? ... How on earth are we going to recognise him? What does he look like? What nationality is he? Is Matigari a man or woman anyway? Is he young or old? Is he fat or thin? Is he real or just a figment of the people's imagination? Who or what really *is* Matigari ma Njiruungi? Is he a person, or is it a spirit?" (*M*, 170). Paradoxically, Matigari's effectivity does not lie in whether his actions are believable to the novel's other characters (and by implication, to the reader), but in the commotion he generates. His fabulous qualities lead to the diffusion and dissolution of his proper name into a common noun, "patriot," which can apply to all the people. The novel depicts this dramatically in the form of a question the people repeatedly ask themselves: "Who is Matigari ma Njiruungi?" That is, who is the patriot? The refrain, which spreads through the entire country each time his parable is transmitted through oral narrative, also serves as an interpellative structure that reincarnates the imagined community of the nation.

But unlike the formally similar "Who are we?" in *Devil on the Cross*, this refrain does not lead to an equivocation in the questioning subject's personality. It is more like a rhetorical question that suggests the answer in advance, where the speaker-cum-addressee is supposed to reply, "I am Matigari," or at least, "I can be Matigari." As long as the people think that Matigari is a messiah who will miraculously save them, the nation will never be reincarnated. It will only be actualized if the proper name is dissolved into a common noun, appropriated by each person through a commitment to patriotic action. The teleological time of nationalist appropriation is a practical-humanist messianism. Matigari tells the children that

> the God who is prophesied is in you, in me and in the other humans. He has always been there inside us since the beginning of time. Imperialism tried to kill that God within us. But one day that God will return from the dead.... He will return on the day when His followers will be able to ... say in one voice: Our labour produced all the wealth in this land.... Let the earth return to those to whom it belongs.... But that God lives more in you children of this land; and therefore if you let the country go to the imperialist enemy and its local watchdogs, it is the same as killing the God who is inside you. It is the same thing as stopping Him from resurrecting. That God will come back only when you want Him to.
>
> (*M*, 156)

Despite the patriarchal nature of Ngugi's vision—Guthera is a Mary Magdalene figure whose role is to aid Matigari—*Matigari* is a more successful attempt at nationalist *Bildung* than *Devil on the Cross* because it draws more hopeful images. In sharp contrast to Gatuiria's indecision and the failed student uprising in the earlier novel, Matigari decides that justice cannot be achieved by peaceful means. He burns down the house of John Boy, Jr., the son of the cook of his former settler employer, who has now become a rich landowner, and vows to build a bigger house with better foundations. Led by chants from the children, the gathering crowd sets fire to the cars and houses of other comprador tycoons. Although Matigari dies at the end of the novel, he is succeeded by Muriuki (the Resurrected), a street child who has retrieved his guns and inherited his mantle.

But this is only a novelistic depiction of how the nation survives and reincarnates itself through the interpellative power of oral narrative. The more important question is whether *Matigari*, the book, has been as successful in interpellating its readers in the real world as the character in its fictional world. In other words, does the novel also successfully embody and perform what it thematizes such that it is a self-recursive cultural prosthesis that prepares the way for the popular reappropriation of the neocolonial state? And is its performance of the nation's survival a full reincarnation or merely a haunting of the state? The book conjured up a specter that haunted the Moi regime, which tried to arrest Matigari and then banned the book. Under such conditions, the theme of survival is necessarily doubled. One must consider how the novel *qua* embodiment of the nation's survival itself survives. Perpetually shadowed by state censorship, the survival of survival becomes problematic enough to cause the teleological time of nationalist appropriation to waver.

Like *Devil on the Cross*, Ngugi wrote *Matigari* in Gikuyu, incorporating elements of orature, popular music, and culture so that through oral performance, it would become organic to the Kenyan people and organize them into a collective subject of resistance. Through his commitment to the nationalist struggle, he tries to solve by personal example the problem of the intellectual as nonrecursive *techne* Gatuiria personified. But despite his best intentions, the combined effect of political exile and censorship has not been salutary. In the first place, as Christopher Wise points out, however much they may try to simulate orature, "authentic" novels are not oral narratives like the West African griot epic because they lack the face-to-face communal setting of the griot's performance and the dynamism of the story's repeated regeneration and transformation through collaborative work with different audiences.[36] One can of course argue that novels can be converted into oral narratives through public readings, as *Matigari* presumably was. But even here, censorship generates a ghostly supplement that haunts and undermines the living Gikuyu original even as it enables its survival. The novel survives predominantly in its English translation. But this means that many specific historical connotations that threatened the neocolonial state's rhetoric and activity are lost.[37] For instance, the novel's title loses its Mau Mau allusions and simply becomes the central character's name. But more importantly, the need for an English translation also ironically integrates Ngugi into the global circuit of cultural commodification, which assists the usurpation of the original by its English double. As Simon Gikandi notes:

> The two texts function in a political situation where English is more powerful than Gikuyu.... The eloquent English translation of *Matigari Ma Njiruungi* defeats Ngugi's intention of restoring the primacy of the African language as the mediator of an African experience. The act of translation is hence a double-edged weapon: it allows Ngugi's text to survive and to be read, but it is read and discussed as if it were a novel in English.[38]

Matigari survives uncannily, out of its proper home, and becomes generally inaccessible to its intended audience, the Kenyan masses. But it can only live on by being misdestined to the North Atlantic, where it becomes part of "African national culture," a commodified cultural identity within the international circuit of cultural exchange and consumption. Indeed, the global *academic* industry may even have infected the aims of Ngugi's critical writings from the early 1990s onward. Simon Gikandi suggests that as a political exile Ngugi no longer shares the same communicative sphere as his intended audience, the Kenyan people. Hence, even *Mutiiri*, the Gikuyu journal he started, is "driven not so much by the concerns of Kenyan workers and peasants, but by the rhetoric of American identity politics and postcolonial nostalgia."[39] We should, however, not confuse the uncanniness of the Kenyan national spirit with a celebration of diasporic transnationalism. Ngugi's desire for repatriation is patent. The melancholy irony is that the combined effects of neocolonial oppression, geographical deterritorialization, translation, and the global culture industry are such that national culture necessarily undergoes an accompanying alienation in its attempt to be the people's self-recursive mediation. Intended as linguistic repatriation, the act of writing in Gikuyu subjects the project of homecoming to an expropriating movement.

One can understand the dilemmas of Ngugi's project of nationalist *Bildung* in at least three ways. Following the Third Worldist nationalist position associated with Bandung, one can argue that they indicate the limits of the current conjuncture. Although the nation cannot fully incarnate itself because national reappropriation at the economic, political, and cultural level has not been accomplished, it will be able to transcend the neocolonial world-system in due time. Conversely, one can argue that Third Worldist nationalist appropriation has entered its terminal phase today. Other signs of its impending demise would include the nation's fragmentation by tribal or ethnic conflict, the lack of a historical-material basis for utopian or messianic visions of popular struggle united by socialist ideals such as Ngugi's, and the inherent violence of nationalism, which imposes a false unity that is rapidly undermined by contemporary globalization. The primary rational-choice policy suggestions for solving the African tragedy endorsed by international agencies are either the neoclassical model of a noninterventionist state, market liberalization, and structural adjustment, with the aims of attracting foreign investment and creating an export-oriented industrial economy, or the East Asian model of hyperdevelopment (as opposed to African under-development) under a strong state with an effective bureaucracy, following the examples of South Korea, Taiwan, and Singapore.[40] A recent post–Cold War variation has also stressed the importance of formal democratic reform, which provides a secure environment for foreign investment, and which is sometimes tied to foreign aid.[41]

Although these rational-choice policies differ in content from Third Worldist nationalism, they are underwritten by the same concepts of appropriation and incarnation. Echoing in degrees Kant's faith in world trade and Hegel's statism, they see themselves as better institutional models for the incarnation of freedom. Yet it is not clear that they can alleviate the neocolonial dereliction Ngugi depicts. The Asian economic model lost its shine after the financial crisis of 1997. The intellectual critique of American neoliberalism's hypocritical and destructive nature has been painfully confirmed in the public imagination by the corporate management scandals of 2002.[42] But more importantly, they fail to address the uneven, exploitative character of the global capitalist system. As Giovanni Arrighi observes:

> For the casualties of so-called globalization, first and foremost the peoples of Sub-Saharan Africa ... the real problem is that some countries or regions have the power to make the world market work to their advantage, while others do not, and have to bear the costs. This power ... has ... deep roots in a particular historical heritage that positions a country or a region favourably or unfavourably in relation to structural and conjunctural processes within the world system.[43]

If we accept that a progressive nationalism making demands on the state with the aim of achieving the people's repatriation and reappropriation of their alienated products still remains important in the current conjuncture, we can understand the troubled character of Ngugi's nationalist *Bildung* in yet another way. It can be seen as a *problematization* of the Marxist concept of appropriation, and more generally, the idea of freedom as the power of self-incarnation and self-actualization typified by culture's self-recursive causality. It indicates that repatriation through nationalist *Bildung* is always haunted, that nationalist appropriation is always marked by a certain kind of death. The notion of "the people" finds itself constitutively inscribed within a global force field that it cannot transcend or control in its efforts to return to itself. Even socially sustainable development requires foreign capital, which makes the nation vulnerable to financialization and other foreign prosthetic processes. This sheer vulnerability is constitutive of *Bildung* as self-recursive mediation. Despite his intentions, Ngugi illustrates that the nation survives through a certain corruption. It undergoes alienation when it attempts cultural reappropriation. The dialectic of property and appropriation must be reformulated to take into account what Jacques Derrida has called "paradoxical ex-appropriation, [the] movement of the proper expropriating itself through the very process of appropriation."[44] But since the movement of ex-appropriation exceeds contradiction and negativity, this may require leaving behind dialectical logic itself.

Notes

1. C. L. R. James, *Notes on Dialectics* (London: Allison and Busby, 1948), 131.
2. Ibid., 152.
3. For Marx, labor is a form of autocausality, a process of self-actualization ontologically unique to humanity. Labor's defining feature is the ability to incarnate ideas and actualize the potentiality in nature and the human subject as part of nature. When we produce the material conditions of life, we *rationally* produce our means of subsistence (*Lebensmittel*). See Karl Marx, *Das Kapital, Kritik der politischen Ökonomie, Erster Band* (Hamburg, 1890); *Karl Marx Friedrich Engels Gesamtausgabe*, ed. Institut für Marxismus-Leninismus (Berlin: Dietz, 1973–), 2.10: 162; *Capital: A Critique of Political Economy*, vol. 1, trans. Ben Fowkes (Harmondsworth: Penguin, 1976), 284. Hereafter *K1*.
4. See *Ökonomisch-philosophische Manuskripte (Zweite Wiedergabe)*, *Karl Marx Friedrich Engels Gesamtausgabe*, ed. Institut für Marxismus-Leninismus (Berlin: Dietz, 1973–), 1.2: 390; "Economic and Philosophical Manuscripts," in *Early Writings*,

trans. Rodney Livingstone and Gregor Benton (Harmondsworth: Penguin, 1975), 349: "Activity and consumption, both in their content and in their *mode of existence*, are *social* activity and *social* consumption. The *human* essence of nature exists only for *social* man; for only here does nature exist for him as a *bond* with other *men*, as his existence for others and their existence for him, as the vital element of human actuality; only here does it exist as the *basis* of his own *human* existence." Hereafter *OPM*.

5. *Die Deutsche Ideologie*, in *Marx/Engels Gesamtausgabe*, ed. V. Adoratskij (Berlin: Marx-Engels Verlag, 1932), 1: 5, 57–58; *The German Ideology*, 3rd rev. ed. (Moscow: Progress Publishers, 1976), 96–97.

6. Amilcar Cabral, "Presuppositions and Objectives of National Liberation in Relation to Social Structure," in *Unity and Struggle: Speeches and Writings*, trans. Michael Wolfers (New York: Monthly Review, 1979), 130.

7. For accounts of the Eurocentrism of Lenin's position on non-European nationalism and his support for a tactical concilation with bourgeois nationalism, dissenting voices in the Comintern (Third International) meetings by M. N. Roy and others who favored a more revolutionary form of nationalism, the growing independence of Chinese communism under Mao from Soviet-style internationalism, and the relationship between Communism and nationalism in Latin America and Africa, see Hélène Carrère d'Encausse and Stuart R. Schram, eds., *Marxism and Asia* (Baltimore: Penguin, 1969); Horace B. Davis, *Toward a Marxist Theory of Nationalism* (New York: Monthly Review, 1978), 165–246; and Ronaldo Munck, *The Difficult Dialogue* (London: Zed, 1986), 88–125.

8. Cabral, "Presuppositions and Objectives," 130.

9. Cabral, "National Liberation and Culture," in *Unity and Struggle: Speeches and Writings*, trans. Michael Wolfers (New York: Monthly Review, 1979), 143.

10. See Colin Leys, *Underdevelopment in Kenya: The Political Economy of Neo-Colonialism* (London: Heinemann, 1975); Colin Leys, "Confronting the African Tragedy," *New Left Review* 204 (March–April 1994): 33–47; and Giovanni Arrighi, "The African Crisis: World Systemic and Regional Aspects," *New Left Review* 15 (May–June 2002): 7–36.

11. The *OED* states that as a medical term, it refers to "that part of surgery which consists in supplying deficiencies, as by artificial limbs, teeth, etc." Websters stresses that the original body is "human" and the addition is "an artificial part."

12. Ngugi Wa Thiong'o, *Moving the Centre: The Struggle for Cultural Freedoms* (Portsmouth, N.H.: Heinemann, 1993), xv–vi. Hereafter *MC*.

13. Ngugi Wa Thiong'o, "Moving the Center: An Interview by Charles Cantalupo," *Paintbrush* 20, no. 39–40 (Spring–Autumn 1993): 215. Hereafter "Cantalupo Interview."

14. W. R. Ochieng and E. S. Atieno-Odhiambo, "Prologue: On Decolonization," in *Decolonization and Independence in Kenya*, ed. B.A. Ogot and W. R. Ochieng (London: Currey, 1996), xiv.

15. Jennifer A. Widner, *The Rise of a Party-State in Kenya: From Harambee! to Nyayo!* (Berkeley: University of California Press, 1992), 5–6.

16. See William Acworth, "Interview with Ngugi wa Thiong'o," *Ufahamu: Journal of the African Activist Association* 18, no. 2 (Spring 1990): 42–43.

17. "Cantalupo Interview," 223.

18. Ngugi Wa Thiong'o, "Towards a National Culture," in *Homecoming: Essays on African and Caribbean Literature, Culture, and Politics* (London: Heinemann, 1972), 4, 12. Hereafter *H*.

19. Ibid., 11–12.

20. Ngugi Wa Thiong'o, *Decolonising the Mind: The Politics of Language in African Literature* (Portsmouth, N.H.: Heinemann, 1986), 2. Hereafter *DM*. This symbiosis is also seen in the connection Ngugi draws between Africanization and the socialization of political and economic life and between African communalism and socialism.

21. Ngugi Wa Thiong'o, *Barrel of a Pen: Resistance to Repression in Neo-Colonial Kenya* (Trenton, N.J.: Africa World Press, 1983), 90.

22. Chinua Achebe, *Hopes and Impediments: Selected Essays* (New York: Doubleday, 1989), 45; 139.

23. Ngugi Wa Thiong'o, *Penpoints, Gunpoints, and Dreams: Towards a Critical Theory of the Arts and the State in Africa* (Oxford: Clarendon, 1998), 89. Hereafter *Penpoints*.

24. For a fuller discussion, see Simon Gikandi, "Ngugi's Conversion: Writing and the Politics of Language," *Research in African Literatures* 23, no. 1 (Spring 1992): 131–144; and Modhumita Roy, "Writers and Politics/Writers in Politics: Ngugi and the Language Question," in *Ngugi wa Thiong'o: Texts and Contexts*, ed. Charles Cantalupo (Trenton, N.J.: Africa World Press, 1995): 165–185.

25. Marx, *Die Deutsche Ideologie*, 15; 42 and 20; 49.

26. Ibid., 15; 42.

27. Ngugi Wa Thiong'o, "Europhonism, Universities, and the Magic Fountain: The Future of African Literature and Scholarship," *Research in African Literatures* 31, no. 1 (Spring 2000): 3.

28. Salman Rushdie, *Imaginary Homelands: Essays and Criticism, 1981–1991* (London: Granta, 1992), 301–302.

29. Ngugi Wa Thiong'o, *Devil on the Cross* (Portsmouth, N.H.: Heinemann, 1982), 45–46. Hereafter *DC*.

30. See Muturi's speech in *DC*, 51–53.

31. Ngugi Wa Thiong'o, *Matigari* (Portsmouth, N.H.: Heinemann, 1989), ix. Hereafter *M*.

32. Simon Gikandi notes that "Matigari" was "a reference to leftovers of food or dregs in drinks," but around 1963, it became a signifier for the Mau Mau and referred to recalcitrant independence fighters who remained in the forest, whom the Kenyatta regime regarded as a threat. Simon Gikandi, "The Epistemology of Translation: Ngugi, *Matigari*, and the Politics of Language," *Research in African Literatures* 22, no. 4 (Winter 1991): 161–162.

33. Ibid., 162.

34. See *Juvenile Injustice: Police Abuse and Detention of Street Children in Kenya*, Human Rights Watch Report, June 1997.

35. See Lewis Nkosi, "Reading *Matigari*: The New Novel of Independence," *Paintbrush* 20, no. 39–40 (Spring–Autumn 1993): 197–205; and Simon Gikandi, "The Epistemology of Translation." Both view this as evidence of a crisis of representation in the postcolonial African novel. See also Simon Gikandi, "The Politics and Poetics of National Formation: Recent African Writing," in *From Commonwealth to Postcolonial*, ed. Anna Rutherford, 259–275 (Sydney: Dangaroo, 1992). James Ogude, *Ngugi's Novels and African History* (London: Pluto, 1999) argues that Ngugi has an idealistic view of historical change that is not anchored in reality.

36. Christopher Wise, "Resurrecting the Devil: Notes on Ngugi's Theory of the Oral-Aural African Novel," *Research in African Literatures* 28, no. 1 (Spring 1997): 134–140.

37. This and the following arguments in this paragraph come from Simon Gikandi, "The Epistemology of Translation," 165–167.

38. Ibid., 166. For a fascinating analysis of the Anglocentric nature of academic scholarship on African literature, see Bernth Lindfors, "Sites of Production of African Literature Scholarship," *Ariel: A Review of International English Literature* 31, no. 1–2 (Jan.–Apr. 2000): 153–177. Lindfors notes (1) the lack of conversation between non-African and African scholars; (2) that no book has been written about Ngugi in an African language; (3) that since 1973, Kenyans have only produced six book-chapters on Ngugi, four of which were for books published outside Africa, whereas non-Africans have written sixty-eight book-chapters, most of which were published outside Africa; and (4) that Ngugi is well-known abroad but has not been introduced to other language groups in Kenya.

39. Simon Gikandi, "Traveling Theory: Ngugi's Return to English," *Research in African Literatures* 31, no. 2 (Summer 2000): 194.

40. Following the Berg Report of 1981, the World Bank endorsed the first model in the 1980s, but abandoned it by 1997. See Giovanni Arrighi, "The African Crisis," 5–10. On the East Asian model, see Howard Stein, ed., *Asian Industrialization and Africa: Studies in Policy Alternatives to Structural Adjustment* (New York: St. Martin's, 1995). Some of these ideas have influenced African leaders. See Richard W. Stevenson, "Africa Decides to Flirt with Free-Market Capitalism," *New York Times*, June 2, 2002, available online at http://www.nytimes.com/2002/06/02/weekinreview/02STEV.html.

41. See Rachel L. Swarns and Norimitsu Onishi, "Africa Creeps Along Path to Democracy," *New York Times*, June 2, 2002, available online at http://www.nytimes.com /2002/06/02/international/ africa/02DEMO.html; and Daniel Yergin, "Giving Aid to World Trade," *New York Times*, June 27, 2002, available online at http://www.nytimes.com/2002/06/27/opinion/27YERG.html.

42. See Joseph E. Stiglitz, *Globalization and Its Discontents* (New York : Norton, 2002); Robert Brenner, *The Boom and the Bubble: the U.S. in the World Economy*

(New York: Verso, 2002); and Edmund L. Andrews, "U.S. Businesses Dim as Models for Foreigners," *New York Times*, June 27, 2002, available online at http://www.nytimes.com/2002/06/27/business/27GLOB.html.

43. Arrighi, "The African Crisis," 34.

44. Jacques Derrida, "Politics and Friendship," in *The Althusserian Legacy*, ed. E. Ann Kaplan and Michael Sprinker (New York: Verso, 1993), 223.

3 Transnational Topographies of Power

Beyond "The State" and "Civil Society" in the Study of African Politics

James G. Ferguson

Introduction

The collective project to which this volume is devoted is that of exploring the future of property and the forces of globalization. But one cannot get far in thinking about "the forces of globalization" without encountering what one might call "the *concepts* of globalization." By this I mean both the concepts upon which the process of globalization produces and relies, and the (necessarily overlapping) analytic concepts we scholars use to grasp this process. I have in mind such concepts as "transnational," "multicultural," "flows," "diversity," "privatization," as well as "civil society," which in this essay is my specific concern. The critical interrogation of one of these "concepts of globalization" might prove a productive site for an exchange between the empirical study of social and political processes in southern Africa (where we meet "the forces of globalization" in the flesh, so to speak) and critical theory, with its traditional emphasis on the analysis and historical contextualization of concepts. Like theories, concepts are social creatures; as Said (1983) has reminded us, they take on new meanings and new functions when they travel. And the concept of "civil society" has been doing a lot of traveling lately. In particular, it has become an inescapable feature of the discussion on the state and democracy in Africa.

The fad for "civil society" has been perhaps most in evidence among political scientists, who have been understandably eager to leave behind their cold war paradigms for livelier topics such as democratization, social movements, and what they call "state/society relations." But anthropologists, too, have been bitten by the bug, finding in "civil society" a new and improved incarnation of their old disciplinary trademark, "the local." Rising numbers of anthropology dissertation students are nowadays heading out to "the field," not in search of an intriguing culture or a promising village, but rather an interesting NGO. But if such anthropological engagements are to be fruitful, it will be necessary to devote some critical scrutiny to the common-sense mapping of political and social space that the state/civil society opposition takes for granted. Beginning with the category "civil society" itself, I will try to show how the state/civil society opposition forms part of an even more pervasive way of thinking about the analytic "levels" of local, national, and global—a way of thinking that rests on what I call the *vertical topography of power*. I will argue that calling into question this vertical topography of power brings into view the transnational character of both "state" and "civil society," and opens up new ways of thinking about both social movements and states.

I will not attempt a genealogy of the term "civil society," but will only note a few aspects of the changes in its meaning. Its origins are customarily traced to eighteenth-century liberal thought, and especially to Scottish Enlightenment thinkers such as Francis Hutcheson, Adam Ferguson, and later, Adam Smith, in whose thought the term is associated both with the developing conceptualization of society as a self-regulating mechanism and with concepts of natural law. Better known to many is the Hegelian usage of the term to denote an intermediary domain between the universal ideal of the state and the concrete particularity of the family, a conception famously critiqued by Marx and imaginatively reworked by Gramsci. Today, the term most often comes up in discussions of democracy, especially to refer to voluntary or so-called NGOs—nongovernmental organizations that seek to influence or claim space from the state.

The term "civil society" still had a rather antique cast to it when I first encountered it in graduate seminars on social theory. But since then, it has gotten a new lease on life, chiefly thanks to the dramatic recent political history of Eastern Europe (Keane 1988; Seligman 1992). There, of course, communism had promised to lead to the gradual demise of the state. But instead, the state swallowed up everything in its path, leaving behind no social force—neither private businesses, nor church, nor political party—capable of checking its monstrous powers. It was not the state but rather civil society that had "withered away." In this historically specific context, the old term had a remarkable resonance, and it licensed otherwise unlikely coalitions between actors, from dissident writers to the Catholic Church, who had in common only that they demanded some space, autonomy, and freedom from the totalitarian state.

Coming out of this rather peculiar and particular history, the term "civil society" came for many to be almost interchangeable with the concept of democracy itself—nearly reversing the terms of Marx's famous critique, which had revealed the imaginary freedoms of capitalism's democratic political realm as an illusion, one to be contrasted against the real *unfreedom* of "civil society," conceived as the domain of alienation, economic domination, and the slavery of the workplace. But this new conception—of "civil society" as the road to democracy—not only met the political needs of the Eastern European struggle against communist statism, it also found a ready export market, both in the First World, where it was appropriated by conservative Reagan/Thatcher projects for "rolling back the state," and in the Third World, where it seemed to provide leverage both for battling dictatorships and for grounding a post-socialist mass democratic politics. With little regard for historical context or critical genealogy, and in the space of only a few years, "civil society" has thus been universalized. It has been appropriated, for different reasons (if equally uncritically), by both the right and the left. Indeed, it has become one of those things (like development, education, or the environment) that no reasonable person can be against. The only question to be asked of civil society today seems to be: How can we get more of it?

I will argue that the current (often ahistorical and uncritical) use of the concept of "civil society" in the study of African politics obscures more than it reveals, and, indeed, that it often serves to help legitimate a profoundly antidemocratic transnational politics. One of my aims in this essay, then, is to point out the analytic limitations of the state/civil society opposition, and to trace its antidemocratic political and ideological uses.

But I also have a second, less reactive aim in exploring the specifically African career of the "civil society" concept. For in the course of criticizing the state versus civil society formula, I hope to arrive at some suggestions for other ways of thinking about contemporary politics in Africa and elsewhere. In particular, I will argue that the state/civil society opposition brings along with it a whole topography of power, revealed perhaps most economically in Hegel's famous conception of "civil society" as, in Mamdani's phrase, "sandwiched between the patriarchal family and the universal state" (Mamdani 1996, 14; Gibbon 1993). This conception rests on an imaginary space, with the state up high, the family low, on the ground, and a range of other institutions in between. In what sense is the state "above" society and the family "below" it? Many different meanings characteristically get blurred together in this vertical image. Is it a matter of scale? Abstraction? Generality? Social hierarchy? Distance from nature? The confusion here is a productive one, in the Foucauldian sense, constructing a common-sense state that simply *is* "up there" somewhere, operating at a "higher level." This common-sense perception has been a crucial part of the way that nation-states have sought, often very successfully, to secure their legitimacy through what Akhil Gupta and I have termed claims of vertical encompassment. These are claims that naturalize the authority of the state over "the local" by merging three analytically distinct ideas—(1) superior spatial scope, (2) supremacy in a hierarchy of power, and (3) superior generality of interest, knowledge, and moral purpose—into a single figure: the "up-there" state that encompasses the local and exists on a "higher level."

Such an image, of course, underlies the familiar public-private split and the idea (of which Habermas makes much) of a "public sphere" that mediates between state and citizen. By imagining the family as a natural ground or base of society, the domestic is left out of the sphere of politics entirely, as feminist theories have pointed out. But this imagined topography also undergirds most of our images of political struggle, which we readily imagine as coming "from below" (as we say), "grounded" in rooted and authentic "lives," "experiences," and "communities" (Malkki 1992). Meanwhile, the state itself can be imagined as reaching down into communities, intervening in (as we say) a "top-down" manner, to manipulate or plan "society." Civil society, in this vertical topography, may appear as the middle latitude, the zone of contact between the "up-there" state and the "on-the-ground" people, snug in their communities. Whether this contact zone is conceived as the domain of pressure groups and pluralist politics (as in liberal political theory) or of class struggle in a war of position (as in Gramscian Marxism), this imaginary topography of power has been an enormously consequential one.

What would it mean to rethink this? What if we question the self-evident "verticality" of the relation of state to society, displace the primacy of the nation-state frame of analysis, and rearrange the imaginary space within which civil society can be so automatically "interposed between" higher and lower levels? As we will see, such a move entails rethinking "the state" and looking at transnational apparatuses of governmentality that I will suggest are of special significance in many parts of contemporary Africa, where states are, in significant ways, no longer able to exercise the range of powers we usually associate with a sovereign nation-state or even (in a few cases) to function at all as states in any conventional sense of the term. But it also, and at the same time, entails rethinking received ideas of "community," "grassroots," and "the local," laden as they are with nostalgia and the aura of a "grounded" authenticity. Using the politics of structural adjustment in Zambia and the South African civic movement as examples, I will try to show that both the "top" and the "bottom" of the vertical picture today operate within a profoundly transnationalized global context that makes the constructed and fictive nature of the vertical topography of power increasingly visible, and opens up new possibilities for both research and political practice. First, however, I wish to continue the interrogation of the contemporary conceptualization of the problem of "state/civil society relations" by showing how much it shares, at the level of the topographic imagination, with the older "nation-building" paradigm that it has largely replaced.

The Vertical Topography in the Study of African Politics: Two Variants of a Mythic Structure

I will begin by considering two views of African politics that, sometimes in explicit opposition, often in implicit and confused combination, have dominated the intellectual scene in recent decades. The older paradigm sees nation-building as the central political process in postcolonial Africa, with a modernizing state in conflict with primordial ethnic loyalties. The newer view recommends the rollback of an overgrown and suffocating state and celebrates the resurgence of "civil society," often putatively linked to a process of "democratization." In deliberately presenting a highly schematic and simplified account of their distinctive features, my purpose is to reveal an underlying set of assumptions that they share.

Nation Building

The key premise of the "nation-building" approach to African politics is the existence of two different levels of political integration and a necessary and historic movement from one to the other. The first such level, logically and historically prior, is the local or subnational; this is the level of primordial social and political attachments left over from the premodern past. Originally referred to by such labels as "tribal organization" or "traditional African society," these supposed "givens" of African political life were thought to include structures of kinship, community, and (in some formulations) ethnicity. Later, Goran Hyden would summarize such local "primordial affiliations" under the singularly unfortunate rubric "the economy of affection" (Hyden 1983). Indeed, it should be noted that while such "primordialist" approaches to subnational identities may fairly be described as out of date, they are very far from having vanished from the contemporary scene.[1]

The second level of integration in the "nation-building" scheme is, of course, the national. Emergent, new, and modern nations were understood to be in the process of construction—stepping out, as it were, for the first time onto the stage of world history. With national structures of authority struggling to establish themselves in the face of "primordial" commitments, "nation building" appeared both an urgent task and a historically inevitable process. Yet the generally hopeful tone of the work in this tradition is shadowed by the phantom that stalks "nation building": the specter of premodern resurgences such as "tribalism," or such manifestations of the lingering "economy of affection" as nepotism, corruption, and other banes of "good government." Failed nation building, it follows, can only mean a resurgence of primordial affiliations (still the usual journalistic explanation for civil wars in Africa). State success, on the other hand, means the construction of new bases of authority resting on nation-state citizenship. Above the national level, finally, appears the international, understood largely as (1) a source of "aid" and a helping hand in nation building, and (2) a utopian image of the union of nation-states, with the key symbol of the United Nations as the promise of the universality of the nation form (Malkki 1994).

"Development," in such a view, is the natural reward for successful national integration, just as nation building is the characteristic rhetoric of the developmental state. The strong, activist state thus naturally becomes the protagonist in the optimistic narratives of "national development" that flourish within this paradigm. This view of the world is perhaps sufficiently familiar as to make it possible to move ahead without further elaboration.

State and Society

"State and society"—the self-proclaimed "new paradigm" in the study of African politics—regards the state and its projects with new skepticism, and rediscovers "the local" as the site of "civil society," a vigorous, dynamic field of possibilities too long suffocated by the state. In place of a modernizing national state bravely struggling against premodern ethnic fragmentation, the image now is of a despotic and overbearing state that monopolizes political and economic space, stifling both democracy and economic growth. Instead of the main protagonist of development, the state (now conceived as flabby, bureaucratic, and corrupt) begins to appear as the chief obstacle to it. What are called "governance" reforms are needed to reduce the role of the state and bring it into "balance" with "civil society" (See, from a huge literature,

Hyden and Bratton 1992; Carter Center 1990; Fatton 1992; World Bank 1989, 1992; Rothchild and Chazan 1988; Chazan et al. 1988; Harbeson, Rothchild, and Chazan 1994).

The local level, meanwhile, is no longer understood as necessarily backward, ethnic, or rural. New attention is paid to such non-"primordial" manifestations of the local as voluntary associations and "grassroots" organizations through which Africans meet their own needs and may even press their interests against the state. There is in much of this newer research an unmistakable tone of approval and even celebration—not of the nation-building state, but of a liberated and liberating civil society. Society left to its own devices, it seems, might make political and economic progress; the problem now is how to induce the state to get out of the way and make it more responsive to "civil society's" demands. Hence the connection, repeatedly asserted in the "governance" literature, between democratization, conceived as making space for "civil society," and development, conceived as getting the state out of the way of a dynamic nonstate sector. It is such a link, too, that accounts for the otherwise peculiar idea of a natural affinity between the draconian and decidedly unpopular measures of "structural adjustment," on the one hand, and populist demands for "democratization," on the other—a point I will return to shortly.

The "new" state-and-society approach is often posed as a simple opposition to the "old" nation-building or "statist" model. But the two paradigms are not as different as they might at first appear. In particular, the state-and-society paradigm uses the very same division of politics into analytic "levels" as does the "nation-building" one, altering only the valuation of their roles. The "national" level is now called "the state," the "local" level "civil society." But where the older view had a new, dynamic, progressive national level energizing and overcoming an old, stagnant, reactionary local level, the new view reverses these values. Now the national level (the state) is corrupt, patrimonial, stagnant, out of date, and holding back needed change, while the local level (civil society) is understood as neither ethnic nor archaic, but as a dynamic, emerging, bustling assemblage of progressive civic organizations that could bring about democracy and development if only the state would let it.

The international, too, appears in both paradigms, but with largely opposite functions. International agencies, especially financial ones, appear in the state-and-society view less as state benefactors and providers of "aid" than as the policemen of states, regulating their functioning and rolling back their excesses through "structural adjustment." If the nation-building view imagined the international in the form of an idealistic UN, the state-and-society paradigm pictures a no-nonsense IMF: stern, real-world bankers, speaking what I have elsewhere called the language of economic correctness (Ferguson 1995).

The implications for "development" are clear, and again, are nearly the reverse of those of the nation-building approach. For the state-and-society paradigm sees development not as the project of a developmentalist state, but as a societal process that is held back by the stifling hold of the state; "structural adjustment" is needed to liberate market forces to work their development magic. Where the first paradigm saw the development problem as too much society, not enough state, the second sees it as too much state, not enough society.

By now it should be clear that the two views bear a remarkable resemblance to each other, even as they are manifestly opposed. Indeed, everything happens as if the second model were, as Lévi-Strauss might say, a very simple transformation of the first. Through a structural inversion more familiar, perhaps, to analysts of myth than of politics, we are left with two paradigms that are simultaneously completely opposed to one another, and almost identical (see figure 1, below).

The Topography of State and Civil Society

It is obvious that there exists a range of phenomena in contemporary Africa that is not captured in the old nation-building optic that sees politics as a battle between a modernizing state and primordial ethnic groups—hence

FIGURE 1 Two Paradigms, Two Analytic Levels

	NATION BUILDING	STATE AND SOCIETY
NATIONAL	*national integration*	*the state*
	modernity: +	modernity: -
	democracy: +	democracy: -
	development: +	development: -
	progress: +	progress: -
LOCAL	*tribal, primordial attachments*	*civil society*
	modernity: -	modernity: +
	democracy: -	democracy: +
	development: -	development: +
	progress: -	progress: +

Key:
modernity (+/-): up-to-date, new / backward, old
democracy (+/-): promoting democracy / inhibiting democracy
development (+/-): creates economic growth / obstacle to growth
progress (+/-): dynamic, progressive / stagnant, antiprogress

the recourse to the idea of "civil society" to encompass a disparate hodgepodge of social groups and institutions that have in common only that they exist in some way outside of or beyond the state. Indeed, while the term "civil society" is often not defined at all in contemporary Africanist literature, most authors seem to intend the classical Hegelian usage that, as I pointed out, imagines a middle zone of "society" interposed between family and state. Others speak more specifically of civil society as a frontier of contact where a politically organized and self-conscious "society" presses against and sets the bounds of "the state."[2]

But while definitions of "civil society" in this literature are usually broad and vague, in practice, writers move quite quickly from definitional generalities to a much more specific vision that is restricted almost entirely to small, grassroots, and voluntary organizations, leaving out of the picture some rather important and obvious phenomena. One is never sure: Is the Anglo-American Corporation of South Africa part of this "civil society"? Is John Garang's army in Sudan? Is Oxfam? What about ethnic movements that are not so much opposed to or prior to modern states, but (as so much recent scholarship shows) produced by them? Or Christian mission organizations, arguably more important today in Africa than ever, but strangely relegated to the colonial past in the imagination of much contemporary scholarship? All of these phenomena fit uncomfortably in the "state" versus "civil society" grid, and indeed cannot even be coherently labeled as "local," "national," or "international" phenomena. Instead, each of these examples, like much else of interest in contemporary Africa, both embodies a significant local dynamic and is indisputably a product and expression of powerful forces both national and global.

The state, meanwhile, when apprehended empirically and ethnographically, itself starts to look suspiciously like "civil society." Sometimes, this is literally the case, such as when NGOs are actually run out of government offices as a sort of moonlighting venture. (A Zambian informant of mine once remarked, "An NGO? That's just a bureaucrat with his own letterhead.") Perhaps more profoundly, as Timothy Mitchell (1991) has argued, the very conception of "state" as a set of reified and disembodied structures is an effect of state practices themselves. Instead, recent work on actually existing state practices (e.g., Gupta 1995) suggests that states may be better viewed not in opposition to something called "society," but as themselves composed of bundles of social practices every bit as "local" in their social situatedness and materiality as any other.

Such work suggests that to make progress here, we will need to break away from the conventional division into "vertical" analytic levels that the old "nation-building" and the new "state-and-society" paradigms share. In the process, we will break out from the range of questions that such a division imposes (how do states rule, what relations exist—or ought to exist—between state and society, how can civil society obtain room to maneuver from the state, etc.), and open up for view some of the transnational relations that I will suggest are crucial for understanding both ends of the vertical polarity. Let us consider what a focus on transnational contexts has to tell us, first about the putative "top" of the vertical topography ("the state") and then about the supposed "bottom" ("grassroots" civic organizations).

The Top

If, as neoliberal theories of state and society suggest, domination is rooted in state power, then rolling back the power of the state naturally leads to greater freedom and ultimately to "democratization." But the argument is revealed to be fallacious if one observes that, particularly in Africa, domination has long been exercised by entities other than the state. Zambia, let us remember, was originally colonized (just a little over a hundred years ago) not by any government, but by the British South Africa Company, a private multinational corporation directed by Cecil Rhodes. Equipped with its own army and acting under the terms of a British "concession," it was this private corporation that conquered and "pacified" the territory and set up the system of private ownership and race privilege that became the colonial system. Today, Zambia, like most other African nations, continues to be ruled in significant part by transnational organizations that are not in themselves governments, but work together with powerful First World states within a global system of nation-states that Frederick Cooper has characterized as "internationalized imperialism."[3]

Perhaps most familiarly, international agencies such as the IMF and World Bank, together with allied banks and First World governments, today often directly impose policies upon African states. The name for this process in recent years has been "structural adjustment," and it has been made possible by both the general fiscal weakness of African states and the more specific squeeze created by the debt crisis. The new assertiveness of the IMF has been, with some justification, likened to a process of "recolonization," which implies a serious erosion of the sovereignty of African states (e.g., Saul 1993). It should be noted that direct impositions of policy by banks and international agencies have involved not only such broad, macroeconomic interventions as setting currency exchange rates, but also fairly detailed requirements for curtailing social spending, restructuring state bureaucracies, and so on. For many African countries, rather significant and specific aspects of state policy are being directly formulated in places like New York and Washington.

Such "governance" of African economies from afar represents, as critics have not failed to point out, a kind of transfer of sovereignty away from African states and into the hands of the IMF. Yet since it is African governments that remain nominally in charge, it is easy to see that they are the first to receive the blame when "structural adjustment" policies begin to bite. At that point, democratic elections (another "adjustment" being pressed by international "donors") provide a means whereby one government can be replaced by another. But since the successor government will be locked in the same financial vice-grip as its predecessor, actual policies are unlikely to change. Indeed, the government that tries to change policy can be swiftly brought to its knees by the IMF and its associated capital cartel, as the Zambian case illustrates vividly. In this way, policies that are in fact made and imposed by wholly unelected and unaccountable international bankers may be presented as democratically chosen by popular assent. Thus does "democratization" ironically serve to simulate popular legitimacy for policies that are in fact made in a way that is less democratic than ever (Ferguson 1995).

The Bottom

Civil society often appears in African studies today as a bustle of grassroots, democratic, local organizations. What this ignores is, of course, as Jane Guyer puts it, "the obvious: that civil society is [largely] made up of *international* organizations" (Guyer 1994, 223).[4] For the local voluntary organizations in Africa, so beloved of "civil society" theorists, very often upon inspection turn out to be integrally linked with entities at the national and transnational level. One might think, for instance, of the myriad South African "community organizations" that are bankrolled by USAID or European church groups (Mindry 1998), or of the profusion of "local" Christian development NGOs in Zimbabwe, which arguably are both the most local, "grassroots" expressions of civil society and are parts of the vast international bureaucratic organizations that organize and sustain them (Bornstein 2001). When such organizations begin to take over the most basic functions and powers of the state, as they very significantly did, for instance, in Mozambique (Hanlon 1991), it becomes only too clear that NGOs are not as "NG" as they might wish us to believe. Indeed, the World Bank baldly refers to what they call BONGOs (bank-organized NGOs) and now even GONGOs (government-organized NGOs).[5]

That these voluntary organizations come as much from the putative "above" (international organizations) as from the supposed "below" (local communities) is an extremely significant fact about so-called civil society in Africa. For at the same time that international organizations (through structural adjustment) are eroding the power of African states (and usurping their sovereignty), they are busy making end runs around these states by directly sponsoring their own programs or interventions via NGOs in a wide range of areas. The role played by NGOs in helping Western "development" agencies to get around uncooperative national governments sheds a good deal of light on the current disdain for the state and celebration of "civil society" that one finds in both the theoretical and the policy-oriented literature right now.

But challengers to African states today are not only to be found in international organizations. In the wake of what is widely agreed to be a certain collapse or retreat of the nation-state all across the continent, we find a range of forms of power and authority springing up that have not been well described or analyzed to date. These are usually described as "subnational" and are usually conceived either as essentially ethnic (the old primordialist view, which, as I noted above, is far from dead) or alternatively and more hopefully as manifestations of a newly resurgent "civil society," long suppressed by a heavy-handed state. Yet can we really assume that the new political forms that challenge the hegemony of African nation-states are necessarily well-conceived as "local," "grassroots," "civil," or even "subnational"?

Guerrilla insurrections, for instance, not famous for their "civility," are often not strictly local or subnational, either—armed and funded, as they often are, from abroad. Consider Savimbi's UNITA army in Angola: long aided by the CIA, originally trained by China, with years of military and logistic support from South Africa, and continuous funding from American right-wing church groups. Is this a subnational organization? A phenomenon of an emerging "civil society"? What about transnational Christian organizations like World Vision International, which (as Erica Bornstein has recently pointed out) play an enormous role in many parts of contemporary Africa, organizing local affairs and building and operating schools and clinics where states have failed to do so (Bornstein 2001)? Are such giant, transnational organizations to be conceptualized as "local"? What of humanitarian organizations such as Oxfam, CARE, or Doctors Without Borders, which perform statelike functions all across Africa?

Such organizations are not states, but are unquestionably statelike in some respects. Yet they are not well described as subnational, national, or even supranational. Local and global at the same time, they are transnational—even, in some ways, anational. They cannot be located within the familiar vertical division of analytic levels presented above. Not coincidentally, these organizations and movements that fall outside of the received scheme of analytic levels are also conspicuously understudied—indeed, they seem to be largely invisible to theoretical scholarship on African politics, tending to be relegated instead to the level of "applied," problem-oriented studies.

In all of these cases, we are dealing with political entities that may be better conceptualized not as "below" the state, but as integral parts of a new, transnational apparatus of governmentality. This new apparatus does not *replace* the older system of nation-states (which is—let us be clear—far from the verge of disappearance), but overlays and coexists with it. In this optic, it might make sense to think of the new organizations that have sprung up in recent years not as challengers pressing up against the state from below, but as horizontal contemporaries of the organs of the state: sometimes rivals, sometimes servants, sometimes watchdogs, sometimes parasites, but in every case operating on the same level and in the same global space.

Such a reconceptualization has implications for both research and political practice, insofar as these depend on received ideas of a "down-there" society and an "up-there" state. In particular, I will examine some of these consequences for two sorts of actor with a special stake in the "grassroots": social movements and anthropologists.

"Grassroots" Politics Without Verticality?

What does the critical scrutiny of the vertical topography of power mean for progressive social movements that have long depended on certain taken-for-granted ideas of locality, authenticity, and "bottom-up" struggle? An extremely illuminating example comes out of the practice and self-criticism of the South African civic movement. Organized and politically powerful local civic organizations played a huge role in the struggle for democracy in South Africa. With national political organizations banned, township civics built networks, organized boycotts and demonstrations, educated cadres, and made many townships no-go areas for the white regime's troops and policemen. Civics took up key government functions and sometimes developed remarkably democratic internal institutions. At the height of the anti-apartheid movement, the civics were not just protest groups but something approaching a genuinely revolutionary force—as the apartheid regime itself recognized.

I will here draw on the recent writings of Mzwanele Mayekiso, a township organizer in the Johannesburg neighborhood of Alexandra, and a true heir of Antonio Gramsci (in an age of many pretenders). Mayekiso sees very clearly the shortcomings of much fashionable celebration of "civil society." Simply lumping together everything outside of the state may have had its utility in the struggle against totalitarian rule in Eastern Europe. But in South Africa, he insists, it is disastrous; it conceals the diametrically opposed political agendas of distinct and antagonistic social classes. For Mayekiso, the socialist, it makes no sense to allow the Chamber of Mines and the Mineworkers' Union to be simply thrown together as "civil society," in opposition to "the state." Moreover, the unthinking valorization of "civil society" for its own sake contains the risk of "following the agenda of imperialist development agencies and foreign ministries, namely, to shrink the size and scope of third world governments and to force community organizations to take up state responsibilities with inadequate resources" (Mayekiso 1996, 12). Instead, Mayekiso proposes an eminently Gramscian solution: a determination to work for what he calls "working-class civil society." It is this which must be strengthened, developed, and allowed to preserve its autonomy from the state. Mayekiso cites two reasons for this: (1) to build a base for socialism during a period when a socialist state is not yet a realistic expectation, and (2) to serve as watchdog over the state while pressing it to meet community needs in the meantime.

It is useful to keep in mind that Mayekiso is writing from the position of an extraordinarily successful political organizer. The South African civics have been a formidable force to be reckoned with, not only in the anti-apartheid struggle, where their organization and political energy proved decisive, but also in their postindependence role. The civics have been successfully transformed from agents of all-out resistance to the apartheid state (aiming, among other things, to make the townships "ungovernable") to well-organized autonomous structures ready to lend support to some state campaigns while vigorously attacking and protesting others. SANCO, a national organization of civics that Mayekiso headed, is today a major player on the national scene, and serves as an independent advocate for worker and township interests—all of which makes it at least a bit more difficult for the ANC government to sell out its mass base.

But the postindependence era has also presented some profound challenges to Mayekiso's Gramscian praxis, which he analyzes with remarkable honesty and clearsightedness. In particular, Mayekiso has come to recognize that the policies of the new South African government are constrained not only by the balance of forces in South Africa but also by the forces of transnational capital, which "denude the ability of nation-states to make their own policy." Faced with the threat of a capital boycott, there may be limits on how far even the most progressive South African government can go down the road to socialism. The traditional nationalist approach, based on organizing the masses to put pressure on the government, has no effective response to this situation. Vertical politics seems to have reached its limits.

Such failures of strictly national politics from below lead Mayekiso to a very interesting critical reflection. Recalling the long struggle of the Alexandra Community Organization during the apartheid years, he acknowledges that its success grew not simply from its strong base in the community, but from strategic transnational alliances. In fact, he reports that the ACO received *most* of its funds not from the community or even from within the country, but from international sources. Dutch solidarity groups, American sister-city programs, Canadian NGOs, Swedish official aid, even USAID at one point—all were sources of aid and support for Mayekiso's "local organizing," which (we begin to realize) was not quite so "local" after all. But Mayekiso does not apologize for this. On the contrary, he uses a reflection on the successful experience of the ACO to begin to develop what he calls "a whole new approach, a 'foreign policy' of working-class civil society" (1996, 283). After all, he says "there is a growing recognition that poor and working class citizens of different countries now have more in common with each other than they do with their own elites" (1996, 283), while "the ravages of the world economy are denuding the ability of nation states to make their own policy" (1996, 280). In such circumstances, challenges from below, within a vertically conceived national space, cannot succeed, but "international civic politics is a real alternative to weak nation-states across the globe" (1996, 280).

Traditional leftist conceptions of progressive politics in the Third World (to which many anthropologists, including myself, have long subscribed) have almost always rested on one or another version of the vertical topography of power that I have described. In this view, "local" people in "communities" and their "authentic" leaders and representatives who organize "at the grassroots" are locked in struggle with a repressive state representing (in some complex combination) both imperial capitalism and the local dominant classes. The familiar themes here are those of resistance from below and repression from above, always accompanied by the danger of cooptation, as the leaders of today's struggle become the elites against whom one must struggle tomorrow.

I do not mean to imply that this conception of the world is entirely wrong or irrelevant. But if, as I have suggested, transnational relations of power are no longer routed so centrally through the state, and if forms of governmentality increasingly exist that bypass states altogether, then political resistance needs to be reconceptualized in a parallel fashion. Many of today's most successful social movements have done just that (as the example of the South African civics in part illustrates). But academic theory, as so often, here lags behind the world it seeks to account for.

To be sure, the world of academic theory is by now ready to see that the nation-state does not work the way conventional models of African politics suggest. And the idea that transnational networks of governmentality have taken a leading role in the de facto governance of Africa is also likely to be assented to on reflection. But are we ready to perform a similar shift in the way we think about political resistance? Are we ready to jettison received ideas of "local communities" and "authentic leadership"? Critical scholars today celebrate both local resistance to corporate globalization as well as forms of grassroots international solidarity that some have termed "globalization from below." But even as we do so, we seem to hang on stubbornly to the very idea of a "below"—the idea that politically subordinate groups are somehow naturally local, rooted, and encompassed by "higher-level" entities. For what is involved in the very idea and image of "grassroots" politics, if not precisely the vertical topography of power that I have suggested is the root of our conceptual ills? Can we learn to conceive, theoretically and politically, of a "grassroots" that would be not local, communal, and authentic, but worldly, well-connected, and opportunistic? Are we ready for social movements that fight not "from below" but "across," using their "foreign policy" to fight struggles not against "the state" but against that hydra-headed transnational apparatus of banks, international agencies, and market institutions through which contemporary capitalist domination functions?

Consider a recent article in the *Los Angeles Times* (1996) on the worldly engagements of the Zapatistas of Chiapas, Mexico. The Zapatistas, we learn, have been discovered by the jet-set and become celebrities. Oliver Stone was photographed receiving the trademark wool mask and pipe from subcommander Marcos during a recent visit to the guerillas' headquarters. Danielle Mitterand, widow of the former French president, recently dropped by. And so on. Most shockingly, Marcos himself has apparently appeared in a fashion spread for the Italian clothing firm Benetton. The subcommander appears in camouflage dress, the glossy photo captioned: "You have to go to war. But what will you wear? Camouflage visual dynamic: light, photogenic... ideal for the soldier who goes from war to war and who doesn't have time to change." Benetton even offered to be the official outfitter of the Zapatistas, but here Marcos drew the line. "Compañeros," he told reporters solemnly (through his mask), "we have decided that it is not suitable to wear sweaters in the jungle."

If this strikes one as funny (as it did me), it is useful to think about exactly what the joke is. For at least part of the humor in the story comes from its suggestion that a group of supposed peasant revolutionaries have, in their inappropriate appetite for Hollywood celebrity and Italian clothing, revealed themselves as something less than genuine ("from fighting to fashion"). After all, what would a "real revolutionary" be doing in a Benetton ad or lunching with Oliver Stone? But this reaction may be misplaced. As Diane Nelson (1999) has recently argued, First World progressives need to rethink their ideas of popular struggle and to prepare themselves to learn from Third World transnational "hackers" with a sense of media politics as well as a sense of humor—and from movements that offer us not a pure and centered subject of resistance, but (like the subcommander) a quite different figure: masked, ambivalent, impure, and canny. Like the South African civics described by Mayekiso, the Zapatistas present us not with authentic others fighting for a nostalgic past, but with media-savvy, well-connected contemporaries, finding allies horizontally, flexibly, even opportunistically—but effectively. For there is obviously real political acumen in the Zapatista strategy. Celebrity attention and world press coverage may well help to protect Chiapas communities against potential aggression; the cost to the Mexican state of political repression surely rises with the amount of press coverage (and public relations damage) that it entails. More profoundly, the *image* of destabilization through guerrilla warfare, properly circulated, is perhaps the Zapatistas' most potent political weapon. Capitalism is built on perceptions, and Mexican capitalism is built on an especially precarious set of perceptions—particularly, on the idea that it is an "emerging market" on the path of the "tigers" of East Asia, a carefully nurtured perception that has supported a huge burst of speculative capital investment in the Mexican economy from the United States and elsewhere. The real damage to the Mexican economy (and thus to the Mexican ruling class) may not come so much from the Zapatistas' actual raids as from the effect that the *fear* of such raids has on the Mexican stock market and on the all-important "confidence" (as they say) of the international bondholders who have the Mexican economy in their pocket. A guerrilla war conducted in images on the pages of an international fashion magazine, then, may not be so out of place after all. Indeed, it may well be the most tactically effective sort of warfare that the terrain will support.

The globalization of politics is not a one-way street; if relations of rule and systems of exploitation have become transnational, so have forms of resistance—along lines not only of race and class, which I have emphasized here, but also of gender, sexuality, and so on. Gramsci's brilliant topographic imagination may be a guide to this new political world, but only if we are willing to update our maps from time to time. The image of civil society as a zone of trench warfare between working people and the capitalist state served the left well enough at one moment in history, just as the vision of a self-regulating zone of "society" that needed protection from a despotic state served the needs of an emergent bourgeoisie in an earlier era. But invoking such topographies today can only obscure the real political issues, which unfold on a very different ground, where familiar territorializations simply no longer function. Rethinking the taken-for-granted spatial mapping that is invoked not only in such terms as "the state"/"civil society" but also in the opposition of "local" to "global" (and in all those familiar invocations of "grassroots," "community," etc.) in these times becomes an elementary act of theoretical and political clarification, as well as a way of strategically sharpening—and not, as is sometimes suggested, of undermining—the struggles of subaltern peoples and social movements around the world.

Toward an Ethnography of Encompassment

Just as a rethinking of the vertical topography of power has special consequences for political practices that depend on unexamined tropes of "above" and "below," it also contains special lessons for forms of scholarship that have traditionally found their distinctive objects in vertically conceived analytic "levels."[6] Working through these conceptual issues, I suggest, might well point in the direction of promising new directions for research. For making verticality problematic not only brings into view the profoundly transnational character of both the state "level" and the local "level," it also brings the very image of the "level" into view as a sort of intensively managed fiction.

To say this is to point toward an enormous ethnographic project (which, in collaboration with Akhil Gupta, I am only beginning to explore), that of exploring the social and symbolic processes through which state verticality and encompassment are socially established and contested through a host of mundane practices. On the one hand, such a project would entail the ethnographic exploration of the processes through which (insofar as state legitimation goes smoothly) the "up-there" state gets to be seen as (naturally and commonsensically) "up there." The spatialization of the state has usually been understood through attention to the regulation and surveillance of the boundaries of nations, since the boundary is the primary site where the territoriality of nation-states is made manifest—wars, immigration controls, and customs duties being the most obvious examples. But while this is a rich area of investigation, it is only one mode by which the spatialization of states takes place. The larger issue has to do with the range of everyday technologies by which the state is spatialized and by which verticality and encompassment become features of social life, commonsensical understandings about the state that are widely shared amongst citizens and scholars. The policing of the border is intimately tied to the policing of Main Street in that they are both rituals that enact the encompassment of the territory of the nation by the state. These acts represent the repressive power of the state as both extensive with the boundaries of the nation and intensively permeating every square inch of that territory; both types of policing often demarcate the racial and cultural boundaries of belonging and are often inscribed by bodily violence on the same groups of people. Nor is this simply a matter of repressive state power: state benevolence as well as coercion must make its spatial rounds, as is clear in, for instance, the ritual touring of disaster sites by aid-dispensing U.S. presidents. It is less in the spectacular rituals of the border than in the multiple, mundane domains of bureaucratic practice that states instantiate their spatiality. Rituals of spatial hierarchy and encompassment are more pervasive than most of us imagine them to be; an ethnographic focus allows these everyday practices to be brought more clearly into focus.

At the same time, however, it is part of my argument that new forms of transnational connection increasingly enable "local" actors to challenge the state's well-established claims to encompassment and vertical superiority in unexpected ways, as a host of worldly and well-connected "grassroots" organizations today demonstrate. If state officials today can still always be counted on to invoke "the national interest" in ways that seek to encompass (and thereby devalue) the local, then canny "grassroots" operators may trump the national ace with appeals to "world opinion" and e-mail links to the international headquarters of such formidably encompassing agents of surveillance as "Africa Watch," "World Vision," or "Amnesty International." Where states could once counter local opposition to, for example, dam construction projects, by invoking a national-level interest that was self-evidently "higher than" (and superior to) the merely "local" interests of those whose land was about to be flooded, today, "project-affected people" are more likely to style themselves as "guardians of the planet," protectors of "the lungs of the earth," or participants in a universal struggle for human rights, and to link their "local" struggles directly to transnationally distributed fields of interest and power. Such rhetorical and organizational moves directly challenge state claims of vertical encompassment by drawing upon universalist principles and globally spatialized networks that render the claims of a merely *national* interest and scope narrow and parochial by comparison. The claims of verticality that I have reviewed here (claims of superior spatial scope, supremacy in a hierarchy of power, and superior generality of interest, knowledge, and moral purpose) have historically been monopolized by the state. But today these claims are increasingly being challenged and undermined by a newly transnationalized "local" that fuses the grassroots and the global in ways that make a hash of the vertical topography of power on which the legitimation of nation-states has so long depended.

What this implies is not simply that it is important to study NGOs and other transnational nonstate organizations, or even to trace their interrelations and zones of contact with "the state." Rather, the implication is that it is necessary to treat state and nonstate governmentality within a common frame, without making unwarranted assumptions about their spatial reach, vertical height, or relation to "the local." What is called for, in other words, is an approach to the state that would treat its verticality and encompassment not as a taken-for-granted fact, but as a precarious achievement—and as an ethnographic problem. Such a project would be misconceived as a study of "state-society interactions," for to put matters thus is to assume the very opposition that requires interrogation. Rather, what is needed is an ethnography of processes and practices of encompassment, an ethnographic approach that would center the processes through which the exercise of governmentality (by state and nonstate actors) is both legitimated and undermined by reference to claims of superior spatial reach and vertical height.

Such a view might open up a much richer set of questions than have up to now been asked about the meaning of transnationalism for states. For in this perspective, it is not a question of whether a globalizing political economy is rendering nation-states weak and irrelevant, as some have suggested, or whether states remain the crucial building blocks of the global system, as others have countered. For the central effect of the new forms of transnational governmentality is not so much to make states weak (or strong) as it is to reconfigure the way that states are able to spatialize their authority and stake claims to superior generality and universality. Recognizing this process might open up a new line of approach into the ethnographic study of state power in the contemporary world.

Notes

1. Consider, for instance, that Hyden was able as recently as 1992 to speak (in a widely cited and highly influential article) of local social structures of kin and com-

munity as "ascriptive" and "part of the natural world over which human beings have limited control." The term "primordial," Hyden acknowledges, may be problematic. Instead, therefore, he prefers the term "God-given ... indicating that they have a character that does not lend itself to alteration by human beings at will." Such "god-given" structures are opposed to state and civic structures that are, in contrast, "man-made" (Hyden 1992, 11). The failure to grasp what might be problematic about the term "primordial" here could hardly be more complete. But Hyden's view is not an insignificant one in the world of current Africanist scholarship. Indeed, he is a recent president of the African Studies Association, and usually reckoned one of the most influential political scientists of Africa.

2. For a range of definitional strategies, see the essays in Harbeson, Rothchild, and Chazan (1994), as well as Bayart (1986).

3. I borrow this evocative term from remarks made by Cooper at a workshop on "Historicizing Development" at Emory University in 1993. It should be noted, however, that I am here connecting the term to larger claims about transnational governmentality that I do not believe Cooper intended to make in his own use of the term.

4. Guyer's insightful discussion of the significance of the international affiliations of African "civil society" parallels my argument here in important ways. The fact that she does not use her observations about the transnational character of Nigerian organizations to question what I have called the vertical topography of power, however, is shown with special clarity in her own definition of "civil society" as "those organizations created by nonstate interests within society to reach up to the state and by the state to reach down into society" (Guyer 1994, 216).

5. I am grateful to Parker Shipton for pointing this out to me.

6. Parts of this section are adapted from a recent oral presentation that I coauthored with Akhil Gupta. Many of the ideas in this section should therefore be regarded as jointly authored.

References

Bornstein, Erica. 2001. *The Good Life: Religious NGOs and the Moral Politics of Economic Development in Zimbabwe*. Ph.D. Dissertation, Program in Social Relations, University of California at Irvine.

The Carter Center. 1991. *African Governance in the 1990s*. Atlanta: The Carter Center.

Chazan, Naomi et al. 1988. *Politics and Society in Contemporary Africa*. Boulder, Colo.: Lynne Rienner.

Fatton, Robert, Jr. 1992. *Predatory Rule: State and Civil Society in Africa*. Boulder, Colo.: Lynne Rienner.

Ferguson, James. 1995. "From African Socialism to Scientific Capitalism: Reflections on the Legitimation Crisis in IMF-ruled Africa." In *Debating Development*

Discourse: Institutional and Popular Perspectives, ed. David B. Moore and Gerald J. Schmitz. New York: St. Martin's Press.

Gibbon, Peter. 1993. "'Civil Society' and Political Change, with Special Reference to 'Developmentalist' States." Paper presented to the Nordic Conference on Social Movements in the Third World, University of Lund, August 18–21.

Gupta, Akhil. 1995. "Blurred Boundaries: The Discourse of Corruption, the Culture of Politics, and the Imagined State." *American Ethnologist* 22 (2): 375–402.

Guyer, Jane. 1994. "The Spatial Dimension of Civil Society in Africa: An Anthropologist Looks at Nigeria." In *Civil Society and the State in Africa*, ed. John W. Harbeson, Donald Rothchild, and Naomi Chazan. Boulder, Colo.: Lynne Rienner.

Hanlon, Joseph. 1991. *Mozambique: Who Calls the Shots?* Bloomington: Indiana University Press.

Harbeson, John W., Donald Rothchild, and Naomi Chazan, eds. 1994. *Civil Society and the State in Africa*. Boulder, Colo.: Lynne Rienner.

Hyden, Goran. 1983. *No Shortcuts to Progress: African Development Management in Perspective*. London: Heinemann.

———. 1992. "Governance and the Study of Politics." In *Governance and Politics in Africa*, ed. G. Hyden and M. Bratton. Boulder, Colo.: Lynne Rienner.

Hyden, Goran, and Michael Bratton, eds. 1992. *Governance and Politics in Africa*. Boulder, Colo.: Lynne Rienner.

Keane, John, ed. 1988. *Civil Society and the State: New European Perspectives*. New York: Verso.

Los Angeles Times. 1996. "Zapatistas in Transition from Fighting to Fashion." April 21.

Malkki, Liisa H. 1992. "National Geographic: The Rooting of Peoples and the Territorialization of National Identity Among Scholars and Refugees." *Cultural Anthropology* 7 (1): 24–44.

———. 1994. "Citizens of Humanity: Internationalism and the Imagined Community of Nations." *Diaspora* 3 (1): 41–68.

———. 1995. *Purity and Exile: Violence, Memory, and National Cosmology Among Hutu Refugees in Tanzania*. Chicago: University of Chicago Press.

Mamdani, Mahmood. 1996. *Citizen and Subject: Contemporary Africa and the Legacy of Late Colonialism*. Princeton: Princeton University Press.

Mayekiso, Mzwanele. 1996. *Township Politics: Civic Struggles for a New South Africa*. New York: Monthly Review Press.

Mindry, Deborah. 1998. *"Good Women": Philanthropy, Power, and the Politics of Femininity in Contemporary South Africa*. Ph.D. Dissertation, Program in Social Relations, University of California at Irvine.

Mitchell, Timothy. 1991. "The Limits of the State: Beyond Statist Approaches and Their Critics." *American Political Science Review* 85: 77–96.

Nelson, Diane M. 1999. *A Finger in the Wound: Body Politics in Quincentennial Guatemala*. Berkeley: University of California Press.

Rothchild, Donald, and Naomi Chazan, eds. 1988. *The Precarious Balance: State and Society in Africa*. Boulder, Colo.: Westview Press.

Said, Edward W. 1983. "Traveling Theory." In *The World, the Text, and the Critic*, 226–247. Cambridge: Harvard University Press.

Saul, John S. 1993. *Recolonization and Resistance: Southern Africa in the 1990s*. Trenton, N.J.: Africa World Press.

Seligman, Adam B. 1992. *The Idea of Civil Society*. New York: The Free Press.

World Bank. 1989. *Sub-Saharan Africa: From Crisis to Sustainable Growth*. Washington, D.C.: The World Bank.

———. 1992. *Governance and Development*. Washington, D.C.: The World Bank.

4 Mercantilism, U.S. Federalism, and the Market Within Reason

The "People" and the Conceptual Impossibility of Racial Blackness

Lindon W. Barrett

About 1730 in Bristol it was estimated that on a fortunate voyage the profit on a cargo of about 270 slaves reached £7,000 or £8,000, exclusive of the returns from ivory. In the same year the net return from an "indifferent" cargo which arrived in poor condition was £5,700. Profits of 100 percent were not uncommon in Liverpool, and one voyage netted a clear profit of at least 300 percent.

—Eric Williams, *Capitalism and Slavery*

The dirty, get-on-down music the women sang and the men played and both danced to, close and shameless or apart and wild.... Just hearing it was like violating the law.

—Toni Morrison, *Jazz*

In the still debated *Capitalism and Slavery* (1944), the historian Eric Williams details the economic purchase secured by the circumscription of the lives of African-derived persons never forthrightly admitted in modern certainties of human being. As summarized by the historian Colin A. Palmer, *Capitalism and Slavery* aims to show "how the commercial capitalism of the eighteenth century was built upon slavery and monopoly, while the Industrial capitalism of the nineteenth century destroyed slavery and monopoly" (Palmer 1944, xii). The following attempt to synthesize some of the key modalities of Western modernity and its forms of personhood—phantasmatic, geopolitical, economic, and racial—accepts this premise that the enslavement of African-derived persons is fundamental to the economic and political development of the modern West. The synthesis interrogates what seems the conceptual impossibility of the human being, as well as the loss of the sub-Saharan populations bound to the commercial traffic of the mercantilist era and also bound, in one instance at the conclusion of the mercantilist era, to the Atlantic federation of the former British North American colonies newly vying for the economic values generated in the Atlantic arena. The perplexity is that at stake originally, as the "modern," is the animation of a conceptual *form*—the commodity—as the principle of economic (and general) rationality, in the face of the already fully animate individual and collective *forms*—in human proportions—of racial blackness. Beginning in the fifteenth century, the modern episode exceeds the bounds of economics simply, and discloses the conceptual license overlapping the modern Western market and modern Western reason by means of the material disposition of African-derived populations.

The perplexity, then, is that the *impossibility* of racial blackness seeming to lie within the limits of the economic fundament of the modern West as well as within the limits of modern psychic rudiments belies the signal importance of the emergent circumstances of the concept of racial blackness: the rise of the Atlantic system of trade on which the articulation of the modern depends. African-derived populations, conscripted under the rubric of racial blackness, become the decisive point of nullification in the geopolitical, economic, and phantasmatic confluence that ultimately betrays the large coextensiveness of the modern market, the ideally infinite arena of ideally infinite exchange, and modern subjectivity, the animating turns of the imagination yielding functional self-coherence, "our inaccessibility to ourselves" (Copjec 1994, ix), in the phrase of the Lacanian psychoanalytical critic Joan Copjec. For following the Portuguese descent down the long swath of the West African coast, which accelerates after 1434 (see Thomas 1997), racial blackness forms the enabling point of "dis/integration" for the paradigms of Western modernity and, in this way, seems an eccentricity of the modern, even as the violent formation of the African diasporic communities of the Americas discloses the conceptual *impossibility* to be, on the contrary, that the Atlantic coast of Africa describes the point of possibility for modern "civic animation," or in the words of the postcolonial historian Dipesh Chakrabarty, "the bureaucratic construction of citizenship, modern state, and bourgeois privacy that classical political philosophy has produced" (Chakrabarty 1992, 351).

Because the transforming metropoles along the Atlantic coastlines of Europe and the "New World" forge their exemplary modern profiles by means of the immense surplus values that depend on the depletion and the disordering of the political jurisdictions along the Senegambian, Guinea, and west-central African coastline and the stark regimes of enforced labor in the Americas, the paramount peculiarity of mercantile capitalism seems the selective criteria by which *almost no* "human suffering was too high to pay for the monetary gain from trade in slaves and from the extension of capitalist production into the New World" (Rodney 1970, 121). The conceptual obfuscation, or upshot, is that the economic boon secured and resecured by Europe and some of its outposts at each node of the Atlantic system of trade—the boon radically augmenting European diets, shipping, and markets—massively introduces sub-Saharan Africans and their descendants into the European "New World" or, differently put, into the newest mechanisms of European viability and, as forcefully, into individual and collective European imaginations. The economist G. R. Steele explains that "mercantilism originated during the transition from the feudal economy to merchant capitalism and international commerce, in the sixteenth and seventeenth centuries. A strong central authority was considered essential to the expansion of markets and it was a mercantilist imperative that the power of the state should be enhanced by an accumulation of national wealth" (Steele 1998, 486). In deference to the conceit of modern nationality, mercantilist policies eschew free trade, promoting instead the cultivation, transportation, and processing of the goods circulating in the new Atlantic trade within national (albeit newly geographically distant) jurisdictions. The European annexation of the Americas inaugurating mercantilist policies and the enormous economic significance of the Caribbean basin cannot be overemphasized in the modernizing progress of Europe and its permutations.

The commercial exchanges bolstered by modern national configurations and agencies bind the subject to the market economically and otherwise by means of the values of "the socially necessary labor time" accruing to the modern centers of European commercial supervision and their outposts. The national articulation of the former British seaboard colonies strikingly exemplifies this imaginative, geopolitical, economic, and racial complex. The fundamental proposition (or feint) of the modern, the certain proposition that "human being" configures the market and conversely the market configures "human being," openly informs the constitutive federal postures of the fledgling union of North American territories, insofar as the rhetorical appeal to "the people" of the incipient national formation apparently glosses the aggregate populations of the former colonies, yet still more forthrightly comprehends the Atlantic circuit of goods premising modern forms of exchange. The importance of the seaboard geography of the former colonies, if not the newly national rhetoric, betrays the subvention of the national identity and its visible sign, "the people," in the ideally infinite arena of ideally infinite exchange constituted and secured through the inconceivability of the fully animate African-derived populations providing "the socially necessary labor time" of the intercontinental trade derived from the Americas. The foreclosure of the certain "human being" of the African-derived populations in the Atlantic theatre discloses that modern nationalisms hold fundamentally supranational coordinates never admitted readily. Stated more particularly, insofar as in "the eighteenth century two features of the market economy fascinated contemporaries: the reliance upon individual initiative and the absence of authoritarian direction" (Appleby 1984, 22), this primary misrecognition of the operations of the market negates the human significance of the African and African-derived populations conscripted into the Atlantic theatre. The tumultuous significance of African-derived persons in the Atlantic arena is occluded by the figure of "an invisible flow of goods and payments girdling the globe and crisscrossing the English countryside" (Appleby 1984, 30), radically reforming across the Western hemisphere civic and subjective protocols—modernity—as marked emphatically by the independence of the former British seaboard colonies.

Because psychoanalytic paradigms do not fundamentally rely on the trajectories of history, as Joan Copjec (1994) argues in *Read My Desire*, these interrogations of the modern are not broached primarily in psychoanalytic terms. The overwhelming problem for psychoanalytical paradigms is that, because the emergent subject of "European" modernity is forged during the earliest phases of capital accumulation, mercantile capitalism, the perplexity is at once historical and paradigmatic. Nonetheless, the coincident development of the modern market and modern subjectivity remains an important issue for Marxist paradigms, in which the concept of commodity fetishism designates the coincidence. The economists Jack Amariglio and Antonio Callari, in their consideration of the concept of commodity fetishism, provide a succinct rendition of the Marxist codification of subjectivity. "Marx," they write, "has had a theory of the subject, the theory of commodity fetishism. To the extent that it attempts to conjoin the analysis of commodity production and circulation with a discussion of 'ideology,' commodity fetishism does discuss the peculiar subjectivity typical of capitalist social formations" (Amariglio and Callari 1993, 188). In particular, they point out that the Marxist understanding of "socially necessary labor time" as the essential value masked in commodity fetishism clarifies the subjectivizing force of the modern market, which is to say, the imperatives "naturalizing" the difference between the social conditions of the labor yielding the commodity and the failure of the commodity to resemble those conditions in the exchange.

In this way, "the act of exchange is not simply the site of an economic process but also one of the key locations within capitalism where a symbolic order is particularly constituted and learned" (Amariglio and Callari 1993, 215). The concept of commodity fetishism describes the phantasmatic torque of rational exchanges so as to abrogate the "unnecessary gulf [that] has come to exist between two important areas of theoretical work in contemporary Marxism, with the theory of value (the economics, if you will) on one side and the nature and role of subjectivity (an antieconomism) on the other" (Amariglio and Callari 1993, 186). The ideally infinite arena of ideally infinite exchange of the modern abstracted market forms the most efficient nexus of material and conceptual exchange. In the historical trajectory, the cultural trajectory, and the trajectories of subjection, commodity fetishism depends on and stands for the fantastic *impossibility* by means of which not only the possible seems coherent but, more importantly, the *force* of the actual seems coherent. This nexus is racial in character insofar as the phantasmatic, geopolitical, and economic coincidence yields the declensions of humanity and subhumanity, the attendant disclosure being that "the history of European people on both sides of the Atlantic indicates that responsiveness to the market economy cannot be taken for granted, for it reflects values and ideas even more than material conditions" (Appleby 1984, 47). This is to say that the emergent subject of the European modernity—the relay of the perplexity of commodity fetishism—and the intrigue of mercantilist agendas form coimplicated registers of the social, economic, and cultural reorganizations of Europe and its extensions following the fifteenth century.

By 1830, as one outgrowth of the competition over the economic values trafficked through the Atlantic theatre, the number of novel military and administrative jurisdictions, modern nation-states, emergent in the "New World" includes: Haiti (1803), Argentina (1816), Chile (1818), Venezuela (1820), Mexico (1821), Great Colombia (1822), Bolivia (1825), Paraguay (1826), and Uruguay (1828) (Lopez-Alves 2000). The resulting macropolitical effect—the nation—and the micropolitical effect—the ineffability of "the people" as the collective representation of individual subjects—reveal that "the act of exchange is not simply the site of an economic process but also one of the key locations within capitalism where a symbolic order is particularly constituted and learned" (Amariglio and Callari 1993, 215). As with the feint of commodity fetishism, there is an enabling slippage, the wholly viable misperception that configures the matter of nationality as simply the cohesion or coherence of an "imagined community," in the well-known phrase of Benedict Anderson. In this way, in the exemplary Federalist intrigues of the United States, the articulation of "the people," the effective concept yielding the sign of *national* visibility, conflates the fiscal management of commodity exchange within the strict protocols of modern rationalized accumulation with the legibility of human being. Beyond the macropolitical reorganizations, the affective principle, the feint, is the semblance of discrete viability (whether national or individual), as nonetheless sustained through the reified, ideally infinite arena of ideally infinite exchange.

The Conceptual Impossibility

The geopolitical, historical, and social palimpsest is intricate. The annexation of the Americas and the policies governing the opportunities to raise and traffic enormous quantities of goods in the new Atlantic economies transforms the premodern axes of long-distance trade: the significance of the sea lanes of the Baltic trade, the Mediterranean Sea, the Indian Ocean, and the intercontinental arena of the silk roads. The newly promoted European desires for sugar and other tropical products formalize in the seventeenth and eighteenth centuries the enormous trade circuit termed the triangular trade, fusing the formerly disparate economies of the Americas, Western Europe, and the West African coast from Senegambia, Sierra Leone, the Windward and Gold coasts, and the Bight of Benin, to Benguela beyond the Bight of Biafra—jurisdictions inhabited by Akans, Angolans, Ashante, Bambara, Igbo, Kongolese, Kru, Mandingas, Mende, Oyo, Vais, Yoruba, and others, who are hard pressed by the demands of the European modernity. In the triangular circuit of the new Atlantic economies, European manufactured objects are disposed on the African coast in trade for slaves, who are shipped across the Atlantic as the requisite labor force for the massive production of the cash crops that in the final segment of the circuit are traded under the nationally protectionist policies of the European metropoles to serve the rearticulated desires of mass populations.

The historian David Eltis directly considers the compound economic and imaginative impress disposing of sub-Saharan Africans and their descendants in the European modernity. Rehearsing in particular the unpursued but potentially far greater economic promise of European enslavement in the Americas, he queries "which groups are considered eligible for enslavement" (Eltis 1993, 1400) in the mercantilist era and its aftermath, proposing that the "crux of the matter is shipping costs, which comprised by far the greater part of the price of any form of imported bonded labor in the Americas" (Eltis 1993, 1405). The scope of this argument, rather than being bound by national jurisdictions, is international, in order to demonstrate "that economic motivation should be assigned a subsidiary role in the rise and fall of the exclusively African-based bondage that Europeans carried across the Atlantic" (Eltis 1993, 1401). The shorter voyage from Europe to the Americas, the less closely packed ships of these routes, the lower mortality and morbidity rates in North Atlantic as opposed to South Atlantic transportation, and the accessibility to European convict labor given that major European population centers abut navigable waterways, David Eltis argues, all attest to the far from complete role of economics in the arraignment of mercantilist labor forces. Rather, he states that "the most cursory examination of relative costs suggests that European slaves should have been preferred to either European indentured labor or African slaves" (Eltis 1993, 1404).

The confluence of imagination, economics, and race is plain: "The most that can be said by way of comparison is that the spread of African slavery in the Americas coincided with the spread of forced labor in punishment systems within Europe (transportation in the English case). But no one was in any doubt about the distinctions between the two" (Eltis 1993, 1411). The ultimate point is that the "absence of European slaves, like the dog that did not bark, is perhaps the clue to understanding the slave trade and the system it supported" (Eltis 1993, 1422). The more than simply economic question foregrounds the *imagination* of the European subject as well as attendant political and material forces, the quandary being "that the peoples with the most advanced capitalist culture, the Dutch and the English, were also the Europeans least likely to subject their own citizens to enforced labor," circumstances disclosing that "the celebration of British liberties—more specifically, liberties for Englishmen—depended on African slavery" (Eltis 1993, 1423).[1] Drawing a circumference around the entire Atlantic circuit, David Eltis's argument extrapolates in important ways the thesis of the historian Edmund Morgan's *American Slavery, American Freedom*, broadening it so as to encompass the psychic and political subjectivity of modernizing Europe generally. In sum, the thesis of Edmund Morgan's classic examination of colonial Virginia is "not... that a belief in republican ideology had to rest on slavery, but only that in Virginia (and probably in other southern colonies) it did" (Morgan 1975, 381).

David Eltis's more general rendition of the principle bears noting. If, in the episode of mercantile capitalism, the "early modern Europeans shifted property rights in labor toward the individual and away from the community" (Eltis 1993, 23), then, as clearly, these reorganizations shift property rights in labor (as well as in epistemological and cultural systems) across continental divisions: toward Europe and the Americas and away from the west coast of Africa. The Atlantic accessibility of the African continent provides the means for dismantling the longstanding systems of property rights, of commercial trade, legal and penal systems, and intercultural contact of the self-governing jurisdictions arrayed along the broad continental swath in which "few—perhaps no—West African peoples appear to have been living on the very margin of subsistence during the eighteenth century... [for] research almost always seems to disclose some surplus output and some interregional trade even in the most isolated areas" (Gemery and Hogendorn 1983, 153). In short, the modern transfer of rights toward the European(ized) individual and away from the community has patent inverse effects on the eastern and western arcs of the Atlantic rim. Summarily stated, the fact that the modern "individual" and its revolutionary civic and political protocols *did not precede* the transfer of rights from the community to the individual, or from the eastern to the western arcs of the Atlantic, reveals plainly the powerful turns of the imagination that accrue along the eastern rim of the Atlantic in the modernizing centers of Europe and its outposts—fully in tandem with the vast economic values in question.

The modernity of *individual* psychic positions is forged from the very same enterprise as the modernity of mercantilism agendas as well as their revised, dramatic, and exorbitant nationalisms. For these reasons, the conceit of racial blackness, which indiscriminately catalogues dark-skinned Africans and their descendants, can be understood as a powerful analog of the complex of commodity fetishism, insofar as the extended quarantining of this key population largely and effectively promotes key turns of the imagination that *naturalize* the gulf between the social conditions of the labor yielding the commodity for exchange and the failure of the commodity to resemble those conditions in the exchange—in other words, the powerful dissemblance by which it is not as plain as it might be that rational economic transactions dispossess some of the parties attendant to the exchange. In the most routine protocols of the Atlantic economies, the difference of phenotypes hyperbolically redacts the diacritical positions on either side of the commodity form, positions opposed as *production* and *consumption*. The difference of phenotypes in these turns of mind *naturalizes* and imbricates the subjective and economic feints of commodity fetishism, that "producers" and "consumers" contend equally within the interests of modern market relations. These turns of the imagination are also racialized in key and stark ways for the modern West, because of its radical dispositions of populations according to continental origin. The radical dispositions dichotomized Europe and Africa, consumption and production, supervision and subordination, and reason and unreason as indices of race given the unprecedented proximities of populations: "Although data on the immigration of free persons to the

Americas are much less precise, it seems probable that enslaved African immigrants to the New World outnumbered Europeans by about four or five to one during the eighteenth century" (Blackburn 1997, 384).

That is, as opposed to the occurrences in Europe and the Americas, the personal securities of the populations of the various polities along the coast of West Africa "evaporated to facilitate a trade that was a constant threat to their existence" (Rodney 1970, 259). For instance, Senegambia, the northernmost coastal region disrupted in the vast triangulation of the Atlantic economies, includes the polities of the Bijangos, Mande, and Mandingas, among others, and, although it is the region that supplies the least number of enslaved conscripts to the expansion of capital accumulation, it nonetheless registers fully the effects of the international violence. Beyond the widespread warfare that does not arise necessarily from—but necessarily inflames—regional political animosities, a variety of legal and extralegal threats reorganizes and frustrates quotidian life across the Senegambia: various systems of land tenure based on land stewardship by the nobility (Papels) or reciprocal labor (Balantas) are compromised, penal systems are recalculated in order to broaden and expedite the possibilities of seizure for enslavement, the means of exploiting personal and class rivalries expand enormously, and the enticements to lawlessness, such as kidnapping, alter both personal and organized political calculations. Most importantly, drawing the region into even greater entanglements with the European and "New World" ideally infinite arena of ideally infinite exchange, the enveloping threat to travel and unfamiliar intercourse weakens the internal commercial relations of the Senegambia. The disruption of the political economies along the lower Guinea and west-central coasts, territories of the Angolans, Kongolese, Oyo, Yoruba, and others, is even more acute, providing "ample proof that the economic pull of the American market could force a fundamental change within Africa" (Lovejoy 1979, 57). Lovejoy notes the volume, rapidity, and high consequence of the overwhelming transfer of the African labor forces to the western rim of the Atlantic:

> The largest exporting region in the early seventeenth century was west-central Africa, which continued sending thousands of slaves a year to the Americas, thus consolidating a pattern that had began a century earlier. Senegambia and Benin maintained their relatively modest share of the trade as well, each providing about a thousand slaves a year. Slaves came from elsewhere too. The really dramatic expansion of the Atlantic trade began after 1650, and from then slave exports affected ever larger parts of Africa, not just the Kongo region. In the

> last fifty years of the seventeenth century, more slaves were sold to Europeans on the Atlantic coast than in the previous two hundred years combined. This phenomenal growth was a response to the spread of plantation slavery in the Americas. From the 1640s through the 1660s, sugar spread from Brazil to the lesser Antilles—Barbados, Martinique, Guadeloupe, St. Kitts, Antigua—and these new colonies acquired tens of thousands of slaves. The figure of the third quarter of the seventeenth century was double the previous twenty-five year period, averaging 17,700 per year, while in the last quarter, almost 30,000 slaves were exported annually. By now sugar plantations were being established on Jamaica and Saint Domingue, which rapidly became the two largest producers of sugar. As a result, the dramatic surge in slave exports continued into the eighteenth century, reaching figures in the order of 61,000 slaves per year for the whole century.
>
> (Lovejoy 1979, 46)

It is important to understand that the violence of the Atlantic conscription is neither random nor absolute. Paul Lovejoy notes the closely deliberative aspects of the undermining of the political jurisdictions of the coast: "The introduction of new crops from the Americas increased food production and thereby helped to maintain population levels despite the export of slaves. Advances in commercial institutions, including credit facilities, currency, bulking, and regularized transportation, assisted in the movement of slaves" (Lovejoy 1979, 68). In short, while the intrusive transatlantic contact "implies disorder in the social framework wherever the external trade was important, the effective organization of slave supply required that political violence be contained within boundaries that would permit the sale of slaves abroad" (Lovejoy 1979, 66).

The fact that "the export of about 11.3 million slaves from 1500 to 1800, including the astronomical increase between 1650 and 1800 in the Atlantic sector, could not have occurred without the transformation of the African political economy" (Lovejoy 1979, 66) is corroborated by the economists Henry Gemery and Jan Hogendorn, who construct a hypothetical West African economy as it might have existed outside of the slave trade in order to make a comparison to the actual economic outcomes of the episode. They measure the net economic loss to the region based on figuring five factors: (1) the levels of subsistence production under both economies, (2) the average surplus production per person above subsistence requirements, (3) the longer working life of those transported to and enslaved in the Americas, (4) mortality during slave acquisition and delivery prior to the transatlantic transportation, and (5) the greater economic contributions of the younger, more productive, and more highly conscripted groups of the labor force. They write:

> As noted, any one of these independent factors 1–5 would in itself convert the net impact of the slave trade into an economic loss for West Africa. The implication is overwhelming that when these factors are taken in combination, the economic costs of the trade exceeded its gains on an overall basis. Let us reemphasize that this conclusion is reached without any reference to the massive intangible costs of the trade.
>
> (Gemery and Hogendorn 1983, 161)

Dramatically, there are inverse effects on the other side of the Atlantic. The historian Ronald Bailey describes the importance of the Caribbean, its commodity routes, and African-derived labor forces to both the colonial development and industrialization of New England—never mind, say, South Carolina, the state with the most direct ties historically and economically to the Caribbean basin. Ronald Bailey summarizes the rehearsal as follows:

> I have argued in this article, as others have done, that New England's maritime trade and shipping laid the foundation for, raised the infrastructure of, and funded early industrial development. This was particularly the case for the cotton textile industry between 1815 and 1860. Maritime trade and shipping depended largely on the slave trade on the slave-based Atlantic economic system of the seventeenth, eighteenth, and nineteenth centuries. The early industries, such as shipbuilding and rum distilling, were directly tied to the slave trade and to maritime activities in general. These helped pave the way for the establishment of the cotton textile industry, which, together with the production of the cotton textile machinery, became the leading sector of U.S. industrialization in the nineteenth century.
>
> (Bailey 1990, 402)

The final observation is that "the contribution of the slave trade and New World slavery to the entire process is hard to exaggerate" (Bailey 1990, 403). The historian Robin Blackburn writes:

> The birth of the North American republic had a large impact on the plantation-related trade of the rest of the Americas. United States ex-

> ports to the French, Spanish, Portuguese, and Dutch colonies reached nearly £1 million annually in 1790–92, representing 24 percent of the total.... The tonnage of US shipping registered as engaged in overseas commerce totalled 346,000 tons, twice that of the tonnage of British shipping involved in the Atlantic trade, in 1770; by 1801 the tonnage of US commercial shipping more than doubled to 718,400. Merchants from New York, Boston and Philadelphia traded with all parts of the Caribbean and Americas in sugar, cotton, coffee, cacao, and indigo, much of which was then re-exported to Europe. They offered powerful economic as well as ideological encouragement to creole aspiration to American independence. The total export trade of the United States grew fivefold in the period 1790 to 1807, swelled by its role as entrepot for the plantation produce of the Americas, to reach over $60 million (over £10 million).
>
> (Blackburn 1997, 483)

Still, the full measure of the trajectory of mercantile capitalism and its modernizing transfers of economic values and peoples in the transatlantic circuit rests in the subtleties and protocols of mercantilist capitalism that understand human congress (and progress) as inseparable from the exchanges (and feints) of the unwieldy abstracted market. Differently put, the full trajectory of the modern West is clarified in the revolutionary certainty that functional human being—individual and especially collective—is inseparable from the ideally infinite arena of ideally infinite exchange, an arena that even the broadest modern legislative, military, and rhetorical resources fail to articulate coherently as often as not. The complex is a matter of subjectivity, the full reach of which—paradoxically—is never the discrete subject but, rather, turns on the (ideally collective) imagination by which discrete subjection reforms and adheres to the coveted processes and values of transatlantic (and global) commodity circulation, a rarified intersubjective template questionable only under the most pressed of circumstances.

The beguiling and basic national proposal—the proposal of an ineffable, "psychological bond that joins a people and differentiates it, in the subconscious convictions of its members, from all other people in a most vital way" (Connor 1978)—credits the nation as a centrifugal, if not fully cohesive entity. In 1882, Ernest Renan writes famously: a "nation is a soul, a spiritual principle" (Renan 1882, 26) the outcome of a "great aggregation of men, [which] with healthy spirit and warmth of heart, creates a moral conscience which is called a nation" (Renan 1882, 29). In the subjectivizing premise of the modern nation state, the assumption of basic or fundamental cohesiveness, there is, then, the foreclosure of the recognition of the more openly destructive imperatives and force of national formations. For example, the historian Alfred Cobban writes: "As an agency of destruction the theory of nationalism proved one of the most potent that even modern society has known. Empires or states that were not homogeneous in culture and language were undermined from within, or assaulted from without" (Cobban 1969, 249). Similarly, the sociologist Anthony Richmond observes that "the internal cohesion and social integration of the nation-state depended upon an elimination of previous local, tribal or provincial attachments and the inculcation of loyalty to the larger territorial unit dominated by the secular state" (Richmond 1994, 291). The case seems, however, that the profound reverberations of national formations (and reformations) in the mercantilist era do not apply foremost or finally to the Western communities redrawn within (and as) the national territories but, as fully, to the instrumental bearers of the "socially necessary labor time" who are never calculable strictly, given the transatlantic protocols of mercantile capitalism, by any national designations.

The violence in question, unlike the apparent cohesion it subtends, never merely is equivalent to or circumscribed by the national formation. The insufficiencies and obfuscations of the rubrics of nationalism for effectively scoring this violence is plain, because "simply put, people from one continent forced those from a second continent to produce a narrow range of consumer goods in a third—having first found the third's native population inadequate to their purpose" (Eltis 1993, 1399). Instead of innate sets of psychological bonds or easily calculated moral gestures, the phenomenon of nationalism details the necessity of the *micropolitical* redescription, in addition to the *macropolitical* reformulation, of social power. These redescriptions of power—according to the political economist Susan Strange, "the ability of a person or group of persons ... to affect [the] outcomes that their preferences take precedence over the preferences of others" (Strange 1996, 17)—fix the always vulnerable margins between the conceptual and the inconceivable, between the proximity to and the attenuation of the violence yielding the apparent cohesion in question.

The Civic Premise

The historian John Brewer, in *The Sinews of Power*, summarizes mercantilism, rather than being a coherent set of policies, as an "era in which the relationship between state power and international trade was seen as a problem of exceptional importance, one which was normally formulated as a debate between the interventionist obligations of rulers rather than a matter of free trade" (Brewer 1988, 169). The emphatically modern historical break of the British mainland colonies from their national origins is evident in these imperatives of mercantilism, its matters of state jurisdiction, international trade, and sovereign intervention. The British Sugar Act of 1764, which imposes tariffs on the seaboard colonies that result in the enormous, economically crucial smuggling between the colonies and the Caribbean basin, followed in 1773 by the Stamp Act, which lowers the tariffs in order to make British intervention in the smuggling more viable, remain important points of escalation in the transatlantic tensions that result in the successful independence of the seaboard colonies, as well as the scrupulous, developing alignment of economic and social life as the paramount premise of modern national agency. Mercantilist principles, exacerbating economic jealousies, chafe at longstanding concepts of national agency. The point Brewer demonstrates is that in the seventeenth- and eighteenth-century histories of England, by shaping the international flow of goods and wealth by the means of intercontinental markets, mercantilism articulates and reinforces modern forms of nationality as bureaucratic, administrative entities. The inaugurating episodes of mercantilism, which is defined in opposition to free trade, witness measures such as the British Navigation Acts and the French *exclusif*, measures aiming to ensure that the tropical products cocoa, coffee, indigo, rum, sugar, and tobacco (as well as gold and silver) extracted from New World outposts by means of African-derived labor are shipped exclusively on the vessels of their respective metropolitan centers and then refined and marketed in those metropolitan territories by national agents and industries. At the conclusion of the era, the fledgling United States, as the sign of its emphatic modernity, both redescribes national territories and presents new conceptual forms. The historian Andrew Cayton observes:

> Indeed, many saw the efforts of nationally oriented men to attach people to the new republic as essentially radical innovations designed to undermine traditional social relationships. Not only were Federalists elevating imperial authority above local authority. By privileging abstract impersonal principles above particular personal ties, they were redefining the nature of social and political relationships.
>
> (Cayton 1998, 78)

Given its recalculation of social and political relationships, the specification of "the people" devised in the crisis of the independence of the seaboard colonies provides a historical correlate to the theoretical conceptualizations of the large coextensiveness of the market and the forces of subjectivity. The articulation of national independence dramatically clarifies the enormous material boon, as well as the subjectivizing turns of the imagination secured by means of the Atlantic economies, a historical progress describing the co-implicated investments of the macropolitical and the micropolitical.

At once, the force in question is *macropolitical*, which is to say broadly historical and supranational, enforcing the economic circuits imbricating the West African, "New World," and European polities within the adamant antinomies of race following the sixteenth century. In the era that follows, "in less than one hundred years the world's economic situation had altered completely.... Negro slaves, who were of only nominal value in 1500, had become indispensable to the maintenance and development of this new plantation economy" (Gailey 1970, 119). Concomitantly, the force in question is *micropolitical*, which is to say insinuates and enforces, the interpellation of a

> model of economic life that borrowed its order from ... the newly conceptualized nature of predictable regularity. As this economy absorbed more and more of the attention of men and women it supplied a new identity for them. By the end of the eighteenth century the individual with wide-ranging needs and abstract rights appeared to challenge the citizen with concrete obligations and prescribed privileges.
>
> (Appleby 1986, 32)

For these reasons, it is important to acknowledge that in the British mainland colonies "African slaves, if taken together ... [are] the largest single group of non-English-speaking migrants to enter the North American colonies in the pre-Revolutionary era" (Wood 1974, xiii). The historical progress reveals that, rather than being foremost the vector of human coherence, the modernity of the national formations, especially in the Americas, provides foremost the novel, beguiling means by which individual and communal detachments are created, channeled, and exploited, in the transcontinental arrangements yielding unprecedented demographics and proximities. The matter is not economic simply but rather involves as specifically the turns of the imagination that demand the impossibility—violently secured—of racial blackness being a feature of readily recognized human being.

This is to say that the profound conceptual problems yet pronounced political efficacy of the figure of "the people" are unmistakable in the finally supranational intrigue of the independence of the seaboard colonies and subsequent American Federalist era. The Federalist era ranges from the 1780s, fomenting the debate over supplanting the Articles of Confederation with a new constitution, to the election of Thomas Jefferson to the presidency in 1800. Still, this is to say further that, in the matter of nation building, the aporetic force in question is not simply the military drama of the Revolutionary War but the effects of the African-derived "socially necessary labor time" on which the modern Atlantic market and its various national articulations (and rearticulations) depend. The material and conceptual effects of the African-derived "socially necessary labor time" redoubles the incongruity of the local, federal, and individual renditions of "the people" that mark the political urgencies of the Federalist era. The developing historiography of the Federalist era draws out the perplexity of the figure of "the people" forming the national register of the independent British mainland colonies. The historian Robert Shalhope outlines the work of Bernard Bailyn, Gordon Wood, and J. G. A. Pocock, and their formation of the historiographical "republican synthesis," or the related set of convictions that, insofar as early U.S. history "revealed a continual struggle between the spheres of liberty and power, the American Revolutionaries quickly formed a consensus in which the concept of republicanism epitomized the new social and political world they believed they had created" (Shalhope 1982, 334). Shalhope positions principally the scholarship of Joyce Appleby against the contentions of the "republican synthesis," so as to describe a " major weakness of earlier analyses of republicanism ... namely, a focus on political and constitutional issues to the detriment of economic analysis" (Shalhope 1982, 345). What is clear from the discrepant perspectives, he contends, is that the "American Revolution created a single political nation but certainly did not fashion a cohesive national community" (Shalhope 1982, 354). Appleby, in her own consideration of the historiographical tensions, forthrightly rejects the earlier "insistence that the classical republican paradigm controlled how eighteenth-century men reacted to change," claiming the historical record demonstrates, instead, that the colonial elite "living with sensibilities formed in an agrarian society and struggling to interpret change with an ideology pivoting on the preeminent importance of stasis could only be disconcerted by the intrusive vigor of the [effects of the] market" (Appleby 1986, 31). To this end, the historian T. H. Breen outlines pointedly the shortcomings, or the explanatory limits, of the historiographical investments of the "republican synthesis":

> Intellectual historians encounter a different, though equally thorny set of problems. They transform the American Revolution into a mental event. From this perspective, it does not matter much whether the

> ideas that the colonists espoused are classic liberal concepts of rights and property, radical country notions of power and virtue or evangelical Calvinist beliefs about sin and covenants. Whatever the dominant ideology may have been, we find that a bundle of political abstractions has persuaded colonists living in scattered regions of America of the righteousness of their cause, driving them during the 1760s and 1770s to take ever more radical positions until eventually they were forced by the logic of their original assumptions to break with Great Britain. Unfortunately, intellectual historians provide no clear link between the everyday world of the men and women who actually became patriots and the ideas that they articulated. We are thus hard-pressed to comprehend how in 1774 wealthy Chesapeake planters and poor Boston artisans—to cite two obvious examples—could possibly have come to share a political mentality. We do not know how these ideas were transmitted through colonial society from class to class, from community to community.
>
> (Breen 1988, 75)

In short, as much as the "republican synthesis" advances ideal propositions of historical and narrative continuity, it cannot account for the way in which radically distinct geographical populations as well as social classes arrived at the collective apprehension of a national "people," revolutionary acts of imagination yielding the "mobilization of strangers in a revolutionary cause [that] eroded the stubborn localism of an earlier period" (Breen 1988, 74). This episode that produces finally the federal compact, more than a political theoretical inheritance, turns on novel economic and conceptual priorities.

Brief considerations of the roles of the three authors of the composite *Federalist*, which famously appeals in the 1780s for the new national compact, begin to illustrate the point. The three exemplary figures are Alexander Hamilton, who is the successful architect of the federal economic policy within the first administrations; John Jay, who is a New York lawyer and, like Alexander Hamilton, one of the representatives from New York at the constitutional convention who in *The Federalist* pinions nativist appeals for the new national agency; and James Madison, who is the instrumental figure of the 1787 constitutional convention. The architectural economic strategies of Alexander Hamilton underscore the immediate conceptual force that the relays of commodity exchange hold for the national endeavor. The nativist appeals of John Jay betray the occlusions of the international complex equally necessary to the endeavor. The role of James Madison highlights the representational quandary—yet nonetheless political efficacy—of the rhetorical figure of the people. The imbrications of their positions are fundamental to and productive of the enterprise they conceive and debate.

Alexander Hamilton—"the colossal genius of the new system" (Beard 1913, 100), notwithstanding James Madison's more preeminent role in the details of constitution making—recognizes keenly the neomercantilist dilemma of the incipient national union:

> Believing economic independence was inseparable from political freedom, Hamilton was alarmed by American dependence on British imports. He opposed commercial coercion, fearing that the young nation would be devastated by such a contest. His less confrontational design envisioned ridding the United States of British economic domination by developing American manufacturing. He concluded that American technological backwardness stood in the way of American manufactures and urged the federal government to launch an aggressive campaign to acquire England's protected industrial secrets.
> (Ben-Atar 1998, 59–60)

In the policies sponsored by Alexander Hamilton, the "intrusive vigor of the market" is undisguised: the pursuit of public credit for the federal agency, the establishment of the national bank, the championing of domestic taxation in support of public credit, the redrawing of economic relations with Britain while at the same time supporting rival domestic manufacturing by flouting British patent laws, the championing of a well-funded national military in the service of international force, and the elimination of the federal land grant program for fear of losing to the skilled immigrant workers of the more open South and West—in effect, the twinning of the fortunes of the new republic with the interests and influence of financiers, bankers, merchants, manufacturers, and land speculators. Jeffersonian opposition to these inaugural federal policies is intense, as is the resolve of the governing Federalists under the presidency of John Adams in the few years before the 1800 presidential election of Thomas Jefferson. The observations of Doran Ben-Atar and Barbara Oberg concerning the tense political atmosphere of the early national union are apt:

> Twice in a period of two years [the Federalist] maneuvers brought the nation to the brink of disunion and civil war. Their attempt during the Quasi-War with France to muzzle the opposition with the Alien and Seditions Acts in 1798 moved Jefferson, in the Kentucky Resolutions, to advocate nullification. Two years later, in response to the Federal-

> ists' Burr maneuver, Republican leaders in Virginia and Pennsylvania considered raising an army and marching on the nation's capital to place Jefferson at the helm.
>
> (Ben-Atar and Oberg 1998, 2)

It is important to note that a significant part of the Jeffersonian opposition to the programs of Alexander Hamilton and the initial Federalist administrations draws on the popular opposition to the expansion of the national military in support of international influence, the policy dependent on formalizing domestic taxation as the perpetual supplement to the revenues collectible from customs and tariffs. The local populations, "as their representatives in Congress made clear, and some of them also made clear out of doors, were not prepared to pay taxes to support a powerful military and aggressive posture in foreign affairs" (Sloan 1998, 67). The policies and impress of the first federal administrations compromise plainly the simple figurativeness of the people, particularly as "in principle, central government was antithetical to liberty, which most Americans associated with local self-rule" (Ferguson 1969, 242).

The question of the independent powers of the federal agency subordinates to the international coordination of economic values the individual subjections and subjects on which it depends for its representative basis. The historian James Ferguson places the question of the powers of the federal agency in the international context that determines it more completely. He outlines that, before the complications of the initial intrigues of the independent seaboard states, "an analogous political-economic process affected British development" (Ferguson 1983, 389). The Bank of England, in order to underwrite more ample business credit as well as provide more efficient means of general exchange, is established in 1694, establishing as well as the British innovation of the funded debt, the innovation that provides the national government access to immense funds with the exceedingly generous license that "no pledge was given ever to repay the principal" (Ferguson 1983, 390). The effect—also considered by Brewer (1988)—is that "the ability to borrow, limited only by having to pay interest, was the crucial factor in Britain's victories in eighteenth-century wars" (Ferguson 1983, 391). In Britain and subsequently the independent seaboard states, the alternatives to the expanding system of commercial credit are repudiated. In England, the scheme to employ land banks, which base credit in real property, is forestalled, and in the North American states, the greater powers of federal taxation finally override the policies of "currency finance," in which governments raise capital by issuing their own paper money or certificates redeemable at a later date and, since guaranteed by the government agency, exchangeable as currency. These policies, undertaken separately by the newly independent states, would allow them to assume the federal debt accumulated in the Revolutionary War and thus curtail the powers of the new federal agency. The retention of the national debt at the federal level, the crucial measure of the viability of the new federal agency and effectively bestowing much wider federal authority, allays the quandary paramount to the Federalist vision: the concern that "Union was a league of states rather than a national system because Congress lacked the power of taxation" (Ferguson 1969, 244). The quizzical specification of the people that is the rhetorical hallmark of the struggle remains deeply troubled—ultimately overwhelmed as a viable appeal—since "in the closing years of the Revolution, the Nationalists under the aegis of such leaders as Robert Morris, Gouverneur Morris, and Alexander Hamilton started a secondary revolution directed against the political-economic establishment of the American states" (Ferguson 1983, 411). The federal agency garners its sovereignty by diminishing the former, wider prerogatives of the more local state agencies.

These indeterminacies of the federated or national people, to follow the perspective of Appleby, betray ultimately that:

> No concepts existed for analyzing a trading system that had not only moved beyond the confines of political boundaries but had created wealth essential to the conduct of politics. There was no classical language for understanding a commercial system that was public, progressive, and orderly. However appealing civic humanism was to English gentlemen involved in public issues, it did not help persons who sought to understand the private transactions that were determining the shape and direction of the Anglo-American economy.
>
> (Appleby 1986, 31)

Further still, beyond the discrepancy of the local and federal imperatives, the new proposition of individual national identity discloses the subjectivizing—rather than merely the individual—puzzle brought into being by the exigencies of the Atlantic economies. The New York jurist John Jay, one of the negotiators of the 1783 Treaty of Paris arranging independence from Britain, the first chief justice of the U.S. Supreme Court, as well as governor of New York, advocates the principle of nativism in support of the new national identity. He presses for the prerequisite of presidential native birth, and in *Federalist* #2 misstates hyperbolically the cultural unity and common sensibilities of the internationally disparate population of the independent mainland states: "This country and this people seem to have been made for each other, and it appears as if it were the design of Providence that an inheritance so proper and convenient for a band of brethren, united to each other by the strongest ties, should never be split into a number of unsocial, jealous, and alien sovereignties" (Hamilton, Jay, and Madison 1787–1788, 38). The hyperbole is undisguised since, in fact, John Jay is familiar intimately with "the already ethnically and religiously cosmopolitan New York City and was himself three-eighths French and five-eighths Dutch, without any English ancestry" (Smith 1998, 23). In other words, John Jay, as does Alexander Hamilton, understands the scrupulous set of international dynamics and equipoise on which the experiment of the new nationality depends. This comprehension is evidenced as much in his characterization of the radically diverse and changing human landscape of the independent states as "one united people" (Hamilton, Jay, and Madison 1787–1788, 38) as it is in his role in negotiating the 1794 Jay Treaty, which brings further economic and political rapprochements with Britain, thereby imperiling U.S. relations with Britain's chief European rival, France. The translation of the *unprecedented* ethnic and racial coordinations of the mainland states into "a people descended from the same ancestors, speaking the same language, professing the same religion, attached to the same principles of government, very similar in their manner and customs" (Hamilton, Jay, and Madison 1787–1788, 38) patently reimagines the diverse immigration to the mainland territories and their dynamic social atmosphere. Bernard Bailyn describes the late eighteenth-century immigration to the North American mainland, revealing the extremities of John Jay's entreaties to the singularity of the new individual national identity:

> The migration to America in the fifteen years between the end of the Seven Years War and the Revolution was remarkable by the standards of the time. Between the end of warfare in the mainland colonies and the disruption of empire in 1775, over 55,000 Protestant and Irish emigrated to America, over 40,000 Scots, and over 30,000 Englishmen—a total of approximately 125,000 from the British Isles—in addition to at least 12,000 from the German states and Switzerland who entered the port of Philadelphia, and 84,500 enslaved Africans imported to the southern colonies. This grand total of about 221,500 arrivals in the fifteen-year period (a conservative figure, yet almost 10 percent of the entire estimated population of mainland America in 1775) meant an average *annual* influx of approximately 15,000 people, which was close to the total estimated population of Boston during these years; and, except, for

> the slaves, the great majority of these tens of thousands of newcomers crowded initially into a few small port towns, almost all of them south of New England.
>
> (Bailyn 1988, 9; emphasis in original)

In short, as do its local and federal assignments, the new subjective assignment of nationality remains as conceptually fraught as it is effective.

Particularly because the Virginia lawyer James Madison registers and calculates keenly the representational antagonisms of the concept of the people, he holds a highly exemplary role in these political and subjectivizing revolutions. James Madison's insights into the delicacy of reimagining the federal compact in the 1780s, as "state rivalries blocked formation of a common front against British trade policies" (Dull 1985, 157), are galvanizing for the new national viability. The historian Jack Rakove observes:

> Far more than was the case at the state level of politics, where the task of correcting the errors incorporated in the first constitutions seemed open-ended, reform of the confederation could proceed only through the pursuit of a carefully delineated agenda. So at least it seemed to James Madison, the most thoughtful and eventually the most influential of these reformers, and to the relatively small circle of like-minded men who shared his interest in national political problems.
>
> (Rakove 1987, 82)

In the unraveling intrigue, James Madison is the leading proponent of the U.S. Constitution, serving as the

> chief spokesman at the Federal Convention for a radically new plan of government ... subsequently champion[ing] the Constitution as "Publius" in *The Federalist* and as a delegate to the Virginia ratifying convention ... [and further bringing] the process of constitution-making to a successful close by guiding through the First Congress the amendments that became the Bill of Rights.
>
> (Hobson 1979, 215)

Hobson remarks on James Madison's motives for, fluctuating opinions of, and compromises accepted in the specific form of government taken by the United States. The two most severe blows to James Madison's political vision at the 1787 convention are the rejection of the proposals "for proportional representation in both houses of the legislature and ... to give the national legislature a 'negative,' or veto, over the laws of the states" (Hobson 1979, 216). James Madison is intent to diminish the local influences represented by the states in deference to the more completely abstracted generality of national influence. For—as registered by the insistent fears of the larger states, like Massachusetts, Pennsylvania, and Virginia by the smaller states, like Delaware, New Jersey, and Rhode Island—forms of interstate conflict and commercial rivalry precipitate in large part the move to the new federated combination, fears James Madison rehearses throughout *Notes of the Debates in the Federal Convention of 1787*. The perspective of the smaller states is argued most strenuously by William Patterson of New Jersey, which is an agricultural state fated to supplement, through the excises and tariffs transacted at their busy ports, the welfare of its commercial neighbors New York and Pennsylvania. The federal agency authorized in the way James Madison champions would meet more effectively these and other matters of interstate rivalry. In sum, the federal agency would be one with authority accruing not only over the several states but, by virtue of their national singularity, also, at best, over the newly reordered competition over the transatlantic flow of property and currency, as well as the rest of the vast North American continent. The envisioned interstate organization and comity aspires to this end above all. As recorded by James Madison in *Notes of the Debates in the Federal Convention of 1787*, John Dickinson, the successful lawyer and one of the representatives of Delaware, who achieves much of his social standing by marrying into "one of the first and wealthiest commercial families" (Beard 1913, 87) of Philadelphia, states the jurisdictional quandary plainly: "We must either submit the states to the danger of being injured by the power of the Nat'l Gov't or the latter to that of being injured by the states" (Beard 1913, 91). The concept of the national "people" is pinioned, rather than clarified or highlighted, in the metonymic tensions that trouble the "nation" and the "state" as coherent markers of identity, not to mention the reportedly disinterested organization of social and political power. The proposal of the veto power that would discipline fully the local legislative determinations of the aggregate national populace redacts powerfully, this is to say, the conceptual peculiarity of the notion of the people.

It is important to grant that, as disclosed by the conclusion of *Notes on the Debates in the Federal Convention of 1787*, the unanimous approval of the new constitutional document is foremost symbolic and carefully orchestrated—particularly by Benjamin Franklin, Alexander Hamilton, and James Madison. If the magnitude of the U.S. federal powers is not as great as he first imagines, James Madison recognizes nonetheless in the compromised document that is the product of the 1787 convention the adequate means to the bolder federation of the states. Hobson describes the trajectory of James Madison's changes of perspective as follows:

> On the very eve of his debut in *The Federalist*, Madison was highly dissatisfied with, not to say, contemptuous of, the proposed government. The October 1787 letter [to Thomas Jefferson] was a strong dose of nationalism that contrasted sharply with "Publius's" celebration of the Constitution and indeed with all of Madison's subsequent writings. After this full and candid critique he ceased his advocacy of the negative on state laws and never again spoke ill of the Constitution.
>
> (Hobson 1979, 233)

The dilemma of the proposed veto—in which the notion of the "people" is vexed between the antagonisms of their state and federated renditions—provides an important measure of James Madison's alterations, or alternately circumscriptions, of mind. That is, the federal veto might attenuate the influence of the larger states yet—as readily as it might exercise it—can do so in no final way. For, with or without the federal veto, given the strength of proportional representation obtaining in the first legislative chamber (then attenuated in the Senate), the scheme retains the always potentially greater influence of the larger states—whether applied alternately as states or as elements of the larger conglomerate. It is unlikely that the representatives of large states would endorse policies directly injurious to the interests of their states, or veto (or sanction efforts to veto) policies directly bolstering the interests of their states. In tandem, particularly, James Madison's defeated proposals of proportional representation in the Senate and the federal veto strengthens the position of the large states. Large states that more fully would constitute the legislative agency would also have a greater power to protect their interests by means clearly distinct from their local political renditions. In all the permutations of authority, the influence of the state of Virginia, the largest Revolutionary state—and the state that James Madison represents—remains well disposed and, as much as the federal veto he champions obfuscates the looming influence of the large states, it exacerbates in doing so the vexations of the concept of the people.

The entreaties of James Madison in support of the new federal compromise are instructive. In *Federalist* #35, beginning by outlining the dangers to government represented by the disparate interests of "the people," James Madison by its conclusion redefines "the people" so as to conflate the concept virtually with the principles and effects of the market, the ideally infinite arena of ideally infinite exchange. James Madison's focus is taxation:

> There can be no doubt that in order to a judicious exercise of the power of taxation, it is necessary that the person in whose hands it is should be acquainted with the general genius, habits, and modes of thinking of the people at large and with the resources of the country. And this is all that can be reasonably meant by a knowledge of the interest and feelings of the people. In any other sense the proposition has either no meaning, or an absurd one.
>
> (Hamilton, Jay, and Madison 1787–1788, 217)

Evidenced by the juxtaposition of "the general genius, habits, and modes of thinking of the people at large" and "the resources of the country," "the people," as a national formula for self-imagination, reveals that the appearance of cohesion is merely the beguiling or subjectivizing effect of the new relays of accumulation generated in the modernizing episode of mercantilism. Any notion that otherwise holds "the people" and the market as essentially distinguishable, James Madison emphasizes, risks absurdity. James Madison in the *Federalist*, as he does before the first congress, exposes "the people" as the device of elite colonial subjects forging their advantage and modernity in the revolutionary national expression.

Even as he is an important figure in the Jeffersonian opposition to the administration authorized by the new federal document, James Madison, having served in the Virginia state assembly from 1784 to 1787, arrives at the 1787 constitutional convention with the fear that:

> In republics the majority made the laws but too often these laws, rather than reflecting the public good or general interest of the whole society, ratified the self interests of a dominant faction in that society—whether debtors, creditors, planters, merchants, manufacturers, members of a certain religious sect, inhabitants of a particular region, or some other political, economic, or cultural group. Whenever the opportunity presented itself, there was nothing to restrain a majority faction from seizing control of the government and imposing its designs on the minority.
>
> (Hobson 1979, 222)

James Madison's motives for, fluctuating opinions of, and compromises accepted in the specific form of government taken by the United States turn always on the absolute representative impossibility of the figure of the people, even as it certifies and ideally humanizes the relays of wealth and power that in the late eighteenth century remain, as yet, radically or relatively unassumed (depending on perspective).

The unprecedented political opportunities and calculations on the North American seaboard and its environs ensures that "the era of the American Revolution was a period of political paranoia. Social and political events were seldom conceived to have causes apart from conscious purpose, and the purposes of any group organized to have an impact on government were automatically thought of as malignant" (Banning 1974, 171). Banning further argues that the intense climate of the Revolutionary era yields the precipitous stature of the new, compromised constitutional document. In the aftermath of its framing, the constitutional document that James Madison worries over is seized as an exceptional resource in the political rivalries it licenses to unfold. "Paradoxically, then, it was the appearance of a deeply felt opposition to the policies of our first administration, which assured the quick acceptance of the Constitution that had been committed to its care. More than the government itself, the opposition had to have an unchallengeable constitution on which to rely" (Banning 1974, 187). The new constitutional document is arrayed against the policies, in large part, of Alexander Hamilton, who represents New York at the 1787 convention and, as the first Secretary of the Treasury (resigning in 1795), is the triumphant strategist of the fledgling national economic policy.

> During the first year of the new government, while Jefferson made his way back from France, Madison acted as congressional leader of the forces who meant to assure a strong and independent executive power. He parted with the administration only on the questions of discrimination and national assumption of the debt, policies Virginians considered sectionally unjust. On these issues, however, both Madison and Jefferson were willing to compromise for the sake of federal union. The two Virginians did not move firmly into a more general opposition until they were confronted with Alexander Hamilton's proposal of a national bank. Then, already troubled by what seemed to them a growing sectional bias in the laws, they saw in the broad construction of federal powers which Hamilton advanced in support of the bank a powerful blow at the barriers against an indefinite expansion of federal authority and, with it, the enhancement of the dangerous power of a northern majority.
>
> (Banning 1974, 180)

Hobson codifies the opposition as follows:

> Despite its extended sphere, the government proved more susceptible to faction than [James Madison] had foreseen in 1787. The threat of oppression, moreover, came not from a *majority* faction (whose dangers his previous warnings had dwelled on almost exclusively) but from a highly organized and influential "moneyed interest" that had somehow seized the reins of power and was adroitly maintaining its control through "corruption." To combat the Hamiltonian system of funded debts, banks, and encouragements for manufactures, Madison adopted a strategy of opposition that necessarily forced him to retreat from his high nationalism of 1787 (even to the point of flirting with the doctrine of "state interposition" in 1799).
>
> (Hobson 1979, 234–235)

The exemplarity of James Madison, Alexander Hamilton, and John Jay is not to fix the feints of the rhetorical and nationalizing "people" as original to any personality, but to underscore that as the sign of its emphatic modernity the fledgling United States redescribes national territories and presents new conceptual paradigms, attending always to the immense transatlantic economic values generating the series of macropolitical confrontations for well over a century, as in: the First and Second Anglo-Dutch Wars (1652–1654, 1664–1667), the Nine Years War (1689–1698), the War of Spanish Succession (1702–1713), the War of Austrian Succession (1740–1748), the Seven Years War (1756–1763), and the American Revolution (1776–1783). The forthright glosses of the "people," as does the macropolitical context eliciting the concept, give modern forms of commercial exchange the priority shaping the renewed coordination of the former mainland colonies.

The "People"

Literary critic David Kajazian acknowledges the queried role of taxation in the political vision in which commodity exchange remains the unassailable end of the new national formation of the British mainland colonies and, moreover, its self-representations. He states:

> On July 4, 1789, four months into its first session, the U.S. congress celebrated thirteen years of formal U.S. independence by passing its first tariff bill. The bill placed duties of 5–15 percent on approximately

> thirty different goods, ranging from nails to carriages, with the highest rates reserved for "articles of luxury." When Madison proposed this "endeavor" with the first non procedural words uttered in the new congress, he represented the tariff as a means of restoring the lost unity of the nation.... For Madison, "The deficiency in our Treasury" threatens the "union" with disintegration into the implicitly plural and antagonist realm of the Representatives' "constituents." In response, he calls the Representatives "first attention" and "united exertions" to a national economic policy. However, Madison suggests that this tariff will do more than fill the treasury, it is precisely a *national* policy because it promises to transform these potentially plural and antagonistic "constituents" into unified subjects abstracted from their particularities and antagonisms and represented as formally equivalent units of a national population—units he elsewhere calls "citizens" who will engage in lively economic exchange.
>
> (Kajazian 2000, 130)

The imaginative torque and the relays of order confirmed in the settlement of federal taxation for the seaboard enterprise pivots on racial blackness as the impossible point of consideration for the viability of national identity. Because "as merchant capital flooded the Atlantic theatre after the sixteenth century, European mercantilist measures emerged almost immediately to regulate that flood, to give it social and political shape" (Kajazian 2000, 131), "the people," the revolutionary form of social organization promulgated by the union of the former seaboard colonies, the newest and most preeminent of these social and political shapes, discloses the intercontinental circuit of commodity exchange and its articulation of the vastly abstracted "market," which are more conceivable than the vast numbers—particularly the racialized numbers of—its increasing compass of the conscripts conflated with the market.

As the Federalist era demonstrates, the United States is, above all, a concept, with its conceivability, effectively the matter of the turns of the imagination, resting finally on the programs of force that, as the fundamental characteristic of European modernity, fails the report of force. This conceptual turn is fundamental, as documented by the historian Howard Ohline, who outlines the constitutive role of the African-derived "socially necessary labor time" yielding—beyond the material artifacts of the Atlantic economies—the inaugural compromises and coalitions of the revised experiment in the seaboard nationality. Ohline examines the role of interest-group politics, "the tendency of individual congressmen to pursue the priorities of his constituents while shaping the policy of the nation as a whole" (Ohline 1980, 335–336), in order to argue that, "afraid of alienating possible southern support for assumption of state debts, no northerner consistently supported the first abolitionist attempt to transform Revolutionary antislavery ideals into the explicit policy of the national government" (Ohline 1980, 336). The political compromise in question arises when petitions to define Congressional powers over slavery and Alexander Hamilton's recommendations concerning public credit are considered by the national representatives on the same agenda in 1790. The principle that "humanity unconnected with material interest was not within the limits of republican legislative actions" (Ohline 1980, 342)—which is used to refute the abolitionist entreaties of the Quakers, who have no immediate connections to slave property—is evident as well in the regional alliances producing the policies that both foreclose the assumption of the national debt by the states and federal abolitionist measures. "The reason that historians have failed to understand that northerners, too, were engaged in special-interest politics in 1790 is that they have looked at the issue entirely in terms of slavery versus antislavery" (Ohline 1980, 357). Northern representatives and their commercial interests, understanding that in "a country in which the operative fiscal systems were those of thirteen local and diverse entities, a federal debt was anomaly," understand further that "loss of the debt portended disaster to the Nationalist movement. Without a debt there would be little reason to ask for the [federal] taxing power, since ... paying the debt was about the only thing that Congress would need much money for" (Ferguson 1969, 245–246). Ohline summarizes the national compromise and coalition of the distinct interest groups:

> As republicanism helps one to understand why Americans accepted slavery in a society dedicated to freedom, special-interest politics helps one to understand why congressmen who claimed to be antislavery accepted slavery as they constructed a modern political system bound together by economic self-interest. The belief of northern congressmen that the national government should foster economic stability and growth created a functional relationship between slavery and economic measures.
>
> (Ohline 1980, 359)

The open fiat on which the new guarantor of national viability, federal taxation, depends designates racial blackness as the conceptual and political, if not *human*, point betraying the premises and dilemmas of modern political community. The civic proposition of self-coherence granting national identity as its most hyperbolic form proceeds from the conscription of sub-Saharan Africans and their descendants into the severest routines of the Atlantic commercial cycles, as well as the severest routines of individual and administrative European imaginations. The disposition of racial blackness constitutes the impossible point of human conception in the enterprise—foreclosed as the unnamed violence of human visibility.

The priority given modern forms of economic exchange in the specification of "the people" reiterates that both actually and figuratively, "the people," historically and paradigmatically, depend on the massive production and movement of the cash crops cocoa, coffee, indigo, rum, sugar, and tobacco, which elicit the international competition waged over the economic values of the Caribbean basin—competition sponsoring and orienting modern national formations. In not merely the historical but also the paradigmatic move, the reasoning in question forcefully determines racial blackness to be the ideal, adamant recognition of African-derived peoples as if exploitable, indispensable, fully accounted quantities. At stake originally, as the "modern," is the phantasmatic animation of the conceptual form (the commodity) in the face of the already fully animate individual and collective material forms (in human proportions) of racial blackness. Given the reasoning feint of commodity fetishism and the ideally infinite arena of ideally infinite exchange, other forms of historical and cultural presence remain so too, although not the expansive limits of the market.

Notes

This paper was completed in part under a fellowship from the University of California Humanities Research Institute. I gratefully acknowledge the conveners of the seminar, Kathleen McHugh and Chon Noriega.

1. The torque and quandary are reckonable, to follow the arguments of the historian William Pierson, as a type of aesthetic transaction in which "certain black and white designs can be made to contain two vastly different pictures, the observed pattern depending upon which color our mind perceives at a particular moment to be dominant.... What would happen if we shifted our normal perspective so as to make our nation's black legacy, a primary point of reference? Just as in the visual image, the patterns of American history would instantly seem to reverse themselves. Such a process would not change the history, but it would offer a flash of Afrocentric insight—how changed the world could be if only we thought differently about things, at least for a moment" (Pierson 1993, ix).

References

Amaragilio, Jack, and Antonio Callari. 1993. "Marxian Value Theory and the Problem of the Subject: The Role of Commodity Fetishism." In *Fetishism as Cultural Discourse*, ed. Emily Apter and William Pietz. Ithaca: Cornell University Press.

Appleby, Joyce. 1984. *Capitalism and a New Social Order*. New York: New York University Press.

———. 1986. "Republicanism in Old and New Contexts." *William and Mary Quarterly* 43: 20–34.

Bailey, Ronald. "The Slave(ry) Trade and the Development of Capitalism in the United States." *Social Science History* 14: 373–414.

Bailyn, Bernard. 1988. *The Peopling of British North America: An Introduction*. New York: Vintage.

Banning, Lance. 1974. "Republican Ideology and the Triumph of the Constitution, 1789–1793." *William and Mary Quarterly* 21: 167–188.

Beard, Charles. 1913. *An Economic Interpretation of the Constitution of the United States*. Repr., New York: The Free Press, 1986.

Ben-Atar, Doron. 1998. "Alexander Hamilton's Alternative: Technological Piracy and the Report on Manufactures." In *Federalists Reconsidered*, ed. Doron Ben-Atar and Barbara B. Oberg. Charlottesville: University of Virginia Press.

Ben-Atar, Doron, and Barbara B. Oberg. 1998. "Introduction: The Paradoxical Legacy of the Federalists." In *Federalists Reconsidered*, ed. Doron Ben-Atar and Barbara B. Oberg. Charlottesville: University of Virginia Press.

Blackburn, Robin. 1997. *The Making of New World Slavery: From the Baroque to the Modern 1492–1800*. London: Verso.

Breen, T. H. 1988. "'Baubles of Britain': The American and Consumer Revolutions of the Eighteenth Century." *Past and Present* 119 (May): 73–104.

Brewer, John. 1988. *The Sinews of Power: War, Money, and the English State, 1688–1783*. Cambridge: Harvard University Press.

Cayton, Andrew R. L. 1998. "Radicals in the 'Western World': The Federalist Conquest of the Trans-Appalachian North America." In *Federalists Reconsidered*, ed. Doron Ben-Atar and Barbara B. Oberg. Charlottesville: University of Virginia Press.

Chakrabarty, Dipesh. 1992. "Provincializing Europe: Postcoloniality and the Critique of History." *Cultural Studies* 6, no. 3: 337–357.

Cobban, Alfred. 1969. *The Nation State and National Self-Determination*. New York: Crowell.

Connor, Walker. 1978. "A Nation is a Nation, is a State, is an Ethnic Group, is a . . ." *Ethnic and Racial Studies* 1, no. 4: 379–388.

Copjec, Joan. 1994. *Read My Desire: Lacan Against the Historicists*. Cambridge, Mass.: MIT Press.

Dull, Jonathan. 1985. *A Diplomatic History of the American Revolution*. New Haven, Conn.: Yale University Press.

Eltis, David. 1993. "Europeans and the Rise and Fall of African Slavery in the Americas: An Interpretation." *American Historical Review* (December): 1339–1423.

Ferguson, E. James. 1969. "The Nationalists of 1781–1783 and the Economic Interpretation of the Constitution." *Journal of American History* 56: 241–261.

———. 1983. "Political Economy, Public Liberty, and the Formation of the Constitution." *William and Mary Quarterly* 40: 389–412.

Gailey, Harry A. 1970. *History of Africa, Vol. I: From Earliest Times to 1800*. Malabar, Fla.: Krieger Publishing Co.

Gemery, Henry A., and Jan S. Hogendorn. 1983. "The Economic Costs of West African Participation in the Atlantic Slave Trade: A Preliminary Sampling for the Eighteenth Century." In *The Uncommon Market: Essays in the Economic History of the Atlantic Slave Trade*, ed. Henry A. Gemery and Jan S. Hogendorm. New York: Academic Press.

Hamilton, Alexander, John Jay, and James Madison. 1787–1788. *The Federalist Papers*. Repr., ed. Clinton Rossiter. New York: Penguin, 1961.

Hobson, Charles. 1979. "The Negative on State Laws: James Madison and the Crisis of Republican Government." *William and Mary Quarterly* 36: 215–235.

Kazanjian, David. 2000. "Race, Nation, Equality: Olaudah Equiano's *Interesting Life* as a Genealogy of U.S. Mercantilism." In *Post-National American Studies*, ed. John Carlos Rowe. Berkeley: University of California Press.

Lopez-Alves, Fernando. 2000. *State Formation and Democracy in Latin America: 1810–1900*. Durham: Duke University Press.

Lovejoy, Paul E. 1979. *Transformations in Slavery: A History of Slavery in Africa*. Cambridge: Cambridge University Press.

Madison, James. 1787. *Notes of Debates in the Federal Convention of 1787*. Repr., New York: Norton, 1987.

Morgan, Edmund S. 1975. *American Slavery, American Freedom: The Ordeal of Colonial Virginia*. New York: Norton.

Morrison, Toni. 1992. *Jazz*. New York: Knopf.

Ohline, Howard A. 1980. "Slavery, Economics, and Congressional Politics, 1790." *Journal of Southern History* 46: 335–360.

Palmer, Colin A. 1944. Introduction to *Capitalism and Slavery*, by Eric Williams. Chapel Hill: University of North Carolina Press.

Pierson, William D. 1993. *Black Legacy: America's Hidden Heritage*. Amherst: University of Massachusetts Press.

Rakove, Jack. 1987. "From One Agenda to Another: The Condition of American Federalism, 1783–1787." In *The American Revolution: Its Character and Limits*, ed. Jack P. Greene. New York: New York University Press.

Renan, Ernest. 1882. "*Qu'est qu'une nation?*" In *Nationalism*, ed. John Hutchinson and Anthony D. Smith, trans. Ida Mae Snyder. Oxford: Oxford University Press, 1994.

Richmond, Anthony. 1994. *Global Apartheid: Refugees, Racism, and the New World Order*. Oxford: Oxford University Press.

Rodney, Walter. 1970. *A History of the Upper Guinea Coast, 1545–1800*. Oxford: Clarendon Press.

Shalhope, Robert E. 1982. "Republicanism and Early American Historiography." *William and Mary Quarterly* 39: 334–356.

Smith, Rogers M. 1998. "Constructing American National Identity." In *Federalists Reconsidered*, ed. Doron Ben-Atar and Barbara B. Oberg. Charlottesville: University of Virginia Press.

Sloan, Herbert E. 1998. "Hamilton's Second Thoughts." In *Federalists Reconsidered*, ed. Doron Ben-Atar and Barbara B. Oberg. Charlottesville: University of Virginia Press.

Steele, G. R. 1998. "The Money Economy: Mercantilism, Classical Economics, and Keynes' General Theory." *American Journal of Economics and Sociology* 57, no. 4 (October): 485–498.

Strange, Susan. 1996. *The Retreat of the State: The Diffusion of Power in the World Economy*. Cambridge: Cambridge University Press.

Thomas, Hugh. 1997. *The Slave Trade: The Story of the Atlantic Slave Trade: 1440–1870*. New York: Simon and Schuster.

Williams, Eric. 1944. *Capitalism and Slavery*. Chapel Hill: University of North Carolina Press.

Wood, Peter H. 1974. *Black Majority: Negroes in Colonial South Carolina from 1670 Through the Stono Rebellion*. New York: Norton.

Part II

Posthuman Futures

Literature, Art, and the Politics of Personhood

5 Divided Origins and the Arithmetic of Ownership

Marilyn Strathern

I

Introduction

Anthropologists do not generally go about their business thinking that their subject matter is a contingency. Yet that invariably becomes the case when the ethnographic record—however vast—or models of social structure—however illuminating—are brought into relation with other bodies of material. They are hardly alone in this. Insofar as bodies of knowledge form systems, other efforts must lie outside: part of the environment, not part of the system.

One body of knowledge that perpetually strives toward the systemic is law. Indeed, this reflection on contingency is prompted by Anne Barron's (1998) discussion of the influences that in 1991 were brought to bear on the Australian Federal Court that upheld (against his will in this case) the appropriateness of copyright as a property relation between an Aboriginal artist and his carving of a sacred emblem. In asking how this legal recognition had come about in the first place, she discusses a number of what she calls contingent issues, issues that in her view belonged to the environment, not to the system. They included the newly discovered artistic value of Aboriginal "art," not to speak of the thoroughly contingent place that, in her opinion, the genius of the Romantic individual holds in respect to copyright law in general. Copyright in this case was allowed to the artist as the originator of the work without invoking any stronger sense of creativity or merit. There are many cultural arenas of debate—and assumptions about the individuality of genius occur over and again in intellectual property discussions—that supply people rhetoric with which they may approach the law without being the basis of law. Of interest to the student of culture may well be the very fashioning of that rhetoric.

The boundaries are not always clear.[1] Two Australian legal theorists and feminists observe just that, in considering whether persons can ever be property (Davies and Naffine 2001). Property law, they argue, is surrounded by assumptions that act out the idea that one can have property in persons, or aspects of persons, even though the law is built on its denial. (They discuss mainly U.S., Australian, and British jurisdictions.) Indeed, they suggest that these days, property in persons may be assumed in the very arena that legal thinkers once took as the radical divide that separated persons from things: self-ownership.[2] Insofar as persons (as subjects) own themselves, no one else can own them (as objects). Now this state of affairs is at once interesting and unsettling for the anthropologist. It may be a contingency that one could ask similar questions of many of the kinds of societies anthropologists study, including those of Aboriginal Australia. But if the rhetoric then brings such societies into the orbit of debate, they are likely to get pressed into other people's agendas. Thus, regardless of what national regimes of law do or do not allow, the international community may have its own interests in whether or not persons are treated as property.[3] This is a contingency, in other words, of some effect.

To be blunt, the question of whether one can talk of persons possessing one another has dogged my own anthropological—and feminist—sensibilities for a long time. Ownership begins to look propertylike in societies such as those of Melanesia, where payments pass hands for all kind of services and rights that people acquire in one another, where suitors expect to pay bridewealth and killers hope to escape revenge by handing out huge sums. In the coarse vocabulary of money, men and women may speak of buying and selling brides and of buying off the victim's kin.

Of course, there are many ways in which people can negotiate interests without having property rights over one another, just as there are diverse ways in which they might be said to "own" one another. What makes the question newly interesting are recent debates that have sprung up in relation to a particular type of property: namely, intellectual property. Along with them has come an arithmetic of sorts, that is, the "discovery" that while there must be an identifiable originator of a work or product on whom the right is conferred (and this holds for works that meet the criteria either of copyright or patent), it is a contingency of some ethical moment that many others may also be involved in the working or supplying of raw material (e.g., Jazsi 1994; Woodmansee 1994; Biagioli and Galison 2003). If rights confer the opportunity of reward, the argument goes, these others should be rewarded too, whether or not they are recognized as owners. The "others" may be counted as many other individuals involved in making the thing in question, or as a collectivity with prior interests in a "commons."

Now this is the moment, as Davies and Naffine gesture at the end of their book, at which materials from beyond the Euro-American tradition may start to acquire comparative value. And this is where we may be reminded of the reason why the Aboriginal artist was trying to withdraw from a copyright agreement: it had led the license holders to whom he had sold it then sublicensing the design, and others moved in to protest. The others included people he would count as kinsmen. It was clear that members of his clan both had claims to the design and claims over him: the design had originated in the clan, and the clan determined the conditions of its reproduction. I do not wish to step into the mire of what is collective or communal here;[4] the interests of a body of people may be conceived as either singular or plural depending on context—and depending on whether one counts the claims or counts the people.[5] I focus instead on one type of multiplicity, where more than one person means there is more than one (type of) claim being put forward. With respect to intellectual property rights, that in turn would imply more than one kind of originating activity. I believe that this focus could in the long run throw light on Euro-American assumptions about property in persons. However, the immediate enquiry springs out of Melanesian materials.

I wish to pursue a strong form of multiple claims in relation to certain Melanesian societies, all from lowland Papua New Guinea. In Davies and Naffine (2001, 172–173), following Pottage (1998), they discuss composite claims put forward in relation to a cell line developed from blood samples collected from that country; one of the "inventors" named in the ensuing patent had been active as a facilitator, not as a scientist. However, the materials I consider concern Papua New Guineans in their relations with one another. They offer some striking examples of multiplicity in the way they count persons, and it is persons vis-à-vis their origins whom they are thinking of. The origins are vested in parenthood and kinship relations: different types of claims yield different kinds of rights. This introduces a deliberate contingency into my narrative. Melanesia aside, what has kinship to do with anything? In their own society, of course, English speakers might use the language of ownership for kin, though explicitly without connotations of property rights (e.g., Edwards and Strathern 2000). Nonetheless, kinship is interestingly absent from the lawyers' questions about persons as property.

In all the material they consider, Davies and Naffine may have thought kin relations too far removed from their legal and quasilegal concerns, or that "owning" ("my" child) in such a context was merely a matter of identification (as in "my" boss) or a reflex of belonging (as in "my" team). However, the crosscultural point is that elsewhere, many claims on both persons *and things* that begin to look property-like, even claims taking one to court, as in the Aboriginal case, are premised on the rights that kin have in one another.

The present narrative creates a question about multiple origins, then, from a blatantly heterogeneous set of "contingent intersections" or "discontinuous particularities"; the aim is to "enable their intelligibility to be appreciated differently" (Barron 1998, 42–43; after Foucault and Levinas). There are greater and lesser contingencies here: severally Euro-American anxieties about property in persons and the role of the originator in intellectual property rights, along with the nature of Papua New Guinean kinship transactions and the way people envisage their origins in one another. Clearly, the concerns do not add up, but taken together, perhaps the intelligibility of each is slightly increased.

II

Counting People: Murik

Imagine a party of NGO-driven Euro-American experts wanting to ascertain precise genealogical relationships. This could be in the context of advice over claims for natural resource extraction, possibly envisaged as royalties or as recompense for indigenous knowledge (cf. Posey 1996; Toft 1998). The experts assume there will be no "community leader"—in any case it is part of their anthropologically informed critique of multinational corporations that these extractors of resources do not pay attention to local divisions—and will be sensitive to the fact that it is easy to overlook women's claims. So in order to give women space to speak, they decide to collect information from husbands and wives separately.

If they were to go into a Murik village, as it existed in the Sepik river area twenty years ago (Lipset and Stritecky 1994), they might have some surprises. They would no doubt be attuned to the difference between biological and social kinship, would not expect people to have any knowledge of genetics, and would be on the lookout for classificatory kin. Having done their homework, they would be aware that these Papua New Guinean people allocate children to bilateral kin groups on both the mother's and father's side. Indeed, knowing that all four of the child's kin groups may make claims on it, they would also be aware of the importance of nurture in the way claims were established. So they would probably settle for the simplest kind of information, beginning with questions about the children people had. Here they might well be startled to find that husbands and wives can disagree. Each has his or her own version, and while often these tally, this is not always true: not just the names and sex of children differ but so do the numbers. They do not count the children in the same way.

Oddly enough, the actual fieldworkers of twenty years ago who reported this were looking for *more* disagreement than they found. They had come with a theory of knowledge that posited that the sexes articulated cultural knowledge differently and that genealogical divergences would appear in their kinship discourses at large (Lipset and Stritecky 1994, 3, 18). Instead, they found considerable agreement, and the divergences in counting boiled down to two sets of differences. Murik men mentioned their adopted children more often than women, while women mentioned children who had died more often than men. I want to suggest that this piece of arithmetic needs a general mathematical solution. That is, it is not a question of people not able to add up properly or adding together incommensurables, but of the observer having to rewrite the sum as an equation: to rewrite the "one" world that the observer sees, in which children are potentially countable, as "two" worlds, perceived separately by men and women, in which children are divided from parents in different ways.

In this example and those which follow, I have deliberately veered away from societies with what are known in an older literature as unilineal descent groups, that is, where people are clearly differentiated by the exclusive groups to which they are affiliated by ancestry through one parent alone.[6] Unilineal descent gives too quick an answer to the way people in Papua New Guinea can perceive origins. Ancestry appears as an origin in the idiom of an exclusive grouping that already presupposes belonging and the sense of ownership this brings,[7] and I want to arrive at some understanding of ownership rather than start with it.

Let me put the positive side. What attracted me to the Murik account was Eduardo Viveiros de Castro's (1992; 1998) thesis of Amazonian perspectivism. By contrast with the commonly understood sense of perspective in which a person's point of view creates an object ("out there"), Amazonian perspectivism creates the subject. For the original condition of humans and animals, he explains, is not animality ("nature") but humanity ("society"). Amazonian perspectivism implies that any being that takes a point of view sees itself as human and as a person, and differences between points of view lie not in minds—which are all the same—but in bodies, and here all "humans" see some bodies as animal and others as human like themselves. To be a person is to register the point of view a subject takes. In the Melanesian analogue I earlier thought I had found (Strathern 1999, 249–56), the pertinent divide would not be between humans and nonhumans but between different kinds of humans, such as the persons of a son and a sister's son.[8] Their divergent affiliations axiomatically ensure that being a son is not the same as being a sister's son; the perspectivist point would be that these positions are not relative views on the (same) world but point to radically distinct states of being in nonsimilar worlds. Paternal kin claim their child in a very different way from maternal kin. My example had explored gender, but it had also rested on the presence of group affiliation. For a division between the father's side and the mother's side on which the distinctiveness rests—that is, the division between parents—is iconic in descent group systems. The advantage of the Murik material is that it sidesteps group assumptions about maternal and paternal connections yet locates an intriguing difference in how mothers and fathers view their children. We could even say, after Viveiros de Castro, that it is not that they count their children differently, but what they count as children are different entities.

This probably seems a rather elaborate way in which to comment upon men's and women's marginally diverse renderings of childbirth. Why not just accept them as holding different perspectives in the Euro-American sense of self-referential "unique" points of view to put alongside numerous other self-referential and unique points of view (Strathern 1999, 251)? The Euro-American stance implies diverse ways of "knowing" the one world we all share but describe from our different viewpoints. However, knowing that knowledge matters when it comes to intellectual property, we might wish to dig a bit deeper.

Analogous Worlds

What attracted me to Viveiros de Castro's Amazonian perspectivism is the clarity with which he locates it as a matter of ontology, not epistemology. It is not about what one knows but about how one is, about the nature of the body with which one inhabits the world and apprehends it. The body is the organ of perception, perspectives being different according to the body one has. The reference to the body includes its affects, dispositions, and capacities (Viveiros de Castro 1998, 47; reiterated by Pedersen 2001, 420). In short, across species, there is spiritual or intellectual unity, corporeal diversity. Now the Melanesian case does not present us with the viewpoints that humans and nonhumans have on one another, and the parallel with Amazonian perspectivism must be tentative. But there is a kind of bodily "perspective" that does suggest differences of an ontological order.

As it happens, Lipset and Stritecky (1994, 15–17) themselves dismiss some of the more obvious reasons why Murik men and women should count their children differently, arguing that the disparity is not just about women recalling stillbirths or men boasting about their social power. The reason they put forward has to do with the bodily interior of each and the influences that internal bodily powers have on others. It is simply that women are not bothered about mentioning dead babies, whereas men are very bothered indeed: men are held responsible for the death of children at birth, since this is a sign that they have failed to follow pregnancy protocols. Adultery, for instance, puts the husband's interior body into a state that is lethal for the young child. When it comes to adoption, women tend to mention children adopted in, but not children adopted out. To men, the traffic is all part of their larger nurturing roles (which they liken to mothering, specifically suckling),[9] including helping others by sending them children. It is women who see the children they have lost as truncating the kind of nurture they offer ("cutting the breast"). Like the observance of protocols at birth, the authors argue, women's nurture requires management of the interior body, for the nubile or parturient female body is otherwise dangerous to adults in general. Very crudely, the signs switch: men mother (nurture) adults and are dangerous to children; women mother (nurture) children and are dangerous to adults. In this equation, the different *effects* that men and women have lie in their being—a matter not so much of managing knowledge as of managing the consequences of their bodily condition. The conditions are specific. Thus, liability for danger comes from female bodies in the form of young women of childbearing age, and from men's bodies when their wives are pregnant. Insofar as such internal dispositions shape the world that people perceive exists around them, these dispositions have ontological status.[10]

But in what sense are they different effects? Is this a case of what Pedersen calls analogous identification (Pedersen 2001, 413; after Viveiros de Castro 1998; cf. Wagner 1977)? We may recall the perspectivist contrast of spiritual unity/corporeal diversity. In the Murik instance, male and female bodies seem alike in their inner capacities to influence others (inner unity), yet see themselves in bodies differentiated along another axis altogether, namely, other person's bodies in particular states of childhood or adulthood (reproductive diversity). For with some drama, the Murik reveal a difference between male and female persons through this other difference between persons, that between adults and children.[11] Temporality, or stage of growth, introduces crucial distinctions, so that under certain (temporally bounded) conditions, men's and women's bodies have differentiated effects on others.[12]

It is clear that more than one kind of originating activity is going on. First as child and then as adult, the person owes their health and vitality to the care that others take, and that care is of one of two kinds: observing rules or bestowing nurture. The inner powers of parents—both male and female—set different influences into motion depending on the reproductive stage the child/adult is at. In turn, the exterior form allows specific social origins to be claimed at certain moments.

Thus Murik men and women alike may claim the privilege of decorating children's bodies. Decorating takes place, for instance, at the climax of a series of rituals that confer entry into a ceremonial group, with its titles and insignia, and is the privilege of the title-holding senior of the group, male or female. Indeed, the capacity to bestow certain named ornaments is described by the ethnographers as a right, and one exercised somewhat competitively. First-born children in particular find themselves subject to the claims of more than one kin group that may be competing for the child (Lipset and Stritecky 1994, 5, 7). Note that these are not unilineal descent groups but ceremonial groups that may use ties through either sons (or brothers) or daughters (or sisters) to claim affiliates. Far from group affiliation being settled at birth, then, allegiance is established only once growth to adulthood is assured. The affiliation of the child is "claimed" by its seniors wishing to bestow their ornaments upon it. We may conclude that the design of the ornaments "tells" you which group the child belongs to—and insofar as they declare the child's subject position, then the child, so to speak, belongs to the ornaments.

Counting Ancestors: Omie

So how many bodies are made present when persons manifest their capacities as though they had both inner and outer versions and when they move through stages which may, as when maturation rites are performed, alter bodily states, temporally or permanently? Or when bodies also hold the imprint of their diverse kinship origins? The Murik child could be claimed by groups on either its mother's or its father's side, and it is his or her body that they in turn claim in decorating it. Where the bodies of children are held to take after the bodies of parents, procreation can introduce a further dynamic.

If persons derive substance from both maternal and paternal kin, each generation has to take into account the fresh combination/division introduced by the new bringing together of the child's two parents.[13] But to reproduce the *same* bodies in each generation, you have to reproduce the same number of origins. This is an explicit aim of some Papua New Guinea kinship systems[14] that consistently produce new generations out of old ones with the same number of antecedents. They achieve this by deliberately shedding earlier connections. Far from the multiplying effect of Euro-American genealogies, each generation can point to an identical number of ancestral origins.

Some peoples bypass the mathematics altogether. They cut through the issues of multiplication and division by simply declaring that women belong to their mother's groups and men to their father's. Such systems are rare in the ethnographic record.[15] Exclusive affiliation along gender lines seemingly flies in the face of the usual kinds of accommodations for combining group membership with reproduction based on parental pairing. However, in one famous case of "sex-affiliation," the symmetry of same-sex identification leads to the extreme claim by the ethnographer that the sexes in themselves form "distinct social groups."[16] Writing about the Omie of Papua New Guinea as things were some thirty years ago, Marta Rohatynskyj[17] observes:

> It is clear that the sexes comprise two distinct groups. Men reside in collectivities on land with which they are identified through a set of *ma'i ma'i* [land specific totems] and the *anie* [plant emblems]. Interspersed among them are isolated women who, in consistently not bearing the *anie* of the groups within which they reside, stand as a whole in opposition to the groups formed by men.
>
> (1990, 449)

She goes on to argue that men and women are equally persons and equally involved in group reproduction. This is through their *anie* affiliation, for women take their mothers' and men their fathers'. And they have the same kinds of emblems because, it is reported, they also have the same kinds of bodies: Omie women have their mothers' bodies and men their fathers' bodies.

Omie can think of themselves, then, as having *either* one (same sex) parent *or* as having two. In other words, they can count the number of parents they have in one of two ways. Rohatynskyj herself (1990, 434) opens her account by saying that it is the sex of the child that determines group affiliation. From the child's perspective there is no alternative: each person has only one same-sex parent (male and female are analogous here). At the same time, the group affiliation that follows from this divides parents quite radically into two kinds. The opposite sex parent plays quite different and quite distinct roles; children may show his or her imprint on their external features, for instance. But the overwhelming nature of the same-sex tie means not only that the same-sex parent and child belong to each other (are identified with each other) but that it is the vital substance of that parent alone that causes the child to come into being and gives it an origin. Rohatynskyj (1990, 439) refers to this as *ownership*. As she glosses it, the one is the cause of the other.

It is worth noting that the same-sex parent is duplicated, through marriage rules it is not necessary to spell out here, in that the girl is also, through this other route, identified with her mother's mother and the boy with his father's father. (Those who share the same plant emblem are spoken of as living together, and here men take precedence; men's ties to the land introduce an important asymmetry between adjacent generations, which the marriage rules resolve in alternate generations.)[18] This shows in maturation rituals, some of which assume that male and female bodies are externally analogous, boys and girls having their septum pierced in the same way, and others of which diverge in order to ensure the appropriate development of internal capacities. Hence boys undergo rebirth at the hands of men, who refashion their insides through dietary and other rules, the fledglings emerging from the initiation nest to take the place of their grandfathers (father's fathers).[19] As they come out, senior men sing songs that the candidates' grandfathers composed personally, and from this moment the juniors are able to use their grandfather's totemic names. Girls are taken care of by senior women, taught appropriate bodily comportment, and (though the ethnographer does not say so) we may read their own capacity to give birth as their inheritance of their own mother's and mother's mother's capacity.[20] The generations are united by the vitality they show.

Perhaps there is a similarity here to identifications made elsewhere, and radically between dead and living. Pedersen's (2001) analysis of certain southern North Asian societies is germane. These people depart from the Amazonian type of human/animal perspectivism also found in northern North Asia, but instigate a perspectivism of sorts across interhuman relations, and specifically, relations between living persons and dead ancestor spirits. It takes shamans to move across the divide and see through ancestral eyes. In the Melanesian cases, there may be an equally dramatic denouement (part of a performance), but it is one staged *as* a stage in the reproductive process that reveals the unity of ancestors and descendants. An altered external body (the now mature child) points to the flow of internal powers across the generations. This is emphatically an embodied power: grandchildren "appear" as their grandparents.[21] Put otherwise, the grandchild makes the grandparent appear.

Owners and Makers

Let me return to the issue of ownership. Rohatynskyj used the term ownership when she described a parent being the cause of his or her child, by which she meant the cause of its being and condition in the world (and the battle for a child to be born as either its mother's offspring or its father's takes place, she observes, hidden away, within the womb). Yet there can be no "original" in the infinite series D—M—MM, only the same state replicated.[22] Perhaps we can regard the opposite sex parent as a kind of negative presence, in which case its active elimination is the relational act that confers the same-sex parent's ownership.

Among its attributes, and like the songs sung at a boy's coming-out ceremony, the *anie* emblem presents an image of what it is of the person that can be replicated in the next generation.[23] The emblem belongs to more than one body, but is only produced through a particular body, that is, in being borne by a living person. So it is an image of his antecedents that a person owns, or equally, we may say it is the image that owns the person (that is, through which they own the person). The *anie* endures: a succession of persons come to "hold" it, but the *anie* makes them all one (the son is both father and grandfather). If the same person (S—F—FF) is counted innumerable times, separate persons (S—F—FF) are equally counted as one. "The one" may be singular; its power derives from its having passed through several bodies.

Now there is an issue of moment in the similarities this has with Amazonian perspectivism and its emphasis on ontologically rather than epistemologically informed points of view. From the position of Amazonian perspectivism, an epistemological viewpoint produces not diverse ways of being but diverse representations of the world. We may borrow the latter vocabulary to include persons' representations of themselves in the world. This is one sense in which Euro-Americans understand intellectual products.[24] Yet the ornaments and songs and habits of comportment that these Papua New Guinea people produce are not "representations." They are more like demonstrations or certificates, a point to which I shall return.[25] Or they are like body products that people produce in the course of their production of one another. Crook (1999, 237) recounts the dramatic gesture with which a senior man from Bolivip (Papua New Guinea), in wishing to convey what and how he was transmitting to the ethnographer, feigned an incision in his thigh—he had given over part of himself, meat, muscle. More generally, "knowing" the protocols is not sufficient, for they cannot be "represented" in models for people to follow; in coaching the next generation, the seniors' job is not done until they have witnessed juniors acting out the protocols. The seniors are originators of the bodily transformations the juniors undergo.

What rescues this analysis from another Euro-American binarism (mind/body) is the perspectivist question about whether such bodies inhabit one or many worlds. Or rather, how many different *kinds* (Astuti 1995) of bodies there are. It would be absurd to argue that bodily distinctiveness alone means that people inhabit different worlds. But it is the case, across Papua New Guinea, that people deliberately attempt to make new bodies in order *to be* in a new world. Hirsch (2001b) argues the point forcefully. Melanesians devise new ways to be persons, giving evidence of an ability to transform themselves in order to make themselves subjects in and have an existence in a transformed world. He gives a telling example from the days of "first contact" in Fuyuge, when people killed several pigs in order to convert a certain kind of headdress from a man-killing one to a pig-killing one. This transformation of the ornament meant that the headdress could continue to be worn but would give the body quite new connotations. No longer would its appearance point to prowess in killing people, but to the fact that its bearers were "persons of a 'new' kind, those who knew the 'law'" (Hirsch 2001b, 245). More generally, people's understanding of transformations in their lives also affects their interpretations of what it means to be the origin of something. Among recent transformations is a new language for the process (of transformation) itself, which gives it an intellectual cast: focus is on the "knowledge" involved.

Rohatynskyj's (1997, 2001) description of present-day Omie is very apposite here. Omie now work with the notion of themselves as a group with a unique culture (1997, 439), and this culture has become an "origin" of their self-accounts. In this context, people talk about what happens to knowledge (in English), such as the knowledge their seniors have vested in the anthropologist. To the anthropologist, her findings are inevitably representations; to the Omie, whether as a reliable guide to the working out of land claims or as a source of mischief used by the unauthorized, they are rather more than that. But "knowledge" offers a new idiom in which to talk about new transformations, including people's perceptions of themselves as people with a "culture," much of which in turn consists of "(cultural) knowledge." Betrayal or loss of culture/knowledge is a language Papua New Guineans routinely adopt for their present condition (cf. Kirsch 2001). When talking of the disappearance of traditional songs, Omie thus lament, "we have lost our customs" (Rohatynskyj 1997, 450). This is not the place to consider the nuances of Melanesian "custom";[26] globally speaking, part of its power is the status that the concept of cultural knowledge has in the international community. "Knowledge" pervades the language of UNESCO and WIPO.[27] In standing for what people transmitted to one another in the past, however, its usage may obscure an intergenerational dynamic where, in the eyes of some (usually seniors), other people (usually juniors) appear to have lost interest in tradition (Sykes 2000).[28] It may also obscure an ongoing shift—or evolution, with the Euro-American inflection of slow incremental build-up—from an ontological to an epistemological sense of perspective.

New-generation Omie no longer recognize the same-sex affiliations, *anie*, and the totemic species through which people's claims on one another had once rested so firmly. In turn, the ethnographer must ask questions about the nature of the transactions by which she came to acquire cultural knowledge from the Omie, what her ownership of it means, and what then she must do with its form embodied in narrative on tape (Rohatynskyj 2001).[29]

Propagating Images

Songs and narratives are forms of expression that Euro-Americans may class as intellectual products. I have embedded some Papua New Guinean examples in what seems like another description altogether—of the way in which persons reproduce themselves over the generations. That is deliberate. In this part of the world, kinship relations offer a crucial clue to how such expressions are owned. Indeed, when people are identified as members of kin groups, these groups are being defined precisely by the interest they have in their members' reproductive capacity; they "own" persons through the perpetuation of the identity (name, insignia) that the person carries for them. More universally, we can talk of such persons as owning a reproductive interest in other persons. This is what axiomatically divides kin from nonkin, nonkin by definition having no such interest. I now wish to argue that what people can own in such persons is also what they can own in artifacts, namely, regenerative capacity.

A case can be made for considering a range of tangible as well as intangible artifacts here, including ornaments and decorations, although I have in mind particularly items that circulate in exchange relations. These may be generative in the weak sense of creating or sustaining relationship, but they may also be regarded as capable of magically multiplying themselves, as root crops planted in the ground multiply. The owner's own regenerative capacity is demonstrated to the extent that he or she exercises the power to reproduce the artifact. That in turn, the ownability of something, becomes one of its attributes. A case can also be made for claiming that these particular conditions have broad currency across Papua New Guinea. And while the data presented so far have been largely historical, they are not out of place in understanding much contemporary practice. Omie may have dropped *anie* and *ma'i ma'i* from the way they think about one another, but they are very much concerned about the form that various "cultural expressions" take, including songs.

Items such as songs circulate readily between persons and groups.[30] And across Papua New Guinea they may do so precisely because of the mystical burden they carry in reference to fertility and potency. It is widely the case that although these forms of expression are in one sense detachable from persons, their reference to persons is emphatically part of their value. In other words, the origin of such artifacts in the lives of others contributes to their distinctiveness and importance. Conversely, they demonstrate the reproductive power of those lives: the transferal of possession is at once an example of it and a sign of it. This description (Leach 2000, paraphrased) comes from the Madang area of mainland Papua New Guinea:

> In 1998 people in a village called Goriong decided they wanted to purchase the tune, words and carvings of a particular Tamberan [ancestral] spirit from the neighbouring village of Seriang. Ten men who claimed to be the descendants of the originator of the spirit voice lined up to receive payment. The Goriong purchaser called each by name and placed money and other items in his hands, as well as handing over a live pig. The men took the pig back to Seriang and cooked it and distributed it among the villagers. Thus the transfer of the spirit voice was made public.

The transaction enabled the Goriong to sing and dance in the name of this spirit. Since they had made a payment, they became entitled to pass it on in turn and profit from the payments it would bring them. This contrasts with situations where someone may ask permission to use a song or dance but acquires only use-rights, and cannot refer to themselves as "owner" as the Goriong were now entitled to do. In the process, the Seriang lost nothing: they could still use the Tamberan (ancestral spirit) voice for their own celebrations.[31] What is important is that the songs are rendered in a way that maintains their integrity. They evoke memories of the dead and are highly charged for their original owners, and the new owners should do nothing to defame or mock the Tamberan spirit.[32]

The form that is eventually displayed may thus be an original and a derivative at the same time. The new owners acknowledge the source from which the Tamberan voice came, for it is a Tamberan that originated at a particular place that they dance and sing. Transactions at the moment of transfer not only secure the release of the practices for use but multiply its origins; both those who had it and those who obtained it may be considered sources of the new practices (even if not to the same degree). Beyond these originators, what is also brought into being are multiple destinations for the creation, in the people who will witness the display. The propagation of objects *means* attachment to new people (Demian 2001).

That such items can be transacted introduces a further possibility in the reproduction of persons: other people's generative power can be appropriated for oneself. So there is a form of generativity that can be transferred independently of the propagation of an "originary" group. In addition to the logic of same-sex affiliation (if the "same" power is replicated over and over again, so too is reference to its origin) there is the logic of dual parenthood: when origins are divided between persons, there need be no end to the process of division and to the number of borrowings and transfers that are recalled, although it is likely that distant antecedents will drop off. For interest is not just in the things acquired through transactions: explicit value is put on maintaining flow itself. This was notably enunciated by Nick Araho (Whimp and Busse 2000, 186–188), in his summary of a discussion at a seminar on intellectual, biological, and cultural property held in Port Moresby in 1997:

> Borrowing information between groups characterises Papua New Guinea; nobody should interfere with that. The sharing of information ... only requires permission or the exchange of certain gifts. Thus, no actions should be taken that might stop the flow of information exchange through traditional channels.

Borrowing, sharing, and exchanging are all effected through payments; keeping the flow going acquires generative connotations of its own. An ability to release generativity is bound up in the "right" to pass things on to others.

III

Intellectual Products?

The comparisons with intellectual property are becoming evident. I have been accumulating instances from this Melanesian material where one might draw parallels with items that in Euro-American legal regimes can become property subject to intellectual property protection. In addition to songs and names, we have encountered carvings, performances, moral rights (in the integrity of a piece of work), and personal images or emblems, and we could even regard groups as having a proprietary identity to protect. Although they are made visible and manifest, many depend on performance to be so, so that they only appear for a while and in the interim exist as memories of designs, patterns, movements. Moreover, there are contexts in which control over reproduction is restricted. The primary comparison would be with copyright, although many limits to this comparison spring to mind.[33] The Papua New Guinean lawyer Lawrence Kalinoe (2000) notes one bias that copyright would introduce. When contemporary artists draw on traditional art forms, such as Tamberan songs, copyright would appear to be the means to protect their artistic expressions. But while copyright declares their originality, as it is often said, it does not deal with the other side of the equation—the simultaneously derivative nature of the work and its multiple origins.[34]

However, that draws too quick a comparison between indigenous protocols that govern the transmission and transaction of performances, artifacts, and so forth, and regimes that seek to protect the products of intellectual work. We have already seen that loss of "custom" nowadays may be glossed as loss of (traditional/cultural) "knowledge." It may be necessary to scrape off that gloss. Kalinoe (2000) has argued the case for considering the protection of various items of value, especially the class that he calls sacred (such as those with ancestral value—ancestral not because they are antique but because they are the living presence of ancestors in their descendants, which guarantees continuity of inner power). Significantly, his proposal is that these should be treated, for legal purposes, simply as property—emphatically *not* as intellectual property.[35] This is worth pursuing.

The ethnographic record from Melanesia could have supplied many examples to convey the substance of the data presented here. Most notably, all the items just mentioned (songs, names, carvings, performance, moral rights, emblems, and proprietary identity) could be bundled up in the single instance of Malanggan carvings in New Ireland and their accompanying displays.[36] The instance would be doubly germane with respect to the designs worked on the carvings themselves, in that the way these figures are guarded from unauthorized imitation have compelled observers to use the vocabulary of intellectual property rights, especially copyright. Malanggan figures would also summarize some of the other features we have found. They recall the inner and outer bodies of the Murik in that the New Ireland carvings are prototypically regarded as an external body for the departed presence of a deceased person whose potency is retained within; they echo the emergence of the Omie child/grandfather, for the sculpture gives an imagistic form to the name of an ancestor that, detached from the deceased's body, can then be passed on to a child;[37] they point to the general difference between a history of exchanges and current ownership (the carved plane refers to the former and the painted patterns upon it to the latter), and to a consistent orientation toward the future, in that the designs reflect anticipated claims for which the recipients make payments. Above all, the image is owned by and retained in the memory of those who have the right to reproduce it.[38] But the one issue I wish to bring forward from Susanne Küchler's extensive study of Malanggan is her comment that "Melanesia is a particularly clear example of a culture within which intellectual property is not an analogue of material property" (1999, 63). Given the mix of tangible and intangible items here, we might well ask what she means by that. The answer will open up the question of whether it is useful, in fact, to think of any of them as intellectual products.

The context of the remark is a discussion (begun by Harrison 1992, 1995) about the nature of mental resources in Euro-American societies of "the modern industrial economy," which lay stress on "material resources and productive capacity" (Küchler 1999, 62). The reproduction of mental products is here governed by a legal system in which intangible efforts have to be embodied in things for rights to be exercised over them. The contrast is with regimes, as in Melanesia, which have the kind of approach to the flow of information enunciated by Araho (Whimp and Busse 2000). Küchler describes intermittent Malanggan performances over a person's lifespan as part of "a shared knowledge technology [that] assures the continuing generative and reproductive capacity of its intangible resources" (Küchler 1999, 63). She has in mind here the deliberate ephemerality of items produced for display, where (in her words) ownership centers less on the object as a material product than on the right to project or produce an image out of a repertoire of soon-to-be absent images. Particularly true of the Malanggan carvings, what is created to be passed on is not the thing itself (which is destroyed) but "an inherently recallable image." Her principal point is that the image is created as a *mental* resource precisely through the disappearance of the object.

The phrase "knowledge technology" is apt. My understanding is that the Malanggan image is created as a *resource*, an entity that can be reproduced again, often a generation hence, by the way it is recalled. So the knowledge in question is the memory that holds the image in people's minds. Another way of putting this would be to say that "knowledge" becomes a means to further reproduction (rather than an end in itself), the image being held in suspension, an outcome of what was seen in the original display when the rights were acquired or reconfirmed. Is it in this sense inert? The mind (memory) of the holder-owner houses it as a kind of body part almost—while it may animate the person, the image as such is not affected by its location. It is perhaps not too extreme to suggest that being in the mind confers no further attributes or identity on the image: its mental or intellectual or intangible condition does not add anything. Although the image that is eventually reproduced will be negotiated from various anticipated claims on it, the holder-owner is not supposed to innovate on what he or she recalls. Indeed, that is heavily frowned upon. The end or aim, I infer, is the eventual reproduction of the memory as an image, not as knowledge.

In other words, there is nothing particularly "intellectual" about the fact that the image, like the words of a song or the design of an ornament, is held in the head,[39] and there is nothing to be gained in separating out a class of intellectual property.[40] This also means we might be wary of those contexts in which "knowledge" is too easily brought forward as a gloss for intangible objects. It is at least worth hypothesizing that the regimes of old Melanesia (the phrase is Alfred Gell's) treat knowledge practices as a means, literally as practices, not as an end or as objects with value to circulate.

Ownership of Persons?

Harrison's and Küchler's contrast between regimes holds, but we can add a proviso. Whether or not rights in these Melanesian forms of expression are treated as material property depends on what is material about property. Recall that the starting point of the discussion was the Euro-American presumption that intangible efforts must be embodied in material things for them to be apprehended as property in the first place (e.g., Sherman and Bently 1999, 47; Bainbridge 1999, 45).[41]

I return to the exegesis offered by Davies and Naffine, and their interest in modern renditions of Hegel's forms of appropriation.[42] "Property is seen as an extension of the person and as a means by which the person can relate freely and transparently with others. Property is seen to mediate our social relationships" (Davies and Naffine 2001, 6). Drawing in particular on the work of Radin (1993, 1996) for her advocacy of "property for personhood," they quote her observation that in order "to achieve proper self-development—to be a person—an individual needs some control over resources in the external environment" (Davies and Naffine 2001, 7). The property that a person uses in his or her self-construction, they go on to say, is in effect a relationship to an external thing that contributes to "a person's feelings of well-being, freedom, and identity."[43]

If property is part of the way in which people in modern industrial economies (Euro-American societies) connect to the world, then it must both shape and take the shape of the way the world is perceived. To the extent that the world is thought of as an assemblage of material things, it follows that property can only be claimed over material things. Property in this view *is* the condition of appropriating things from the world. It also follows that an idea (say) can only be claimed as an expression of a person's exertions and intellect when it is found in a "thing." A more generalized version of this is that any human activity, including bodily exertion, can find expression in external things,[44] but by being embodied in something else, is expressed in a condensed and abstracted form (e.g., labor manifests an immediate bodily capacity, but what is incorporated in the products of labor is an abstraction, as for example when it is theorized as "labor power" in terms of social usefulness). However, there is a special inflection to mental activity, for the exercise of the intellect is closely associated with the exercise of the will, the distinguishing mark, in this world view, of personhood (e.g., Davies and Naffine 2001, 104). The idea that must be incorporated in an artifact (thing) before it can be legally owned renders the mind's effects as separate from the body's, exactly as the individual's will is given expression and realized in a world separate from him or herself. In short, in this view, inner energy is projected onto the world, which returns evidence of it to its originator, as signs of the person (creative, productive outcomes of personal activity).

This line of thinking hardly needs further rehearsal. The point to draw from it is that we are not dealing with a simple contrast between owning things as material objects and the kind of situation (as described for Melanesia) where there is no such restriction of materiality in the flow of tangible and intangible assets. Rather we might see, in the Euro-American insistence on intangibles that can only be owned as concrete things, something of a comparable reproductive moment. What is being reproduced? Minimally, what is reproduced is "the self" and its view on the world. This is true over and again. And it applies equally to that part of the external world that involves other persons: whatever encounters there are with social others, the reactions they elicit are absorbed back into the individual as its own feelings and sentiments. In other words, this (Euro-American) form of materiality is the condition under which perspective, a person's point of view, creates an object ("out there"). We could conclude that what is material about property is a function of an epistemological grasp of the world, that is, of knowing it as an object (for example, of contemplation). The contrast is with the kind of perspectivism that creates the subject. What would then be material about the tangibles and intangibles of Melanesian reproduction is arguably the fact that perspective is an ontological way of being that alters the condition of the person ("creates the subject") so that everything in the perceived world (tangible or intangible) defines and contributes to that state of being.

If property, in the sense of the capacity to appropriate, is part of how Euro-Americans reproduce themselves, so too is knowledge. For what has to be returned to the self comes both as things for bodily consumption and as abstract qualities that enhance the equally abstract self, which is exactly where knowledge belongs. Knowledge of the world is a powerful means of connection to it (and, concomitantly, of distinction from it). Yet as we have already seen, for Euro-Americans it is much more than a means: knowledge about the world is returned to the person who (already) knows enough to seek it. Its end in fashioning subjectivity makes it something of an end in itself. For the mind reappropriates that connection to the world as intangibles appropriate to how the mind is thought of itself (as so many thoughts, concepts, percepts, scapes, perspectives, and so forth). Needless to say, I am speaking both culturally and synthetically.

As a consequence, Euro-Americans do value certain things as outcomes of the intellect. It does matter that there is a mental or intangible dimension to the products of that body location we think of as the mind. The translation from idea or effort into material object *and back again* marks the boundaries of the person. The cultural corollary is that one cannot have property in those generative powers themselves, in the mental processes, because that would be tantamount to claiming property in persons.[45] It is precisely the perceived intangible nature of their mental processes that protects people from people. Property rights can only be exercised in relation to things in the world, and intellectual property can only apply to material objects that reembody those intangible processes in things. Otherwise put, in these views, creativity is not axiomatically embodied in the body, but either in the mind or in things in the world.[46] Euro-Americans substitute the bodies of things for their own.

The Melanesian data have pointed to people conceiving of owning what can also be transmitted and exchanged by virtue of being embodied not in things but in (other) persons: human capacities and regenerative powers, such as the "strength" or "life force" that as a name becomes redistributable after death.[47] The Malanggan name is given form as an image that is itself considered to be generative (Küchler 1999, 66), in a quasiprocreative sense, and is passed on (transmitted and sold) in the form of rights to reproduce, to duplicate, the original. But one might wonder whether in the Melanesian case also it is the right, not the potency, that is owned and transmitted. However, that would be to ignore the lengths to which people go to turn potency into a visible and appropriatable phenomenon (Demian forthcoming).[48] It would also ignore a crucial difference. The Melanesian "right" to reproduce is sustained not by a legal apparatus but by the person being in the appropriate and necessary ontological state to exercise the right—as sister's son, heir, purchaser, initiate, or whatever (Kalinoe 2000). Moreover, the very exercise of the right is an instance of what it confers. Making "duplicates" *is* (to reproduce) the capacity for creation. Euro-Americans, on the other hand, value the right as having if not legal then a moral or ethical sanction, and it is this that allows its exercise to the benefit of the holder; the source of creativity is not passed on—it is left intact in the person of the original author or inventor.[49] We come back to the Euro-American significance of "intellect." Once embodied in a thing, mental processes can have further generative force only by being processed freshly (by the originator or by another) through someone's mind.

So far I have been deploying the term used by several writers, "property," although we may ask what is propertied about the kinds of Euro-American ownership relations being considered here. One answer has to be that the holder of property rights and the subject of legal rights run together. The counterpart to the specific material thing in which efforts are embodied is the concrete person who can be a bearer of rights. Personal concreteness is given form through individuality (but see Sherman and Bently 1999), so we arrive at the further well-rehearsed point that exclusive interests define the individual's sphere of activities.

> Property in things other than oneself has been said to enhance personhood, because it establishes an extended sphere of noninterference with one's person.... Property and personhood have also been linked in a more intimate manner by the assertion that persons may also be said to have property in themselves. Common to both approaches has been a desire to show how property interests express and secure the autonomy of the individual and hence their very personhood.
>
> (Davies and Naffine 2001, 6)

The arithmetic here—the singular, recursive character of the origins of a person's actions in that very person—is evident.

Single and Multiple Origins

In asking if persons are property, Davies and Naffine (2001, 99) observe that the law—English, Australian, American, European law—"fails to supply a sensible, credible understanding of our embodied selves." The concept of the legal person cannot cope, for instance, with pregnant women or with the body at death. One of the problems is that it cannot count. (It is not just the law. No one can.) The reason is evident: it is the body that normally bestows indivisibility on the person. So the law is baffled by a body within a body; it does not know how many persons a pregnant woman is, and resolution in terms of parts and wholes pleases no one.[50] Death creates a different problem, which is that the person's will lives on in disembodied form (in their testimonies and documents), and its wishes have to be given a finite life. The law has to kill off this disembodied personality, an uncanny echo of the way some Melanesians have to kill (the memory of) the dead through deliberate forgetting, by rendering the deceased absent (cf. Battaglia 1990). However, there seems a swifter resolution to the number of persons there now are, since with the departure of the rational, sovereign will from the corpse, the authors argue, lawyers find little of the person there and tend to treat the corpse as a thing. But this brings its own anxieties about others, the deceased's relatives among them, laying claims to it. In short, "the possessive legal individual is rendered incoherent by the cultural and biological facts of reproduction" (Davies and Naffine 2001, 92).

I return to the numbers in a moment. First I note that the possessive in the "possessive individual" (famously after McPherson 1964) refers to the simultaneous condition of being a proprietor and of being property as a result of having property in oneself—a conceptualization that is of course a (cultural) contingency as far as the law is concerned. In some views, that property in oneself (self-ownership) is the guarantee of the freedom with which the will is exercised.[51] As noted at the outset, it is held that insofar as persons own themselves no one else can own them. The Melanesian material suggests that we parse the question about property through a more general question about embodiment. (Questions about persons and property thereby "disappear" from the account.)

Insofar as no one else can own what is self-owned, then persons must be embodied *either* in themselves, their own persons, *or* in artifacts and external objects—not in "other" persons. (The view that creativity regarded as a product of the intellect is embodied in the mind rather than the body, rendering the body "other" to the mind, plays, we might say, on an internal division of the person into self and other.) It is embodiment in things of the world that lays the conditions for property rights and for all the equivocations Davies and Naffine voice in the way people want to use the language of property rights for self-embodiment as well.

We have already noted a peculiarity about this Euro-American form of embodiment, in that the incorporation of a person's efforts into things does not render those things personlike. On the contrary, they are detached from the generative or creative potential that remains within the person. The person has produced out of himself or herself an entity that now exists autonomously in the world as a "thing." If the claims through property are to keep those things within the person's orbit, they must rest on a reconceptualization of the productive process consonant with the "antinomy between objects and subjects of ownership ... [which means that] subjectivity cannot reside in objects, as such, nor objectivity in subjects, as such" (Barron 1998, 55). The connection is simple. The producer[52] is imagined as the *origin* of the product. Conversely, there can be no property claim to a work (the reference is to copyright) "without some author who can be said to originate it" (1998, 55).

Once imagined thus, there is no need to demonstrate anything more complex. This is the burden of Barron's explanation of how the Australian courts ever came to endorse copyright in an ancestral design. All that was necessary was to show that it was the artist and no one else who refashioned the design. She writes: "In law, originality is simply the description of a causal relationship between a person and a thing" (1998, 56). It follows (in this view)[53] that the law is less concerned with establishing the nature of creativity than with determining whether this or that person can demonstrate he or she was the originator. Other claimants may of course be potential ones or exist as anticipated competitors, but they are the absent multitude against which any one person asserts originality.

There is no need to repeat the point that Euro-Americans equate sources of potency with an origin in the person as a singular entity, and the person is in this respect literally indivisible. It further follows that origins (in the sense pursued here) cannot be divided. What then do we make of the arithmetic in the observation that the Australian artist was "an individual of several persons" (Barron 2001, 45, quoting Saunders and Hunter 1991, 479)? Anthropologically, I would put it that the Euro-American "individual" is the person in its indivisible, embodied state, here taken for granted. The "several persons" correspond to the different social positions that the artist holds. Barron lists them: author of the work (a legal status), a skilled artist (by reputation), an honored citizen of Australia and local hero (acknowledged by the Northern Territory Government who had purchased his work), a successful entrepreneur (known through his dealings), as well as an Aboriginal person (whom some felt had desecrated a ritual object), and a member of a clan (whose ancestors were involved). To his legal status, then, are added many other possible statuses on which he could act. They are contingent to the law; nonetheless, such positions affect the way the law's justice is perceived. This echoes the claims currently being made in relation to intellectual property rights elsewhere, which is how to acknowledge all those multiple others who participate in the productive process, except that here, the multiple others are aspects of the one individual. Origins are singular, even if there may be many of them.

Applied Maths

Now the view on the world that creates the world as object and the viewing self as subject creates a problem as far as other persons are concerned: what to do with everyone else—how to count them in? If that problem is among those that still drive the extended Enlightenment project of "making society," let me comment on a tiny movement in it. Property offers one obvious solution: keep others at bay. It is two other related solutions on which I linger for a moment. The first is rendering one person as several persons, as in the case of the artist. The second is sustaining a division between what is essential and what is contingent, for this allows several persons to be involved in producing things, and even to seek acknowledgement and reward, without being co-owners of the primary rights in the thing concerned.

Rendering one person as several persons abstracts the notion of person in terms of roles and statuses, and there may be as many of these as there are social niches to be filled. They can be added to over and again. But they do not add up. A glance at Barron's list shows that they are not commensurate entities in the first place, that the list is infinite (can be broken down into countless parts), and that the principal form of coherence is the individual's biography (his embodied life). A person moves between different domains as different persons; they overlap, but that is all. This is equally true of the claims that are made to acknowledge coworkers who are not co-owners in a creative process. There may be a division of labor between all those involved in producing a book, the publisher, the binder, the printer, and so forth, but each has competence in their own sphere or domain, which means that each can deploy the same skills for numerous other books as well. In each instance, they add their skills to the author's, but the contribution of each remains discrete and recognizable in the publication, the binding, or whatever. A similar additive perception of multiple workers allows scientific investigators to build on one another's work, so that they can distinguish the unique efforts of a team of inventors, who may publish as coauthors, from either the (contingent) technicians, funders, and others necessary to the outcome or else the work of antecedent or competitive teams to which the inventors "add" the essential original input. This arithmetic enables multiple other persons to be recognized as inhabiting the same world, without compromising anyone's unique perspective. Everyone has their own unique perspective and is the origin of a singular view, and knowledge of this fact allows one to be added to another without expectation of closure or summation.

Another way of putting it is to say that however many others inhabit one's world, and however many different or specialized or exclusive domains there are in which one operates, all the pointers of one's activity point to oneself. All that can be said is that the perspectives overlap; the signs do not change. It was one of the discoveries of twentieth-century anthropology[54] that, by contrast, in many social regimes, people imagine finite worlds in which there is a kind of "division of labor" between persons that stresses the dependency of each person's status on that of others. A shift of perspective does change the signs. An extreme example is exemplified in what we have learned by applying the insights of Amazonian perspectivism to Papua New Guinean divisions between persons.

I return to the formulation that being a son propels one into a different world from that one inhabits as a sister's son. In the world created between a son and his father, and I take a canonical example and speak in male terms, the mother's brother may be identified with his sister as a male mother. When someone instead acts as a sister's son (toward his mother's brothers) his own father is still in that world. He has not disappeared, but the signs have changed. The values put on the relationship are different. The father now appears (say) as an in-law to the mother's brother. The world is changed not simply because the son comes to see his father through different eyes (his MB's), but because the mother's brother has made a different subject out of him. He is now the son not of his "father" (F) but of his MB's sister's husband. This is hardly an alteration of perspective that the person can will into being. It is an ontological switch effected through the being and presence of the other relative.[55] One cannot in this situation "add" other persons (new individuals become assimilated to positions already given). Another kind of mathematics is called for, one that describes the equations by which different sets of signs appear. The limitation of this perspectivism of course is that all one can do is change the signs: if one is not this, one is that.[56]

The Murik men and women who give different values to adopted or dead children or the Omie assimilation of the boy to his grandfather are not confused about how many persons there are or what generation people belong to. To the extent that this kind of mathematics applies, the point is that there is no ultimate or single origin.[57] Persons, subject positions, are created by the relations in which they must engage (Leach 2003). When, as they do, people emphasize specific "origins" ("roots"), this is to select particular relationships out of many, to give one priority over others. To use language appropriate to the Australian artist's copyright suit, for example, Barron (1998, 50; after Morphy 1991; cf. Kalinoe forthcoming) notes the different kinds of "rights" kin have in one another's ancestral designs. Thus someone may have the right to reproduce a painting from his mother's clan, or indeed from his mother's mother's clan, and will be consulted by them when they reproduce their own, even though his origins in that clan do not give him the rights that descendants of the father can claim. It is not a contingent or a subsidiary authority, but one that belongs to its own distinct order of relationships by which the person is "owned."[58]

Imagining how copyright ownership could be mapped onto Aboriginal concepts of clan ownership of images and designs, Barron observes that "even if it could, the unification of copyright ownership in a single entity, albeit a collective one, would not mirror the distribution of rights among individual members of the clan [in their relations with members of other clans]" (1998, 72).

A judge, trying to convey how very "other" Aboriginal concepts were from those found in the law of property, concluded a famous land claims case[59] with a remark he could have found in more than one anthropological text (and see the comments above apropos Murik ornaments and Omie emblems), stating that the clan belongs to the land rather than the land belongs to the clan (quoted in Barron 1998, 54). The same could be said of sacred paintings. An artist belongs to the painting rather than the painting to the artist. For a painting executed in reference to ancestral images contains within it its conditions of reproduction. Like the Malanggan, it shows in its very designs who has the right to paint it. You have to be a person in an appropriate relationship to others who also have claims (not necessarily the same as yours) and who thus have claims over you. In this manner, the design authorizes the painter.

IV

It is exactly this kind of modulation of authority with which Jacob Simet, Director of the PNG National Cultural Commission, has been concerned (Simet 2000, 2001a), in relation to the Model Law on protection of cultural property in the Pacific.[60] This directive makes an excellent case for setting up protection mechanisms outside intellectual property regimes, but does so by insisting on the absolute claims of "traditional owners."[61] These are identified as groups. In implying they are singular in nature, and by implication homogeneous, it addresses the problem of collective ownership in terms which remain familiar counterfactuals to Euro-American private property thinking: "community ownership," "communal moral rights," and "cultural [as opposed to economic] or communal rights."[62] The radical issue presented by the data from Papua New Guinea (and Australia) is how to accommodate multiple rights when they derive from incommensurable orders of relationship. Simet (2000, 78) observes of Tolai:

> One idea which might easily form part of the development of a mechanism for protection of indigenous knowledge is the assumption that all traditional knowledge is communally owned. [In fact] ... people were very particular about acquisition, ownership, transfer, protection and use of knowledge. Only some kinds of knowledge belonged to the public domain, while the rest belonged to individuals and social groups.

And as he goes on to explain (Simet 2001b), Tolai individuals and groups are enmeshed in diverse relations with one another. A telling example is the way in which the signs of a clan's identity are distributed between its masks (*tubuan*) and the magic (*palawat*) that makes the masks effective vehicles of power. The *tubuan* is held by a clan member who acts as manager for the clan; the *palawat* is held by a nonmember, who acts as a custodian on behalf of the clan and deploys the magic on its behalf. Clan members cannot use their own magic themselves.[63]

These groups and individuals are not the "several persons" of Enlightenment arrangements of society. Persons exercise different kinds of authority depending on the relations that summon them, and are made into different persons in the course of it. So contrasting types of multiplicity come into view. If we talk of multiple origins in relation to Euro-American works, then multiplicity comes from the way persons are added to one another's enterprises. If we talk of multiple origins in relation to their Melanesian counterparts, then multiplicity comes from the way people divide themselves from one another. Singularity (individuality) is an outcome, not an origin.

This attempt at a comparison exposes an asymmetry in my account. Some might find the substance of intellectual property issues in certain systems at odds with—as too contingent to—attention to kinship in others. I am not comparing like with like. Quite so. Precisely because the focus is on the "things" people produce in the one case and on the "persons" they produce in the other, I am drawn to the parallel. Very differently construed as they are, one can nonetheless compare ideas of ownership imagined in intellectual property relations and Melanesian notions of owning persons through kin ties. That is not where the asymmetry is. Asymmetry emerges if one takes what appears superficially similar. For if one looks closely, it is the "kinship" in the Euro-American case that appears fundamentally at odds with the Melanesian "kinship" material.[64] Davies and Naffine's observation about embodiment in Western law is highly relevant. The arena of family and kin relations is also where the Euro-American arithmetic that creates distinct objects and singular originators falters. Kin are bound up with one another in dependencies that make counting difficult, where belonging is a kind of ownership but not quite, where persons both are and are not embodied in other persons, and where notions of property can only introduce complicating rather than simplifying factors.

Notes

Acknowledgements: I am most grateful for the invitation from UC Irvine's Critical Theory Institute in the spring of 2002, and the stimulus of discussions there. Conversations with Eduardo Viveiros de Castro started this off; without the interest of colleagues from Papua New Guinea, notably Lawrence Kalinoe, Andrew Moutu, and Jacob Simet, there would have been less incentive to continue. The paper was written under the auspices of PTC, "Property, Transactions, and Creations: New Economic Relations in the Pacific," a three-year investigation funded by the UK Economic and Social Research Council (Award R000 23 7838). It shows the obvious influence of PTC colleagues: I warmly thank Eric Hirsch, co-convener, and Tony Crook, Melissa Demian, Andrew Holding, Lawrence Kalinoe, Stuart Kirsch, James Leach, and Karen Sykes. Anne Barron, James Leach, Alain Pottage, and Eduardo Viveiros de Castro all kindly commented on a draft, for which many thanks indeed.

1. Understood as signs of "overlap and intersection" (Barron 1998, 44). Note that Barron intervenes in a debate which asserts *either* that the author defined by copyright is a Romantic individual *or* that there is no connection at all. She argues that the connection is one of resemblance between different systems of practice: that is, a contingency. Sherman and Bently draw out the role that ideas about creativity played in earlier developments of intellectual property rights, and argue that in pre-twentieth-century thinking, the intangible was thought of not so much as a thing as an action or performance—the productive effort—embodied in material form (Sherman and Bently 1999, 47–48). (My thanks to Alain Pottage for this reference, and for his comments on the paper.) Insofar as it is arguable that this is still an element

in contemporary thinking, the position of Davies and Naffine, which I take up for its reading of an Euro-American approach, is controversial.

2. Because persons owned themselves (or God did), no one else could exercise ownership over them. The authors are concerned to point up the flexibility of the law, the contradictions it tries to accommodate, and its limits.

3. The issues are likely to be mediated by human rights concerns. See the case of Miriam and the NGO (Strathern 2001, forthcoming). There are, of course, ethical and other questions to be framed that do not bear directly on the law at all.

4. This has been one of the running concerns of the PTC project (see acknowledgements, above). The discussions by Blakeney (1995, 2000) and Weatherall (2001) deals with aspects of the Australian situation, with reference to communal ownership.

5. The basis of the claims *and* the nature of the rights may differ—one can imagine different reasons for making a claim but similar rights of possession and disposal being conferred. The "joint ownership" provisions in Euro-American property law are not helpful to the present case.

6. Given the role that such societies play in earlier accounts of mine, I have set myself a set of apparently contingent materials. I particularly want to acknowledge the input of Tony Crook's (forthcoming) and James Leach's (2003) work on this point. What counts as a group is a separate set of problems, but note that the present discussion does not observe the usual anthropological distinctions between kinship and clanship.

7. That does not mean that people's claims on one another are uniform. In talking about clan interests in the Australian case, Barron (1998) does an excellent job in pointing out how the exact rehearsal of someone's claims will depend on diverse factors in their own life history, the reproductive stage they are at, and allegiances they have elsewhere.

8. The sense in which persons inhabit different life-worlds is not a matter of where you are on a genealogical grid. See, for example, Leach (2003). Pedersen (2001, 413) uses the term "grid" to distinguish totemic difference from animist or perspectival relations.

9. Of course, suckling can be a form of fathering, too (Strathern 1988). The recursiveness of closed or finite perspectives is endless: (one set of) relations become metaphors for (another set of) relations.

10. I owe special thanks to Andrew Moutu (at the National Museum of Papua New Guinea) for teachings on ontology and on the limits of Euro-American epistemology in conceiving "relations." However, as his own work is in progress (*Names Are Thicker Than Blood: Concepts of Ownership and Person Among the Iatmul*, PhD thesis, Cambridge University), I have avoided drawing on it directly and hope I do not trespass inadvertently.

11. The stages are subject to transformation through ritual. Indeed, the converse holds: gender can be used to discriminate between stages of growth, as in rites that make boys pass from one gendered state to another as their bodies grow.

12. Astuti (2000, 93–94) has an important passage on changing perspectives in Vezu, a cognatic/kindred-based Madagascan society (where a person's reproductive stage is crucial to the world of kin groups and descendants he or she perceives).

13. Which in turn involves the suppression of some of what the parent passes on. In unilineal descent group systems, each of the parents, themselves made up of differentiated elements, passes on one of a pair of differences.

14. As in the famous conception-deconception mathematics of the Bush Mekeo; Mosko (1985) is the classic statement.

15. The particular scandal is that they break all the conventions that associate kinship affiliation, not sexual affiliation, with group membership.

16. And to a criticism of the "partible" model of person, which rests on the child recreating the relationship between parents (Strathern 1988), insofar as here the interest of one parent in the procreative outcome is actively eliminated (Rohatynskyj 1990, 437).

17. In addition to published work (Rohatynskyj 1990, 1997) I draw on her contribution to the 2001 PTC conference (2001); permission to cite and quote from the written version is much appreciated.

18. Patrilateral cross-cousin marriage overcomes the asymmetry of residence; when it is followed, grandchildren replace the original grandparental sibling pair residing together in a locality (Rohatynskyj 1990, 439). *Anie* can also refer to "local group" (Rohatynskyj 1997, 441).

19. The assumption is that by this point their grandfather will be deceased, or if not then nearly so (and in any case "ancestral"). Boys acquire the adult male power that at this point can damage women and children, even as contact with women's power would stunt the boys' growth, and their manifestations of fertility are generally dangerous for the opposite sex (Rohatynskyj 1990, 445; 1997, 443)

20. After Houseman (1988).

21. And vice versa. In Amazonian perspectivism, the departure of the body causes problems for living/dead identification—the dead, without bodies to see with, are no longer human (but for an important qualification, which introduces a difference of perspectives between human beings related to the deceased, see Vilaça 2000, 94).

22. A problem with nonrelational logic; as Houseman (1988) demonstrates, reduplication can be a sign of indeterminacy.

23. De Coppet (1981) describes how *'Are 'Are* specifically detach the deceased's "image" from the body at its mortuary ceremony. Note that just as an Omie person acquires names, the land also has names, and a man learns about his land rights through learning the names of the totemic species (*ma'i ma'i*) that reside there. They advertise who has the right to work.

24. To keep with the analytical dynamic of perspectivism and thus keep its antonym epistemology, I would have to widen the referents of "epistemology" such that points of view (representations, knowledge) were just one kind of intellectual product.

25. Note Hirsch (2001a) on Fuyuge origin stories: the "knowledge" is not a representation but an instruction to the knowledge holder to look after, take care of, and

nurture the things, places, and persons referred to in the myths. The analytical division that has here distinguished between systems can also be found within systems. Riles (forthcoming) has almost parallel comments on the way Euro-American law may be taken either expressively or instrumentally.

26. For a recent synthesis based on Vanuatu materials, see Bolton (2003). Blakeney (2000, 251–252) observes that replacing "folklore" by "traditional knowledge" in the intellectual property rights area "significantly changes the discourse," his particular interest being the shift from copyright-related concerns to patent law and biodiversity in response to that part of "traditional knowledge" concerned (for example) with plants and animals in medical treatment.

27. See Hirsch and Strathern (forthcoming). In the draft Model Law for the Pacific (see below), "traditional knowledge" covers all tradition-based innovations and creations, including literary, artistic, and scientific works, along with names, symbols, information, and so forth. In other words, it serves as a powerful portmanteau.

28. In the same way, the discourse of property, Brown (1998) argues, obscures or displaces what should be an extensive moral discussion on the implications of exposing native people's "sacred" knowledge to unwarranted scrutiny.

29. People's interest in their futures go alongside of new ethnographic sensibilities about the ownership of knowledge nurtured from two distinct sources: postcolonial critique and an intellectual property rights–sensitive world. For a robust criticism along these lines of my own research (and that of others) in Mt. Hagen, see Muke (2000).

30. I deliberately make the statement timeless. I wish to convey neither the imputation that it is only "today," with commodification, that such things circulate, nor that "traditional" reasons for such circulation have lost all significance.

31. At the same time, the spirit is now lodged in another network of people and, hidden from view, people may dream of new designs or forms. "Tamberan [spirit] songs are being innovated all the time," and this includes the dreaming of "new" Tamberan, which are made public with the distribution of pork everyone can eat, i.e. among the villagers who become its co-owners (Leach 2000). Although an innovation may have a single creator, it is owned by the residential group, who would together be paid if it were transferred to another.

32. Growth or creativity, the time when people hatch innovations for the designs they own, come from experiences that occur out of public view. Leach contrasts this with the world of local business and marketing enterprises, where no one owns the innovations people try out and everyone rushes to imitate other people's little inventions. Villagers complain that as soon as anyone has a lucrative idea, everyone else follows suit!

33. The literature here includes that cited by Coombe (1998) and Brown (2003). Copyright is apt insofar as it covers the expression of form, and is often taken as a model for the protection of cultural property.

34. An analogue in Euro-American contexts might be conflicting demands on copyright as applying to something both individual and replicable (Sherman and Bently 1999, 55).

35. He writes that finding a suitable regulatory regime for "indigenous cultural and intellectual property and traditional knowledge" can be significantly enhanced if we separate the issues relevant to a regime for the preservation of culture from those relevant to the implementation of intellectual property rights protection. One reason Kalinoe offers for avoiding the intellectual property rights route in the protection of cultural property is because intellectual property rights brings things into the public eye. The limited restriction guaranteed by intellectual property rights protection is nothing compared to the long-term publication entailed when the copyright (say) expires. He is thinking of items that are identified with particular groups—perhaps secret "property" not unlike the Tamberan songs described above—and which should only be revealed under controlled conditions, for example, when the moment for their reproduction is ripe. The public domain aspect of intellectual property rights causes problems for this kind of resource (Brown 1998; Brush 1999).

36. I draw particularly on Küchler (1987, 1992, 1999); also Lincoln (1987). The details and much of the phrasing in what follows come directly from Küchler's various writings, which are always stimulating. Malanggan is also spelled Malangan. For a critical comment on emphasizing display, see Küchler (2003, 170).

37. On this point Küchler observes: "names, as the carriers of a transcending body politic, are considered the property of the ancestral domain, are 'found' and recollected through dreaming [prior to being reproduced again], to be validated and transferred as images" (1999, 66). The named image that is the subject of such rights and that can be exchanged is what kin own of one another.

38. The figures or effigies ("skins") appear as material objects in a particular form (which is their image), and once they have disappeared, what is retained is the memory of this form as an abstract, mental image. Unless otherwise indicated from its context, *image* refers primarily to the latter. Note that what is owned includes the capacity to turn such a memory into a realization and make a new effigy (Küchler 1992, 105, 107).

39. I say head (and mind), but that is already a Euro-American perspective; to say "body" is already a Melanesian view, to render it in the most appropriate but still inadequate vocabulary the English language can offer.

40. Or rather, the gains are primarily those of analytical rhetoric, such as drawing the anthropologist's attention to issues of creativity and authorship.

41. The point applies to both copyright (it is the form of expression that is protected) and patent (an idea materialized in a usable object). The question of intangibility is however the subject of some debate in intellectual property rights law—and the expression/idea distinction differs between the United States and the United Kingdom (Bainbridge 1999, 43–44).

42. My thanks here to Daniel Miller, who has long urged me to grasp this perspective and whose work is much illuminated by it (e.g., Miller 1995). "Hegel argues that in becoming a person one must put oneself into the external world and then reappropriate the self through the appropriation of objects in the world. Taking the world unto ourselves is our method of completing our subjectivity and individuality,

because it involves the purely subjective person externalising their personality and re-grasping it in the form of an external object" (Davies and Naffine 2001, 4).

43. Davies and Naffine note that Radin's emphasis on "property for personhood" compels her to produce an alternative category ("fungible property") to cover property that is interchangeable with other things and exists largely for wealth creation.

44. In law, a necessary condition for dealing with the intangible, which must be turned into an object that "can be incorporated in commodity and subjected to the process of exchange" of the kind with which the law deals (Barron 1998, 56).

45. In liberal (industrial, Euro-American, etc.) societies, people cannot own other people's capacities as such (but see Gray 1991, 299–300).

46. This is why performers who make their body creative —in dance, song, athletics, acrobatics, sports—are exactly, out of routine, performers. Euro-Americans often regard the body antics of other peoples—ritual experts, shamans, monarchs —as "performance."

47. A name separated from the deceased's body can be appropriated and shared by ancestors and living alike. (If we follow Küchler's argument for New Ireland, we would have to argue that land is not material either.)

48. In the Malanggan case, the ethnographer (Küchler 1999, 67) remarks that the names and its imaged form are produced out of a "source" (*wune*), which refers to its originary "womb" or "water source"; the "template" for the construction of an image (1992, 97) and it (the source) are transmitted at the same time.

49. This is quite explicit in intellectual property law: the current distinction in British and European copyright between the economic right acquired through intellectual property protection and the moral right that identifies the author as the originator of the work; the two persons may or may not be the same individual. Rights acquired through patenting may belong to any one of a number of "owners" of the scientific work that went into the invention, which is separate from the reputation that the inventors can acquire through scientific publishing.

50. Treating a fetus as "part" of the person (the mother) resolves the dilemma as to whether "the woman or the foetus is the person" (Davies and Naffine 2001, 91). A Melanesian response would be that the woman makes manifest the multiple embodiment that characterises all persons— persons are made up of persons.

51. Davies and Naffine (2001, 9) quote the observation, for instance, that Western property is based on self-possession as a primordial property right that grounds all others. This axiom holds whether or not the self-owning individual is given in the world (being ultimately owned by God, as per Locke) or has to fashion that condition out of it (through its own struggling, as per Hegel).

52. I use the term to refer to the agent in the process of production, whatever process of making or acknowledging or giving expression is involved.

53. Which is controversial; see note 1, above.

54. Most explicitly in structuralism, but I would see its antecedents in comparative endeavors to classify kinship terminologies or group structures that stumbled on relations between relations.

55. James Leach laid this out in his PhD dissertation (1997, University of Manchester). He writes of the Nekgini speakers of Madang Province: "When Nekgini people use kinship names in their speech, these usages are not classificatory or taxonomic, but are part of the of the process by which persons are made to appear, in the perception of others, as standing in a certain relationship" (2003, chapter 3).

56. Which is not to rule out creativity: people may play with and elaborate on sign switching, and indeed such sign switching runs throughout revelatory practices in Melanesia; a notable example is the Barok demonstration that by switching positions, one can make male appear female and old as young (Wagner 1987).

57. The "one" Omie origin only appears with the reduplicated FF (cf. Houseman 1988).

58. "Ownership" is a strong word in English to use in such a context, but carries an appropriate ontological connotation. As we have seen, what is owned of them may be thought of as their power to reproduce.

59. Compare for instance de Coppet (1985). Famous Australian precedents are Aboriginal land claims, as Barron (1998, 52–53) reminds us. The courts had to confront the fact that people may relate to land *either* as members of a territorial band *or* as members of a clan that has its sacred imprint on the landscape. Neither together nor apart do they add up to "property" in the legal sense. They are two ways of being, a position the court came close to endorsing in interpreting them as two entities with different spheres of activity ("economic" and "spiritual"). The judge could also have been drawing inspiration from the Torrens system of land registration in Australia, by which title relates not to an owner's various holdings but to a holding's various owners (Riles, forthcoming).

60. Under the auspices of UNESCO and WIPO: a Model Law for the Protection of Traditional Knowledge and Expressions of Culture in the Pacific Islands. At the time of Simet's observations in 2001, it was being discussed at various fora, including the South Pacific Commission (e.g., Kalinoe 2001); it has since been adopted.

61. Indigenous systems, the principal architect of the Model Law observes, "are driven by characteristics of trans-generational, non-materialistic, and non-exclusive or communal ownership of rights" that make intellectual property rights inappropriate (Puri 2002). However, the Model Law deliberately uses the term "property" in accord with international usage, thus conferring a "property right" on those who own traditional knowledge and expressions of culture (Part II: Rights of Traditional Owners), and seeks to identify the "true owners" in each case; such owners in this usage include groups or communities.

62. The Model Law is based on an explicit objection to Western forms of private property, and sees the Pacific counterpart as "communal" property. Thus notes to the Model Law in draft form appropriately observe that "in traditional societies rights over a work of art are generally distributed over several individuals or groups of individuals," but then interprets the relevant subject of traditional ownership as a group or community. Hence under "collective ownership" it is noted that "property rights in traditional knowledge and expressions of culture can vest only in a group, clan or

community of Pacific Islanders" or "ownership and control over the reproduction of works is vested in the group, clan or community." Simet (2000) wishes to make a strong distinction between a "community" as a kind of public domain, in which certain types of knowledge circulate on a nonexclusive basis, and clans or groups that assert exclusive claims, as may individuals. But in his view, exclusive access does not mean that the clan or group has authority and control over all its property: aspects of *its* property may be under the control of *others* (nonmembers) who act as custodians or guardians of it.

63. In this matrilineal system, the relevant nonmembers are "children" born to male members of a clan. The reproductive model is evident here (and is mirrored in rules of exogamy: a clan is not autofertile, but depends on other clans for its spouses). Tolai land usage repeats the division between the "owners" of land and the "custodians" of the history associated with it, which is in the safekeeping of nonowner "children."

64. If this were a starting point rather than an ending point, one would at the outset observe that the sphere or scope of kinship in the two contexts is not isomorphic. To compare "Euro-American" (or English) and "Melanesian" (or Murik or Omie), kinship would emphatically and systematically mean not comparing like with like. On the other hand, the two cosmologies that have concerned me here, the one attending to the production of things in the world, the other to the production of people out of people, offer the kind of "comparability" of dynamics that one can hold up to systemic contrast.

References

Astuti, Rita. 1995. *People of the Sea: Identity and Descent Among the Vezo of Madagascar*. Cambridge: Cambridge University Press.

———. 2000. "Kindreds and Descent Groups: New Perspectives from Madagascar." In *Cultures of Relatedness: New Approaches to the Study of Kinship*, ed. J. Carsten. Cambridge: Cambridge University Press.

Bainbridge, David. 1999. *Intellectual Property*. London: Financial Times Management.

Barron, Anne. 1998. "No Other Law? Author-ity, Property, and Aboriginal Art." In *Intellectual Property and Ethics*, ed. L. Bently and S. Mariatis. London: Sweet and Maxwell.

Battaglia, Debbora. 1990. *On the Bones of the Serpent: Person, Memory, and Mortality Among the Sabarl Islanders of Papua New Guinea*. Chicago: University of Chicago Press.

Biagioli, Mario, and Peter Galison, eds. 2003. *Scientific Authorship: Credit and Intellectual Property in Science*. New York: Routledge.

Blakeney, Michael. 1995. "Protecting Expressions of Australian Aboroginal Folklore Under Copyright Law." *European Intellectual Property Review* 17, no. 9: 442–445.

———. 2000. "The Protection of Traditional Knowledge Under Intellectual Property Law." *European Intellectual Property Review* 22, no. 6: 251–261.

Bolton, Lissant. 2003. *Unfolding the Moon: Enacting Women's Kastom in Vanuatu*. Washington: Smithsonian Institute.

Brown, Michael. 1998. "Can Culture Be Copyrighted?" *Current Anthropology* 39: 193–222.

———. 2003. *Who Owns Native Culture?* Cambridge, Mass.: Harvard University Press.

Brush, Stephen. 1999. "Bioprospecting in the Public Domain." *Cultural Anthropology* 14: 535–555.

Coombe, Rosemary. 1998. *The Cultural Life of Intellectual Properties: Authorship, Appropriation, and the Law*. Durham, N.C.: Duke University Press.

Crook, Tony. 1999. "Growing Knowledge in Bolivip, Papua New Guinea." *Oceania* 69: 225–242.

———. Forthcoming. *"Kim Kukuru": An Anthropological Exchange with Bolivip, Papua New Guinea*. London: British Academy.

Davies, M., and N. Naffine. 2001. *Are Persons Property? Legal Debtaes About Property and Personality*. Aldershot: Ashgate Dartmouth.

de Coppet, Daniel. 1981. "The Life-Giving Death." In *Mortality and Immortality: The Anthropology and Archaeology of Death*, ed. S. C. Humphrey and H. King. London: Acedmic Press.

———. 1985. "Land Owns People." In *Contexts and Levels: Anthropological Essays on Hierarchy*, ed. R. H. Barnes, D. de Coppet, and R. J. Parkin. Oxford: JASO.

Demian, Melissa. 2001. "Claims Without Rights: Stable Objects and Transient Owners in Suau." Presented to ASA Conference panel "Intellectual and Cultural Property Rights." Sussex.

———. Forthcoming. "Seeing, Knowing, Owning: Property Claims as Revelatory Acts." In *Transactions and Creations: Property Debates and the Stimulus of Melanesia*, ed. E. Hirsch and M. Strathern. Oxford: Berghahn.

Edwards, Jeanette, and Marilyn Strathern. 2000. "Including Our Own." In *Cultures of Relatedness: New Approaches to the Study of Kinship*, ed. J. Carsten. Cambridge: Cambridge University Press.

Gray, Kevin. 1991. "Property in Thin Air." *Cambridge Law Journal* 50: 252–307.

Harrison, Simon. 1992. "Ritual as Intellectual Property." *Man* n.s. 27: 225–244.

———. 1995. "Anthropological Perspectives on the Management of Knowledge." *Anthropology Today* 11: 10–14.

Hirsch, Eric. 2001a. "Mining Boundaries and Local Land Narratives (Tibide) in the Udabe Valley, Central Province." In *Rationales of Ownership*, ed. L. Kalinoe and J. Leach. New Delhi: UBS Publishers' Distributors Ltd.

———. 2001b. "Making Up People in Papua." *Journal of the Royal Anthropological Institute* n.s. 7: 241–256.

Hirsch, Eric, and Marilyn Strathern, eds. Forthcoming. *Transactions and Creations: Property Debates and the Stimulus of Melanesia*. Oxford: Berghahn.

Houseman, Michael. 1988. "Towards a Complex Model of Parenthood: Two African Tales." *American Ethnologist* 15: 658–677.

Jaszi, Peter. 1994. "On the Author Effect: Contemporary Copyright and Collective Creativity." In *The Construction of Authorship: Textual Appropriation in Law and Literature*, ed. M. Woodmansee and P. Jaszi. Durham, N.C.: Duke University Press.

Kalinoe, Lawrence. 2000. "Ascertaining the Nature of Indigenous Intellectual and Cultural Property, and Traditional Knowledge, and the Search for Legal Options in Regulating Access in Papua New Guinea." Unpublished manuscript, PTC project, Cambridge.

———. 2001. "Expressions of Culture: A Cultural Perspective from Papua New Guinea." Presented to WIPO Sub-Regional Workshop "Intellectual Property, Genetic Resources, and Traditional Knowledge." Brisbane.

———. Forthcoming. "Traditional Knowledge and Legal Options for the Regulation of Intellectual and Cultural Property in Papua New Guinea." In *Transactions and Creations: Property Debates and the Stimulus of Melanesia*, ed. E. Hirsch and M. Strathern. Oxford: Berghahn.

Kirsch, Stuart. 2001. "Lost Worlds: Environmental Disaster, 'Culture Loss,' and the Law." *Current Anthropology* 42: 167–198.

Küchler, Susanne. 1987. "Malangan: Art and Memory in a Melanesian Society." *Man* n.s. 22: 238–255.

———. 1992. "Making Skins: Malangan and the Idiom of Kinship in New Ireland." In *Anthropology, Art, and Aesthetics*, ed. J. Coote and A. Shelton. Oxford: Clarendon Press.

———. 1999. "The Place of Memory." In *The Art of Forgetting*, ed. A. Forty and S. Küchler. Oxford: Berg.

———. 2003. *Malanggan: Art, Memory, and Sacrifice*. Oxford: Berg.

Leach, James. 2000. "Multiple Expectations of Ownership." Presented at PTC conference "Tradition, Knowledge, and Ownership: Transaction and Protection," organised by L. Kalinoe. Port Moresby.

———. 2003. *Creative Land: Place and Procreation on the North Coast of Papua New Guinea*. Oxford: Berghahn Books.

Lincoln, Louise. 1987. "Art and Money in New Ireland." In *Assemblage of Spirits: Idea and Image in New Ireland*, ed. L. Lincoln. New York: George Braziller.

Lipset, D., and J. Stritecky. 1994. "The Problem of Mute Metaphor: Gender and Kinship in Seaboard Melanesia." *Ethnology* 33: 1–20.

McPherson, C. B. 1964. *The Political Theory of Possessive Individualism: Hobbes to Locke*. Oxford: Clarendon Press.

Miller, Daniel. 1995. "Introduction: Anthropology, Modernity, and Consumption." In *Worlds Apart: Modernity Through the Prism of the Local*, ed. Daniel Miller. ASA Decennial Conference series. London: Routledge.

Mosko, Mark. 1995. *Quadripartite Structures: Categories, Relations, and Homologies in Bush Mekeo Culture*. Cambridge: Cambridge University Press.

Morphy, Howard. 1991. *Ancestral Connections*. Chicago: University of Chicago Press.

Muke, John. 2000. "Ownership of Ideas and Things: A Case Study of the Politics of the Kuk Prehistoric Site." In *Protection of Intellectual, Biological, and Cultural Property in Papua New Guinea*, ed. K. Whimp and M. Busse. Canberra: Asia Pacific Press at ANU; Port Moresby: Conservation Melanesia Inc.

Pottage, Alain. 1998. "The Inscription of Life in Law: Genes, Patents and Biopolitics." In *Law and Human Genetics: Regulating a Revolution*, ed. R. Brownsword, W. R. Cornish, and M. Llewelyn. Oxford: Hart Publishing.

Pedersen, Morten. 2001. "Totemism, Animism and North Asian Indigenous Ontologies." *Journal of the Royal Anthropological Institute* n.s. 7: 411–427.

Posey, D. 1996. *Traditional Resource Rights: International Instruments for Protection and Compensation for Indigenous Peoples and Local Communities*. Gland: Switzerland, and Cambridge: International Union for Conservation of Nature.

Puri, Kamal. 2002. "Traditional Knowledge and Folklore, Sustainable Dvelopments." Report from Conference of the U.K. Commission on International Property Rights: How Intellectual Property Rights Could Work Better for Developing Countries and Poor People. London.

Radin, Margaret J. 1993. *Reinterpreting Property*. Chicago: University of Chicago Press.

———. 1996. *Contested Commodities: The Trouble with Trade in Sex, Children, Body Parts, and Other Things*. Cambridge, Mass: Harvard University Press.

Riles, Annelise. Forthcoming. "Law as Object." In *Legal Legacies, Current Crises*, ed. D. Brenneis and S. Merry. Sante Fe, N.M.: School of American Research Press.

Rohatynskyj, Marta. 1990. "The Larger Context of Omie Sex Affiliation." *Man* n.s. 25: 434–453.

———. 1997. "Culture, Secrets, and Omie History: A Consideration of the Politics of Cultural Identity." *American Ethnologist* 24: 438–456.

———. 2001. "Omie Myths and Narratives as National Cultural Property." Presented to the workshop "Becoming Heirs," organised by Karen Sykes, at the PTC Conference "Innovation, Creation, and New Economic Forms: Approaches to Intellectual and Cultural Property." Cambridge.

Saunders, D., and I. Hunter. 1991. "Lessons from the 'Literatory': How to Historicise Authorship." *Critical Inquiry* 17: 479–509.

Sherman, B., and L. Bently. 1999. *The Making of Modern Intellectual Property Law: The British Experience, 1760–1911*. Cambridge: Cambridge University Press.

Simet, Jacob. 2000. "Copyrighting Traditional Tolai Knowledge?" In *Protection of Intellectual, Biological, and Cultural Property in Papua New Guinea*, ed. K. Whimp and M. Busse. Canberra: Asia Pacific Press at ANU; Port Moresby: Conservation Melanesia Inc.

———. 2001a. "Conclusions: Reflections on Cultural Property Research." In *Culture and Cultural Property in the New Guinea Islands Region: Seven Case Studies*, ed. K. Sykes. New Delhi: UBS Publishers' Distributors Ltd.

———. 2001b. "Custodians by Obligation." Presented to the workshop "Becoming Heirs," organised by Karen Sykes, at the PTC Conference "Innovation, Creation, and New Economic Forms: Approaches to Intellectual and Cultural Property." Cambridge.

Strathern, Marilyn. 1988. *The Gender of the Gift: Problems with Women and Problems with Society in Melamesia.* Berkeley: University of California Press.

———. 1999. *Property, Substance, and Effect: Anthropological Essays on Persons and Things.* London: Athlone Press.

———. 2001. "Global and Local Contexts." In *Rationales of Ownership: Ethnographic Studies of Transactions and Claims to Ownership in Contemporary Papua New Guinea,* ed. L. Kalinoe and J. Leach. New Delhi: UBS Publishers' Distributors Ltd.

———. Forthcoming. "Losing (Out On) Intellectual Resources." In *Law, Anthropology, and the Constitution of the Social: Making Persons and Things,* ed. A. Pottage and M. Mundy. Cambridge: Cambridge University Press.

Sykes, Karen. 2000. "Losing Interest: The Devaluation of Malnaggan in New Ireland." Presented to the PTC Colloquium "Intergenerational and Intergender Transactions." Cambridge.

Toft, Susan, ed. 1998. *Compensation and Resource Development in Papua New Guinea.* Canberra: Australian National University, and Port Moresby: Law Reform Commision.

Vilaça, Aparecida. 2000. "Relations Between Funerary Cannibalism and Wafare Cannibalism: The Question of Predation." *Ethnos* 65: 83–106.

Viveiros de Castro, E. 1992. *From the Enemy's Point of View: Humanity and Divinity in an Amazonian Society,* trans. C. V. Howard. Chicago: University of Chicago Press.

———. 1998. "Cosmological Deixis and Amerindian Perspectivism." *Journal of the Royal Anthropological Institute* n.s. 4: 469–488.

Wagner, Roy. 1977. "Analogic kinship: A Daribi example." *American Ethnologist* 4: 623–642.

———. 1987. "Figure-Ground Reversal Among the Barok." In *Assemblage of Spirits: Idea and Image in New Ireland,* ed. L. Lincoln. New York: George Braziller.

Weatherall, Kimberlee. 2001. "Culture, Autonomy, and Djulibinyamurr: Individual and Community in the Construction of Rights to Traditional Designs." *Modern Law Review* 64: 215–242.

Whimp, Kathy, and Mark Busse, eds. 2000. *Protection of Intellectual, Biological, and Cultural Property in Papua New Guinea.* Canberra: Asia Pacific Press at ANU; Port Moresby: Conservation Melanesia Inc.

Woodmansee, Martha. 1994. "On the Author Effect: Recovering Collectivity." In *The Construction of Authorship: Textual Appropriation in Law and Literature,* ed. M. Woodmansee and P. Jaszi. Durham, N.C.: Duke University Press.

6 One Two Three

The Psychic Economy of Multiplicity

Akira Mizuta Lippit

There was no "One, two, three, and away!" but they began running when they liked, and left off when they liked, so it was not easy to know when the race was over. However, when they had been running half-an-hour or so, and were quite dry again, the Dodo suddenly yelled out, "The race is over!" and they all crowded round it, panting and asking, "But who has won?"

—Lewis Carroll, *Alice's Adventures in Wonderland,* 1865

One

"A voice comes to one in the dark. Imagine."[1] Two sentences from Samuel Beckett's *Company* (1980), the first two of his small novel, come to one—to the "one on his back in the dark" and to the one that reads. To more than one one; to which one? To two ones, one inside, the other out. One here, one there. Are they "one and the same," to invoke Étienne Balibar's question?[2] Are they the same one? Beckett's novella engenders a multitude from one: it multiplies persons, tenses, and modes of address from one and to one. One for all, all for one, "devising it all," he says, "for company." ("Company," in the *OED*, is "an assemblage, a collection, or multitude of things.")

To each one comes a voice. Two one. To one, but not necessarily from one. "A voice," an indefinite, singular voice may still be more than one voice. (Certain forms of multiplicity, say Deleuze and Guattari, are "designated by indefinite articles, or rather by partitives," "some voice comes to one," "a voice comes to some one ... ")[3] "Comes to one" can also be understood as "becomes one": a voice that comes to one, that may not have begun as one, becomes one as it comes to one. This voice that provokes imagination, that sparks and charges the imperative to imagine, comes to and becomes one. It comes not to me, nor to you, but to the one that may also be me and you. To a me or you, some me or you in the dark, to some one. This voice illuminates an ambiguity: Imagine that a voice comes to one? Or that a voice comes to one and demands "imagine"? Either one, perhaps, or both ones. Imagine a voice that illuminates the dark, a voice that comes to one.

What makes possible a voice that comes to one in the dark? Imagination, an image or dream? Some dream that makes possible an imperial message, destined for you, for oneself, but caught in the milieu of a throng, of "multitudes so vast; their numbers have no end?"[4] The message, sent to you, will travel for "thousands of years" but remain in the milieu, on its way, in transit. Imagine. But in this scene, says Kafka, you "dream it to yourself," as evening falls; what doesn't come doesn't come to you and not to one. You are not one.

Or perhaps one comes to it, like "a man from the country" who comes to the Law in another of Kafka's parables. Some man, any or one man from the country for whom the Law, or at least the gateway of the Law, exists only for him, "for you," in the language of the "doorkeeper," a singularity formed from a generality. An order of the one, forged from a multitude that comes to it. "*No one else* could ever be admitted here, since this gate was made *only for you*. I am now going to shut it."[5] Only for you, this one and not any other one, for no one else. You are not any one.

The voice that comes to one, comes from another one; a one formed outside of the world that determines this one. A power, one could say, of the one. On pages one and two of her *Psychic Life of Power*, Judith Butler says: "To be dominated by a power external to oneself is a familiar and agonizing form power takes. To find, however, that what 'one' is, one's very formation as a subject, is in some sense dependent on that very power is quite another."[6] A different one that is one all the same, after all. A paradoxical one, says another, Paul de Man, following Pascal. In Pascal, "The status of the *one* is paradoxical and even contradictory: as the very principle of singleness, it has no plurality, no number. As Euclid said, *one* is not a number."[7] And yet, says de Man, "the one partakes of number, according to the principle of homogeneity enunciated by the same Euclid."[8] One is and is not a number; one is and is not one.

> *One* is not a number; this proposition is correct, but so is the opposite proposition, namely, that *one* is a number, provided it is mediated by the principle of homogeneity, which asserts that *one* is of the same species as number.[9]

One is not a number, but a species (*genre*), says de Man. Which is to say, it is a kind of animal, genre, or gender divided from its own by the principle of homogeneity. A schizoid species of number. One and the same, and not the same, all the same.

One is one, and is not one. A becoming one; a one that becomes another one. Not by filiation or evolution, Deleuze and Guattari say, but by contagion, "by transversal communications between heterogeneous populations."[10] What one Sergei Eisenstein (there is another Sergei yet to come), in the age of cinema called "montage." A conflict that generates contact. Among the many conflicts that determine montage, Eisenstein includes "the conflict between the acoustic and the optical in sound cinema."[11] (An image) and a voice come to one in the dark (imagine), and become one like a cinema, some cinema, a "synchresis." "The voice alone is company," says Beckett, "but not enough."[12]

(*n* + one)

More than any other philosopher since Leibniz perhaps, Gilles Deleuze has been identified with a thinking of multiplicity, its structures, modes, figures, geographies, and progenitors. Multiplicity is not a numerical figure for Deleuze, although it always involves a form of arithmetic, a calculation. "The rhizome," say Deleuze and Guattari of their exemplary figure for multiplicity, "is reducible neither to the One nor the multiple. It is not the One that becomes Two or even directly three, four, five, etc. It is not a multiple derived from the One, or to which One is added (*n* + 1)."[13] Neither an origin nor a destination, the rhizome is a "milieu," a middle from which "the One is always subtracted (*n* □ 1)."[14] The one is always subtracted. The rhizome and all other figures for multiplicity are constituted by subtracting one from the milieu. By subtracting the One. But of Deleuze and his association with a philosophy of multiplicity, Alain Badiou says, "Deleuze's fundamental problem is most certainly not to liberate the multiple but to submit thinking to a renewed concept of the One."[15] The rhizome opened by Deleuze (and sometimes Guattari), says Badiou, returns and returns to—comes to—"the univocity of Being." One voice.

In *The Logic of Sense* Deleuze says:

> Philosophy merges with ontology, but ontology merges with the univocity of Being.... The univocity of Being does not mean that there is one and the same Being; on the contrary, beings are multiple and different, they are always produced by a disjunctive synthesis, and they themselves are disjointed and divergent, *membra disjuncta. The univocity of Being signifies that Being is Voice that it is said.*[16]

It is said, Being, in one voice, a single voice that comes to one. But "univocity does not signify that being is numerically one," Badiou insists. "The One is not here the one of identity or of number, and thought has already abdicated if it supposes that there is a single and same Being."[17] One is not *that* one but *another* one, some other one. Someone. "Nor," continues Badiou, "does univocity mean that thought is tautological (the One is the One). Rather it is fully compatible with the existence of multiple *forms* of Being."[18] The one is not a circle, does not determine a circular passage to and from itself. And yet, you should add, one is also one:

> But, as always with Deleuze, going beyond a static (*quantitative*) opposition always turns out to involve the *qualitative* raising up of one of its terms. And, contrary to the commonly accepted image (Deleuze as liberating the anarchic multiple of desires and errant drifts), contrary even to the apparent indications of his work that play on the opposition multiple/multiplicities ("there are only multiplicities"), it is the occurrence of the One—renamed by Deleuze the One-All—that forms the supreme destination of thought and to which thought is accordingly consecrated.[19]

One-All. A reformulation of one, an equation of unequal parts, partitives, all-in-one; a one that is only ever a part of all, and an all that is only ever a part of one. Part One-All, some One-All.

Even if, as Badiou claims, Deleuze's thinking of multiplicity is founded on "a metaphysics of the One," of the One-All, its articulation—its calculation—takes the form of an assault against the mark of One.[20] Nowhere more so than in his rebellion against psychoanalysis. Deleuze and Guattari's two volumes, *Anti-Oedipus* (1972) and *A Thousand Plateaus* (1980)—bound by a common subtitle that names the convergence of economic and psychic symptoms, "Capitalism and Schizophrenia"—form, among other things, a sustained critique of psychoanalysis. One line of assault against psychoanalysis in particular is against Freud's tendency to reduce multiplicity to one, "six or seven wolves" drawn as five, rendered as a single animal, the wolf, for example. "The wolves," say Deleuze and Guattari of Freud's analysis of the Wolf Man, "will have to be purged of their multiplicity."[21] "For him, there will always be a reduction to the One."[22] The wolves have become in Freud's account a lone wolf; whole packs of wolves and human beings condensed to a single hybrid animal-man. Six or seven wolves that come to one in the dark (imagine).

Essential to Deleuze and Guattari's critique of Freud is an emphasis on the arithmetic of psychoanalysis, its modes of counting and accounting, its general economy. Of the wolf count in Freud's analysis, Deleuze and Guattari say:

> The Wolf is the pack, in other words, the multiplicity instantaneously apprehended as such insofar as it approaches or moves away from zero, each distance being nondecomposable. Zero is the body without organs of the Wolf-Man. If the unconscious knows nothing of negation, it is because there is nothing negative in the unconscious, only indefinite moves toward and away from zero, which does not at all express a lack but rather the positivity of the full body as support and prop.[23]

The unconscious that Deleuze and Guattari propose against Freud depends on the figure of a zero, of some zero, of a zero sum, against which every distance, nondecomposable, establishes a unique multiplicity. (Zero, says de Man, is "absolutely heterogeneous to the order of number.")[24] Multiplicity, which is to be distinguished from the multiple and the one, "the abstract opposition" between them, and any form of dialectics, takes the form, they say, of a mathematics in which one is always subtracted, n – one.[25] For Deleuze and Guattari, the subtraction of one is not a negation, but a distance, the minus sign a line of escape.

But why isn't this equation reversible; shouldn't a fuller multiplicity, a greater intensity follow from the possibility of adding *and* subtracting one from a form of zero composed both by the formulas n – one and of n + one, none, or no one? Not as equivalent actions that balance one another, that balance the books, but as lines of movement and intensity, nondecomposable distances to and from one? Wouldn't this facilitate what Deleuze calls transversality? And in A *Thousand Plateaus*, Deleuze and Guattari offer a revised arithmetic: "If you change dimensions, if you add or subtract one, you change multiplicity; it is in no way a center but rather the enveloping line or farthest dimension, as a function of which it is possible to count the others."[26]

The case of psychoanalysis, Freud's accounting and arithmetic, his psychic economy, is more complex, perhaps, than Deleuze and Guattari acknowledge. In its very foundation, psychoanalysis bears the mark of a surplus formation. An unreconciled addition haunts Freud's neologism "psychoanalysis." It concerns the erroneous "o" added to the newly-coined term. Horst Gündlach, in his essay "Psychoanalysis & The Story of 'O': An Embarrassment," explains Freud's grammatical lapse:

> The first word in the compound "psychoanalysis" is "psyche," soul, which belongs to the first declension and has the stem "psycha".... If the word to be added begins with a consonant, you substitute the end "a" of the stem of the first word by an "o." This produces words like "psychology," "psychotherapy, "psychopathology," "psychophysics," etc.... If the word to be added starts with a vowel, you elide the end "a" of the stem of the first word. This produces words like "psychagogics," "psychanopsia," "psychasthenia," "psychiatry," etc.[27]

The correct synthesis, notes Gündlach, should be "psychanalysis." Freud's mistake was widely noted at the time, Gündlach continues, and came to be something of an embarrassment.[28] According to Gündlach, during the first decade of psychoanalysis, the surfeit "o" was sometimes kept intact, at others eliminated, in publications and in private correspondence. But the very surplus is marked by confusion, or is itself a mark of confusion, the graphical sign of a doubled excess: "O" or "0," One or none? According to the very logic of psychoanalysis, developed by Freud in his case study of the Wolf-Man—specifically with regard to the letter/number "V"—the graphic symbol "O" must be read both as the letter "O" and the number "0."[29] As an alphanumeric code; a circle or circuit from letter to number and back. (Sometimes an upper case "i," "I" can appear as the numeral "1.") An excess "O" has been added, or a zero—nothing—has been added. (Zero, says Brian Rotman, indicates "the virtual presence of the *counting subject* at the place where that subject begins the whole activity of traversing what will become a sequence of counted positions."[30] A zero-sum consciousness.) Two systems, one alphabetic, the other numeric; two systems in one.

"O" and "a," *fort* and *da*. "o-o-o-o" (*fort*) and *da*, gone and here. An economy of absence and presence, invisibility and visibility, subtraction and addition, but also of substitution, an "o" for an "a" (*psycho* for *psycha*). (In this sense, or nonsense, the word "unconscious" could be read in French and English, "*un*," one or a, "one conscious" or "a conscious.") Anti-Oedipus, A-O, an Oedipus, one Oedipus, what Deleuze and Guattari call with a rupturing hyphen, "*an-omalie*."[31] A-o, "all-one." (It was "Anna O" [Berthe Pappenheim], another A-O, whose hysterical symptoms included the displacement of her own language from German to English, who named psychoanalysis the "talking cure," a cure that comes to but also from one in the form of a voice.) A conscious, one conscious, all conscious (or some conscious). "I think where I am not, therefore I am where I do not think," says Jacques Lacan, reading the one conscious offered by Descartes against the logic of *fort/da*.[32] I add and subtract *ergo sum. I think therefore I am here and not here.*

Two

From *Company*: "Use of the second person marks the voice. That of the third that cankerous other. Could he speak to and of whom the voice speaks there would be a first. But he cannot. He shall not. You cannot. You shall not."[33] No first person, only a second and third. You are not one. A second person, a second voice. The one to whom "a voice comes," some voice comes, some univocity of Being, the univocity of some Being, perhaps, is not you, it only says "you." Or not yet you. You are not yet one. Of the "secret proper name" and "the absolute idiom" that would end psychoanalysis, or at least, the session, Derrida says: "the ideal pole or conclusion of analysis would be the possibility of addressing the patient using his or her most proper name, possibly the most secret. It is the moment, then, when the analyst would say to the patient 'you' in such a way that there would be no possible misunderstanding on the subject of this 'you.'"[34] Like the secret words or *cryptonyms* that Nicolas Abraham and Maria Torok find in the Wolf Man's accounts, hidden from even himself.[35] ("The hearer. Unnamable. You," says Beckett.[36] Zero.[37]) A you that comes to you as one, unnamable. Transference, one could say, offers a fantasy of the elimination of difference. It comes to one, all-one. An economy of the one, of one, but a partitive economy of some ones. Two ones, a second one, you (as another one).

For Blanchot, "a plural speech"—one speech as two—is the domain of mortality. "I think of what Apollo affirms when, through the mouth of the poet Bacchylides, he says to Admetus: '*You are a mere mortal; therefore your mind must harbor two thoughts at once.*' In other words, a multiplicity of speech in the simultaneity of one language."[38] One language, two thoughts (at once), a multiplicity of speech. A company of one. Any instant of mortal speech, any one utterance or voice, is only ever partitive, divided, schizo—one voice is only ever some voice. Blanchot says of Admetus, condemned to dialogue:

> Being two, thinking and speaking by twos in the intimacy of dialogue, would be an ingenious means for Admetus, given his status as a mortal condemned to simultaneous thoughts, to make himself Apollo's equal and even his superior, since his ever present duality, be it that of two persons, maintains the movement of thought that is necessarily excluded from a being that is one.[39]

"The founder of dialogue," afflicted with a split conscious, a consciousness that is not one but two, schizophrenic, thinks and speaks in irreducible twos. To speak, speaking two, as two and between two. Each voice some of another one; Admetus always one and (at the same time) someone else. De Man also finds in "man" an originary "dialectic of the infinite." Turning to Pascal's *Réflexions*, de Man says:

> For it follows, says Pascal, that man is double, that the one is always already at least two, a pair. Man is like the *one* in the system of number, infinitely divisible and infinitely capable of self-multiplication. He is another version of the system of the two infinites.... As a metaphor of number, man is one and is not one, is a pair and is infinite all at the same time.[40]

All at the same time, man is like one, which is and is not like itself. You and not you, you and one more you, one and the same, now. "You will end as you now are," says the voice that comes to one in the dark. "And in another dark or in the same another devising it all for company."[41]

One comes to one, and becomes two. "What visions in the dark of light! Who exclaims thus? Who asks who exclaims, What visions in the shadeless dark of light and shade? Yet another still?"[42] In the dark one voice, then another. A conflicted voice, a conflict of voices, of faculties, a war of words with oneself. Whose war, which war? A first, second, or third war? My war and yours, one's war or "he war," as Derrida says to Joyce.[43] Derrida's words to Joyce (who has also come to Beckett in the dark), reveal the stakes of a war that cannot be one: an arithmetic of words and languages, a war of words at work in one book. (The one book, or book of one.) This war involves, for Derrida, the attempt of one language to erase the other language, all other languages. To colonize the other language, the language of the other, of another under one. From the two words that Derrida says to Joyce:

> Erase the typeface, mute the graphic percussion, subordinate the spacing, that is, the divisibility of the letter, and you would again reappro-

> priate *Finnegans Wake* into a monolingualism, or at least subjugate it to the hegemony of a single language. Of course this hegemony remains indisputable, but its law only appears *as such* in the course of a *war* through which English tries to erase the other language or other languages, to colonize them, to domesticate them, to present them for reading from only one angle. But one must also read this resistance to this commonwealth [now known as "the coalition of the willing"], *not only to pronounce oneself but also to write oneself against it.* Against Him. And this is indeed what happens. Between islands of language, across each island. Ireland and England would only be emblems of this. What matters is the contamination of the language of the master by the language he claims to subjugate, on which he has declared war.[44]

A war "not only to pronounce oneself but also to write oneself against" him, against his war, his war against which *he war*. A war that is not one, is never only one, that cannot be one or won, that can never be only one's own or owned. For no one, no wonder.

One reads in Beckett: "Only eyelids move. When for relief from outer and inner dark they close and open respectively."[45] A kind of television—imagine—that becomes one, then two, "devising it all," as Beckett says, "for company." ("You lie in the dark and are back in that light.")[46] TV is made possible by the switch, rendered by the mode of switching, not only between on and off (power), but also between various channels, from one gender to the next (transvestite), from the sex that is not one to the second sex. From one to the other to another, but also to one (two-one), toward one, a signal that comes to one, in the dark, sometimes.

Three

The Wolf Man, says Maria Torok, displayed an "insistence on the number three that accompanied [him] throughout his 'obsessional neurosis'—a number that was never understood, yet never forgotten."[47] Throughout his accounts, secret accounts, numerologies, and psychic economies, the Wolf Man comes to serve as a kind of matrix through which various claims of psychoanalysis converge. A kind of internet.[48] And like the possibilities of being oneself and another, but also a third, on the internet, and as the possibility of being other, of being at once oneself and other, of being others all at once increases, so does the anxiety regarding the preservation of oneself, of being true to oneself. Despite a certain excitement around the possibility of multiple selves, the anxiety of losing oneself—addiction, identity theft, the unconscious of virtual space—also grows stronger. The logic of sociopathology (one who is not one): the more selves, the less of oneself, until even the one disappears. Know thyself, oneself, no one self. Mikkel Borch-Jacobsen says the logic of the self as conscious establishes a temporality of the self: only while the self thinks—is thinking, now—does it exist. At the moment I stop thinking, I no longer am. ("I cannot even say 'I am,' but only 'there is something, something is happening, is lived, is life.'"[49] Some life.) The zero degree of thinking; all or nothing, One-All. "Isn't it precisely this disappearance of the ego," he says, "that 'multiple personality' stages in its own spectacular and derisive fashion? How, in fact, can an absence of ego be expressed, if not paradoxically, by multiplying it?"[50] 0 × one, two, three ... Forever one, for eons.

Borch-Jacobsen cites Bennett Braun's 1979 definition of multiple personality disorder. Braun, a "pioneer" in the diagnosis of MPD, defines the phenomenon as: "One human being demonstrating two or more personalities with identifiable, distinctive, and consistently ongoing characteristics, each of which has a relatively separate memory of its life history.... There must also be a demonstration of the transfer of executive control of the body from one personality to another (switching)."[51] Transfer of executive control from one to another (switching), from one CEO of the BWO to another. Made possible by the switch. One devises two or three or more, according to Borch-Jacobsen, not to protect the one, but to preserve the none, no one. Company devised to hide the absence of even one.

MPD, says Borch-Jacobsen, but also Elaine Showalter, among others, is (or was) an epidemic.[52] "'Multiple personality' is an epidemic," says Borch-Jacobsen, following anthropologist Sherrill Mulhern, "and psychiatrists are its vectors."[53] MPD "has the remarkable property of propagating itself in successive waves."[54] Against the rhetorics of hypochondria, Deleuze and Guattari promote the use of disease as a form of currency: "We oppose epidemic to filiation, contagion to heredity, peopling by contagion to sexual reproduction, sexual production."[55] (The very economy of psychoanalysis, one could add.) A *Thousand Plateaus*, *Mille plateaux*, MP. Contagion suggests an economy of contact, tactile or airborne, slight or extensive, from one to another to one another. A biologic of proliferation, expansion, and acceleration of oneself into the world.

But in the end, at the end of the world, "you as you always were," says Beckett. "Alone."[56] In the company of one, of Deleuze's One-All, perhaps—or, to employ the logic of transversality, the All-One, A-O, *Allone*, alone. Invoking a specular economy of identity (imagine), and the TV trope, Borch-Jacobsen says: "You want to see *who* I am? Well then, watch. I 'switch': I am switching. I am in so far as I switch, for as long as I switch. I switch, I am. *Je switche, je suis. Je switche, je suis.*"[57] From Cartesian *cogito* to remote control, switch to swish, gender to gender (or sex to sex), French to English, one to two (and three and beyond)—TV. *Cogito ergo sum, ergo* some, therefore some. I think therefore I am someone. And also therefore someone else.

Notes

1. Samuel Beckett, *Company* (New York: Grove, 1980), 7.

2. Étienne Balibar, "My Self and My Own: One and the Same?" lecture given at the Critical Theory Institute, University of California, Irvine, February 2003. Among the many complex questions that Balibar engages with regard to oneself and one's own is the specific question of multiple consciousness, raised by Locke in "Of Identity and Difference." Under the assertion that "consciousness alone makes self," Locke speculates: "Could we suppose two distinct incommunicable consciousnesses acting the same body, the one constantly by day, the other by night; and on the other side the same consciousness acting by intervals two distinct bodies?" Aside from the schizophrenic dialectic imagined by Locke—consciousness and body, day and night—he has invoked a form of multiple personality and the possibility of a multiuser body.

3. Gilles Deleuze and Félix Guattari, *A Thousand Plateaus: Capitalism and Schizophrenia*, trans. Brian Massumi (Minneapolis: University of Minnesota, 1987), 9. "*Flat multiplicities of n dimensions* are asignifying and asubjective. They are designated by indefinite particles, or rather by partitives" (original emphasis).

4. Franz Kafka, "An Imperial Message," in *Kafka: The Complete Stories*, trans. Willa and Edwin Muir (New York: Schocken, 1971), 5. Regarding the turn toward the law and the voice of conscience, Judith Butler says: "If the law speaks in the name of a self-identical subject (Althusser cites the utterance of the Hebrew God: 'I am that I am'), how is it that conscience might deliver or restore a self to oneness with itself, to the postulation of self-identity that becomes the precondition of the linguistic consolidation "Here I am." Judith Butler, *The Psychic Life of Power: Theories in Subjection* (Stanford: Stanford University Press, 1997), 108.

5. Franz Kafka, "Before the Law," in *Kafka: The Complete Stories*, trans. Willa and Edwin Muir (New York: Schocken, 1971), 4 (emphases added).

6. Butler, *The Psychic Life of Power*, 1–2. The subtitle of "One Two Three" echoes Butler's title.

7. Paul de Man, "Pascal's Allegory of Persuasion," in *Aesthetic Ideology*, ed. Andrzej Warminski (Minneapolis: University of Minnesota Press, 1996), 58.

8. Ibid (original emphases).

9. Ibid.

10. Deleuze and Guattari, *A Thousand Plateaus*, 239.

11. Sergei Eisenstein, "Beyond the Shot," in *S. M. Eisenstein: Selected Works: Volume 1, Writings, 1922–34*, ed. and trans. Richard Taylor (Bloomington and Indianapolis: Indiana University Press, 1988), 146.

12. Beckett, *Company*, 9.

13. Deleuze and Guattari, *A Thousand Plateaus*, 21.

14. Ibid.

15. Alain Badiou, *Deleuze: The Clamor of Being*, trans. Louise Burchill (Minneapolis: University of Minnesota Press, 2000), 10.

16. Gilles Deleuze, *The Logic of Sense*, ed. Constantin V. Boundas, trans. Mark Lester with Charles Stivale (New York: Columbia University Press, 1990), 179 (emphasis added).

17. Badiou, *Deleuze*, 24.

18. Ibid.

19. Ibid., 10–11 (original emphases). Badiou's citation is from Deleuze's *Foucault*: "Multiplicity remains completely indifferent to the traditional problems of the multiple and the one, and above all to the problem of a subject who would think through this multiplicity, give it conditions, account for its origins, and so on. There is neither one nor multiple, which would at all events entail having recourse to a consciousness that would be regulated by the one and developed by the other. There are only rare multiplicities composed of particular elements, empty places for those who temporarily function as subjects, and cumulable, repeatable and self-preserving regularities. Multiplicity is neither axiomatic nor typological, but topological." Gilles Deleuze, *Foucault*, trans. Séan Hand (Minneapolis: University of Minnesota Press, 1988), 14.

20. Badiou, *Deleuze*, 11.

21. Deleuze and Guattari, *A Thousand Plateaus*, 28.

22. Ibid., 31.

23. Ibid.

24. De Man, "Pascal's Allegory," 59. The heterogeneity of zero begins with its radical differentiation from one. "There exists, in the order of number," says de Man, "an entity that is, unlike the *one*, heterogeneous with regard to number: this entity, which is the *zero*, is radically distinct from one. Whereas one is and is not a number at the same time, zero is radically not a number, absolutely heterogeneous to the order of number" (59). Brian Rotman contradicts this: "If zero is a name it is also none the less a *number*." Brian Rotman, *Signifying Nothing: The Semiotics of Zero* (Stanford, Calif.: Stanford University Press, 1987), 12, original emphasis.

25. Deleuze and Guattari, *A Thousand Plateaus*, 32.

26. Ibid., 245.

27. Horst Gündlach, "Psychoanalysis & The Story of 'O': An Embarrassment," *The Semiotic Review of Books* 13, no. 1 (2002): 4.

28. Thus the French term *psychanalyse*, or the frequent hyphenation (and capitalization, a proper name) of the word in English as "Psycho-Analysis." Many others, says Gündlach, only used the word in quotation marks.

29. In his analysis of an "Infantile Neurosis," Freud charts the movement from the shape "V" to its alphabetical and numerical values. He says: "Many months later, in quite another connection, the patient remarked that the opening and shutting of the butterfly's wings while it settled on the flower had given him an uncanny feeling. It had looked, so he said, like a woman opening her legs, and the legs made the shape of a Roman V, which as we know was the hour at which, in his boyhood, and even up to the time of his treatment, he used to fall into a depressed state of mind." Sigmund Freud, "From the History of an Infantile Neurosis," in *The Standard Edition of the Complete Psychological Works of Sigmund Freud*, ed. and trans. James Strachey (London: Hogarth Press and the Institute of Psycho-Analysis, 1955), 90. Eventually, the butterfly becomes a wasp (*Wespe*), and then the Wolf-Man himself, "S. P." The becoming-animal in Freud's analysis is more complex than Deleuze and Guattari concede: Sergei Pankeiev is not only becoming one wolf from "six or seven," a lone wolf, but also a butterfly-wasp in the process of becoming himself, coming to himself, to one self.

30. Rotman, *Signifying Nothing*, 13 (original emphasis).

31. Deleuze and Guattari, *A Thousand Plateaus*, 244.

32. Jacques Lacan, "The Agency of the Letter in the Unconscious or Reason Since Freud," in *Écrits: A Selection*, trans. Alan Sheridan (New York: Norton, 1977), 165–166. "Je pense où je ne suis pas, donc je suis où je ne pense pas."

33. Beckett, *Company*, 8.

34. Jacques Derrida, "Roundtable on Translation," in *The Ear of the Other: Otobiography, Transference, Translation*, ed. Christie V. McDonald, trans. Peggy Kamuf (New York: Schocken, 1985), 107. Derrida adds, however, that "if the most secret proper name has its effect of a proper name only by risking contamination and detour within a system of relations, then it follows that pure address is impossible. I can never be sure when someone says to me—or to you—says to me, 'you, you,' that it might not be just any old 'you'" (107). In an economy of contamination and detour—"a general structure of the mark"—*you* can always be another *you*. There is always more than one you.

35. Nicolas Abraham and Maria Torok, *The Wolf Man's Magic Word: A Cryptonymy*, trans. Nicholas Rand (Minneapolis: University of Minnesota Press, 1986).

36. Beckett, *Company*, 32.

37. "The name is the trope of the zero," says Paul de Man. "The zero is always *called* a one, when the zero is actually nameless, 'innommable.'" De Man, "Pascal's Allegory," 59, original emphasis.

38. Maurice Blanchot, *The Infinite Conversation*, trans. Susan Hanson (Minneapolis: University of Minnesota Press, 1993), 80 (original emphases).

39. Ibid.

40. De Man, "Pascal's Allegory," 64 (original emphasis).

41. Beckett, *Company*, 8.

42. Ibid., 61. Earlier, "Why in another dark or in the same? And whose voice asking this? Who asks, Whose voice asking this?" (24).

43. "I shall say only two words. I do not yet know in what language, I do not yet know in how many languages. How many languages can be lodged in two words by Joyce, lodged or inscribed, kept or burned, celebrated or violated? ... HE WAR ... I spell them out: H E W A R, and sketch a first translation: HE WARS—he wages war, he declares or makes war, he is war, which can also be pronounced by babelizing a bit (it is in a particularly Babelian scene of the book that these words rise up), by Germanizing, then in Anglo-Saxon, He war: he was—he who was ('I am he who is or who am,' says YAHWE). Where it was, he was, declaring war, and it is *true*. Pushing things a bit, taking the time to draw on the vowel and to lend an ear, it will have been true, *wahr*, that's what can be kept [*garder*] or looked at [*regarder*] in truth." Jacques Derrida, "Two Words for Joyce," in *Poststructuralist Joyce: Essays from the French*, ed. Derek Attridge and Daniel Ferrer, trans. Geoff Bennington (Cambridge: Cambridge University Press, 1984), 145, original emphasis. One could add to Derrida's polyphony of verbs, their conjugations and tenses, another sonic possibility: he wore. A past tense of he wears, which serves in some enunciations as a homonym for war, for wars; an exteriority added to one, which envelopes the one who wears or has worn.

44. Derrida, "Two Words for Joyce," 156 (last emphasis added). In *Archive Fever*, Derrida resumes this line of thought. Following Freud's speculative history of Moses, monotheism, and the metaphysics of one, the One, Derrida describes the violence that issues forth from the one as an effect of its economy: "As soon as there is the One, there is murder, wounding traumatism. *L'Un se garde de l'autre*. The One guards against/keeps some of the other. It protects *itself* from the other, but, in the movement of this jealous violence, it comprises in itself, thus guarding it, the self-otherness or self-difference (the difference from within oneself) which makes it One." Jacques Derrida, *Archive Fever: A Freudian Impression*, trans. Eric Prenowitz (Chicago: University of Chicago Press, 1996), 78, original emphases.

45. Beckett, *Company*, 45.

46. Ibid., 25.

47. Maria Torok, "Afterward: What is Occult in Occultism? Between Sigmund Freud and Sergei Pankeiev Wolf Man," in *The Wolf Man's Magic Word*, 98–99.

48. For more on the relation between multiple personality disorder and "communication technology," see Allucquère Rosanne Stone's performance essay, "Risking Themselves: Identity in Oshkosh," in *The War of Desire and Technology at the Close of the Mechanical Age* (Cambridge, Mass.: MIT Press, 1995), 45–63. See also Mark Poster, who shares initials with the disorder, *What's the Matter with the Internet?* (Minneapolis: University of Minnesota Press, 2001), especially "CyberDemocracy: Internet as Public Sphere?", 171–188.

49. Mikkel Borch-Jacobsen, "Who's Who? Introducing Multiple Personality," in *Supposing the Subject*, ed. Joan Copjec, trans. Douglas Brick (London: Verso, 1994), 61.

50. Ibid.

51. Bennett B. Braun, "Clinical Aspects of Multiple Personality," communication to the annual congress of the American Society of Clinical Hypnosis (San Francisco:

November 1979); cited in Borch-Jacobsen, "Who's Who?", 47. Braun continues: "The total individual is never out of touch with reality. The host personality (the one who has executive control of the body the greatest percentage of time during a given time) often experiences periods of amnesia, time loss, or blackouts. Other personalities may or may not experience this." Cited in Borch-Jacobsen, "Who's Who?", 47. According to Elaine Showalter, "Dr. Bennett Braun, a former president of the ISSMPD, has said that the FBI is trying to assassinate him because he has implicated it in satanic conspiracies involving multiples." Elaine Showalter, *Hystories: Hysterical Epidemics and Modern Culture* (New York: Columbia University Press, 1997), 169. Pioneer and paranoid, then.

52. In *Hystories*, Elaine Showalter locates multiple personality disorder as a "primarily female disorder" (162), although it has become a "popular defense for male serial killers" (163) and a phenomenon prevalent in the United States that has begun to travel outward by contact.

53. Borch-Jacobsen, "Who's Who?", 52.

54. Ibid. Borch-Jacobsen notes the proliferation of both cases and personalities since "Sybil" in 1973: "According to Humphrey and Dennett, there were two hundred known cases of multiple personality disorder in the United States before 1980, one thousand in 1984, four thousand in 1989, and the latest estimates are in excess of thirty thousand" (53).

55. Deleuze and Guattari, *A Thousand Plateaus*, 241. "Propagation by epidemic, by contagion, has nothing to do with filiation by heredity, even if the two themes intermingle and require each other."

56. Beckett, *Company*, 63.

57. Borch-Jacobsen, "Who's Who?", 61.

7 Language of Order(s)

Jenny Holzer in the Public Sphere

Alexander Gelley

The idea of a public subject is today understood primarily in the sense of consumer, voter, or citizen (including noncitizen), in other words, as a collective exposed to various kinds of influence or control. The study of this collective—consumer behavior, demographics, polling—has the primary goal of furthering projects of the state or of the corporate system. The social sciences—political science, statistics, sociology, approaches to mass media—are in great part devoted to facilitating this process, to ensuring its maximal efficiency. Norbert Bolz writes:

> The unity of the public sphere is at present altogether a product of the mass media. A bourgeois public sphere in the sense of the philosophy of the Enlightenment is today nothing but a fetish of sociologists. Properly viewed, the individual has become a function within the network of media systems, that is, a viewer or auditor of an endlessly varied staging mounted by media technologies.[1]

The kind of instrumentalization of the public subject that I am talking about has assumed new force in recent decades. During the 1960s and 1970s—the period of the civil rights movement, student activism, and Vietnam protests—a public subject was much more in evidence: not as a homogeneous entity, of course, but as a potential collective that could be elicited for one cause or another and that claimed the street, square, or college quad as its rightful arena. Indeed, in that period, it seemed as if a public subject could be best identified in terms of the space it laid claim to. The marches and other mass demonstrations of that era provided evidence of a *Masse*—a politically potent collective in a formative state, searching for a way of coalescing into a veritable public subject.

It is in the context of that past era that I want to consider the intervention of Jenny Holzer—one could consider others like Barbara Kruger or Laurie Anderson in similar terms—an intervention that may seem low-keyed, muted, even ineffectual, if we evaluate it by standards of the political activism of that time. But one shouldn't confuse the context with the purpose or goal of the art work. What such a purpose or goal might be is what this paper will explore.

What first drew me to Holzer's work was the experience of being hooked by a phrase in one of her displays. I don't recall the specific occasion. It might have been in response to the "Truisms" or to one of the longer "Essays." It doesn't matter. What counted was this effect of being "hooked" or addressed. You perk up. You pay attention. What caused this? Was it the surprise of seeing a phrase that was not an ad on a street wall or a neon display? Was it some twist, a provocative turn, in the statement itself? Or was it that I responded almost involuntarily to the form of direct address, that I assumed the role of the *you* who was being singled out?[2]

Beginning with her *Truisms*—one-line dicta, moral apothegms—disseminated as posters on public walls in New York City in 1978,[3] Holzer has experimented with the effects of texts in public sites. Her work employs a variety of techniques—print, neon, electronic signage, inscription in stone—and its force owes much to the strategic selection of media and site in each case. But its singularity is particularly due to its use of language, to the distinctive but by no means personal or identifiable *voice* from which the written pronouncements emanate. The effect of a voice, disembodied but insistent, may be concluded first of all from the mode of injunction in which many of the statements are couched. Whether the form is that of a general truth: *MODERATION KILLS THE SPIRIT*,[4] a moral exhortation: *REMEMBER YOU ALWAYS HAVE FREEDOM OF CHOICE*,[5] or a prescription: *PUSH YOURSELF TO THE LIMIT AS OFTEN AS POSSIBLE*,[6] the agency of enunciation simulates an authoritative source, possibly religious or juridical, with the addressee positioned in a subordinate, passive status.

"What invariably catches us off-guard," Michael Auping writes, "is that the message seems so anomalous to the delivery system."[7] Furthermore, its effect is heightened by the twist, the slight but unmistakable deviancy of the statements. They sound like misquoted or badly translated sayings. When proverbs, bits of gnomic wisdom, seem to come from an authoritative source, a lived ethos, they are accepted as definitive, unanswerable.[8] But when the source is elusive, words of wisdom become unanchored, not at home and uncanny: *unheimlich*, in the double sense of that German term. This is the effect of many of the *Truisms*: *VIOLENCE IS PERMISSIBLE EVEN DESIRABLE OCCASIONALLY,*[9] *TEASING PEOPLE SEXUALLY CAN HAVE UGLY CONSEQUENCES,*[10] and *PEOPLE ARE BORING UNLESS THEY'RE EXTREMISTS.*[11]

Holzer makes a practice of collecting scraps from "the basement of language," found language of the streets and crossroads. She has the writer's special knack of "standing watch at the crossroad of discourses," as Roland Barthes put it, and he reminds us that the Latin for crossroad, *trivialis*, "is the etymological attribute of the prostitute who waits at the intersection of three roads."[12] What I have in mind here is trivial talk or idle talk, a "default" mode of speech that keeps going with minimal content. Of course, the referent of language, what it's *about*, can never be altogether voided, but there are degrees of presence or manifestation. Insofar as the referent is attenuated or shrunk, what remains is a kind of hollow or blanched language, evidence not so much of what language is about as to the fact *that there is language*. Jacques Derrida has put the matter in the following terms: "In the moment that the question arises, '*how to avoid speaking?*' it's already too late. It was no longer a question of not speaking. Language has begun without us, in us, before us.... It was certainly necessary to be able to speak to allow the question to be raised, 'how to avoid speaking?' "[13] This is not a particularly abstruse point, although it may well be termed an ontological premise. We find it verified by such common locutions as "shooting the breeze," "nothing special," "wind-bag," and so forth. Jenny Holzer can be ranged with a long list of writers who have made a specialty of activating this kind of palaver. Of course, it is a highly localized art. What Flaubert could do with *Bouvard and Pecuchet* was restricted in time and place. Holzer shows full awareness of this when she says, "I have both consciously and unconsciously identified with that American tradition of free speech, dirty speech, all kinds of speech, nutty speech."[14]

This buzz or murmur of language, Hegel's "prose of the world," is recurrently excavated, distilled, and actualized for purposes of amusement, critique, or provocation, but its effectivity is contingent and short lived. Hal Foster has written aptly of the group of artists who emerged in the 1970s:

> The most provocative American art of the present is situated at such a crossing—of institutions of art and political economy, of representations of sexual identity and social life.... This work does not bracket art for formal or perceptual experiments but rather seeks out its affiliations

> with other practices (in the culture industry and elsewhere); it also tends to conceive of its subject differently.[15]

In stressing art's "affiliations with other practices (in the culture industry and elsewhere)," Foster helps us understand the particular thrust of a project like Holzer's. She has adapted forms of discourse such as address, order, injunction, interpellation—forms particularly apt in staging the interplay of the political and the ethical, the individual and the collective. Such pairings are to be taken not as contrastive but rather as overlapping binarisms, useful for disclosing the gradations that they span.

Holzer's distinctive contribution has been to find new ways of turning a public space—street, wall, neon billboard, bench—into an installation site, so that the familiar features of the scene—the noise, the crowd, the signage, advertisement, traffic signals—are suddenly reconfigured. Her public work tries to slip through the protective shield of the city dweller and catch her off-guard. One glances at a giant electronic sign and expects to find a commercial message, but instead there is *TURN SOFT & LOVELY ANYTIME YOU HAVE A CHANCE,*[16] or on a park bench, one looks at an inscription that looks like a commemorative plaque and instead finds:

> CRACK THE PELVIS SO SHE LIES RIGHT.
> THIS IS A MISTAKE. WHEN SHE DIES
> YOU CANNOT REPEAT THE ACT. THE
> BONES WILL NOT GROW TOGETHER
> AGAIN AND THE PERSONALITY WILL
> NOT COME BACK. SHE IS GOING TO SINK
> DEEP INTO THE MOSS TO GET WHITE
> AND LIGHTER. SHE IS UNRESPONSIVE
> TO BEGGING AND SELF-ABSORBED.[17]

It might be useful to think of contemporary public space in relation to literary genres. We find nothing surprising in the description of the Forest of Arden in *As You Like It*: "tongues in trees, books in running brooks, / Sermons in stone" (2.2). It is our familiarity with pastoral conventions that allows us to interpret the "voices" and "writing" in this forest as appropriate to the setting. Is there any more "natural" environment in contemporary capitalist society than a mall, a department store, or a supermarket? These sites, as we well know, are designed to enhance the receptivity of the public for the primary, indispensable duty of bourgeois society: to shop, more specifically, to act like good consumers, which means to ensure that the existent commodity system will be maintained and, in fact, advanced. Correlatively, the store windows, brand names, billboards, electronic monitors, neon installations—in short, this enveloping medium that we traverse daily addresses us in its characteristic language and images, an idiom as native to us as are the "tongues in trees, books in running brooks, sermons in stone" in a pastoral context. My point here is fairly obvious: we absorb the present-day environment saturated by commodity culture as our natural ambiance; its messages, both explicit and implicit, are the accepted doxa of daily life, the white noise that needs no interpretation since it is part of the taken-for-granted world we live in. How can this murmur, this buzz (both auditory and visual) be interrupted? Well, of course, a bomb can do that. Terrorism or anarchism can pretty much ruin the routine of the quotidian and lead us to scrutinize it in a new manner. But I have in mind a different kind of interruption, something more like becoming aware of our status in relation to *das Man*, the *They* of Heidegger's *Being-in-the-world (In-der-Welt-sein)*. Interrupting the everyday need not be violent. It could come about through infiltration, diversion, or jamming.

As noted earlier, the term "the public" or simply "public" as a modifier (as in *public space, public sphere, art in public places,* etc.) is a contested concept (or set of concepts.) In the more populist mood of two or three decades ago, it elicited an impressive body of commentary and analysis by a variety of theorists, including practicing artists, architects, and city planners. I will cite only Rosalyn Deutsche's remarks from the essay "Agoraphobia":

> While [public authorities] note that public art is difficult to define and stress the incoherence of the contemporary public, they still equate public space with consensus, coherence, and universality and relegate pluralism, division, and difference to the realm of the private.... The assertion [by such public authorities] that public space is the site of democratic political activity can repeat the very evasion of politics that such an assertion seeks to challenge, for this assertion ... can prevent us from recognizing, that the political public sphere is not only a site of discourse; it is also a discursively constructed site. Since any site has the potential to be transformed into a public ... space, public art can be viewed as an instrument that either helps produce a public space or questions a dominated space that has been officially ordained as public.[18]

Public space takes on valence once the publicness is no longer assumed but tested or put into play. Deutsche's book *Evictions: Art and Spatial Politics* provides a number of instances. For example, in New York City in the winter of 1987 and 1988, when Mayor Koch ordered that homeless people living in public places must be examined by authorities and if judged mentally incompetent were to be forcibly hospitalized, the artist Krzysztof Wodickzko, in consultation with several homeless men, developed a prototype of a vehicle that could serve as a mobile home for homeless individuals.[19] This vehicle was elegant yet functional in the style of Bauhaus design. There was no likelihood, of course, that the vehicle would ever be manufactured, much less, if it were, that any municipality would allow it to be parked on the street and used as a shelter. Nonetheless, as Deutsche writes, the Homeless Vehicle Project made a point. It "represents the evicted as active New York residents whose means of subsistence is a legitimate element of urban social structure. It thus focuses attention that structure and, altering the image of the city, not only challenges the economic and political systems that evict the homeless but subverts the modes of perception that exile them."[20]

Holzer's work can be situated within this context, though admittedly anything like empirical verification, a way of testing the practical success of her interventions, would be hard to come by. The general answer might be that the artist's achievement may be gauged by the force of its challenge to the dominant spatial-economic frame, what might be called *Gestell* ("enframing") after Heidegger (though not exactly in his sense). But clearly, that's a circular answer. What is it that determines the "force" or effectiveness of such a "challenge?" What is really being challenged, since nothing changes in the cityscape after one of Holzer's installations has been dismantled? And anyway, her work has been spectacularly successful with the most prestigious public and corporate sponsors of art. They don't seem to feel threatened.

The issue of art's political potential, of its capacity to intervene in society at the level of belief, attitudes, and even action, must inevitably arise with a figure like Holzer. In 1979, early in her career, Holzer was the coorganizer of the Manifesto Show in a gallery on Bleecker Street, in Greenwich Village in New York. It was very much a local affair, and the material exhibited was "a dissonant array of texts"[21] ranging from Tristan Tzara to Hitler (*Mein Kampf*) to Valerie Solanas (*SCUM Manifesto*), along with contributions from artists, friends, and neighbors who were invited, as Holzer recalls, "to write, say, or somehow present as an image what you want to have happen—or don't—what is dearest to your heart, and what makes you furious." Her own contribution was a series called *Inflammatory Essays*, about which she has this to say in response to an interviewer's question:

> I remember that I thought the tone of the *Truisms* was possibly too even, too bland, too balanced. I wanted less balance and I wanted

> the next things to really flame. Then I tried to figure out what kind of form would be uneasy and hot and I went to the manifesto. I'm being kind of flip saying unbalanced and flaming—I also wanted a passionate exposition of the way the world could be if people did things right. I wanted to move between, or include both sides of manifesto-making, one being the scary side where it's an inflamed rant to no good end, and then the positive side, when it's the most deeply felt description of how the world should be. And then I went to the library to find examples of the lunatic ones and the beautiful ones.[22]

The manifesto as a genre is a kind of no-man's-land capable of accommodating utopian aspiration, confession, incitement, imprecation, blasphemy, what have you; it may be an assertion of the most serious intent or a trial of playful fancy. In the scale of rhetorical types, between something like stylistic ornamentation at one extreme and performative enactment at the other, manifesto is clearly closer to the latter. But it is still language and not action, and so always liable to the loopholes, the escape-hatches of writing, of *écriture*.

In her book *Manifestoes: Provocations of the Modern*,[23] Janet Lyon has produced an insightful and informative study that covers instances from the French Revolution (Olympe de Gouges's "Declarations of the Rights of Woman," 1791) to Donna Haraway's 1985 "Manifesto for Cyborgs" and the Lesbian Avenger's 1993 "Out Against the Right: The Dyke Manifesto." Lyon's discussion of Holzer is one of the best I have found. To range Holzer's work, at least some of it, in the genre of manifestoes is, of course, only the beginning of an approach, but it is a useful beginning. Lyon characterizes the *Inflammatory Essays* as "eviscerated manifestoes—free from all explicit or particularized reference—that simulate exactly the rhetorical cadences of any number of political manifestoes." But then, perhaps worried that this description too easily dismisses the performative punch of Holzer's texts, Lyon qualifies, "and yet Holzer's manifesto carries some semantic weight as a manifesto, *even without a context*. That is, its performativity functions as an ubiquitous reminder of the immanence of political insurgency; it is almost as if the contextless manifesto nevertheless so strongly echoes hortatory interpellation that it carries some residue of 'context' with it wherever it appears."[24] I appreciate Lyon's attempt to have it both ways since it reflects, I think, a real aporia regarding the political valence of certain art projects. I also like Lyon's remark: "by exploiting the manifesto's margin of error—between lunacy and social praxis—Holzer displays the 'non-I' in the manifesto's 'we.'" There are plenty of examples of "lunacy" in the repertoire of manifestoes she treats. Some might cite Tristan Tzara's "Dada Manifesto 1918" as a prime example. Others, perhaps, might include *Mein Kampf* or even the *Communist Manifesto*. But perhaps one man's lunacy—or one age's lunacy—is another's prophecy. So we're not dealing with very stable indicators here, and the question of whether "context" is required to take a manifesto seriously and even what constitutes "context" remains undecided.

A preeminent feature of Holzer's work is to put into play what we usually take to be the clear dividing line between a linguistic example (language being cited or quoted) and a performative utterance (the subject being cited or addressed). "Citing" has a large range of implications. It can mean quoting but also invoking and even bringing before the law, as when a policeman gives you a citation. This last instance might more generally be termed the subject of address, the addressee, or, in Jean-Luc Marion's formulation, "*l'interloqué*," the "interlocutory subject."[25]

The issue of context points to the rhetorical gambit that the manifesto undertakes. The force of the manifesto, its realization as "voice," depends less on any identity features in the source than on the indifference or resistance of the addressee, those to whom the manifesto is directed. That is, the manifesto can succeed to the extent that it elicits a response from a social collective that was unaware of its lack. It is not the identity of the addressor but the hidden need of the addressee that provides a standard for the manifesto's effectivity. It seems to me that the peculiar power of many of Holzer's texts has less to do with autobiographical or dramatistic models than with the elusive but insistent challenge that they pose for an audience. *Lustmord* ("The Lust to Kill", 1993–1994), a project developed for the *Süddeutsche Zeitung* and then shown in various installations, may well derive from Holzer's reaction to her mother's death and then to the violence done to women in Bosnia and elsewhere,[26] but this explanation of origin does not explain the shock of its effect, its capacity to arouse guilt, fear, revulsion, or empathy. The skin and body part as bearer of a message here confirms Beatrix Ruf's point that in the work of Holzer and some of her contemporaries the issue of female identity became salient not in personalist terms—Louise Bourgeois' pronouncement "I have too much identity," is cited—but rather by way of "the deconstruction of identity-attributions and of culturally prescribed roles by means of a radical use of the artist's own body and of new, 'uninscribed' artistic media."[27]

I talked earlier about being "hooked" by one of Holzer's displays. In reflecting on this, I made the connection with the notion of interpellation, a key concept in Louis Althusser's theory of ideology. On the surface, this phenomenon of interpellation that Althusser discusses in "Ideology and

Ideological State Apparatuses"[28] seems so obvious, so routine that one only notes it and nods, "Yes, that's something I know. It happens all the time." Someone calls out and you turn, you wonder if it's you who's meant. You've been "hailed." But interpellation in Althusser's sense radicalizes this scene. A policeman, or a voice that sounds like one, calls out, "Hey, you," and those within earshot turn in a mixture of curiosity and fear. "Me? Why me? What did I do?" In that initial response, in turning, or even forcing myself to avoid turning, my status as subject has been spotlighted, suddenly disclosed to myself from the viewpoint of the one who called out, an unidentified voice. This phenomenon is revealing, since it shows that interpellation occurs even when the individual hailed doesn't know the "identity" of the caller. In fact, that seems to be a condition of my response. I perk up. I pay attention. It's as if, of the trillions of files of individuals in a universal registry, mine had suddenly been picked and put on display. I instinctively search in myself for what might be the cause of that call. It is thus that, irrespective of any will or intention, my subject status is exposed. There is a lot that is puzzling here.

In *Mille Plateaux*, Deleuze and Guattari ascribe a founding function to one particular speech mode: not the constative (statement of fact, informational) but the imperative (imposition of a directive, an order). The French locution they use, "*mot d'ordre*" encapsulates a number of meanings that extend this idea: a citation issued by the police, a slogan, an ordering of language for the purpose of imposing order on society. "Language is made not to be believed but to be obeyed, to compel obedience," they write. "The order does not refer to prior significations or to a prior organization of distinctive units. Quite the opposite. Information is only the strict minimum necessary for the emission, transmission, and observation of orders as commands."[29] In this conception of language, the operative agency is not a subject, whether individual or collective, but what Deleuze and Guattari term *collective assemblages*. This notion is required to account for the nonsubjective but social character of enunciation.

To illustrate how a collective assemblage works, let us look at a familiar locution in the language of pedagogy. The term *Bildung* (education, cultivation) refers to the maintenance and transmission of cultural goods. The etymon culture/cultivation also has an agricultural reference. In George Eliot's *The Mill on the Floss*, Mr. Stelling, a curate and teacher, feels that Tom Tulliver's brain is "in need of being ploughed and harrowed,"[30] a fusion of the agricultural and the pedagogic senses of cultivation. What is implicit in this figure—the application of a harrow to the human body—is rendered in literal manner in Kafka's "The Penal Colony." The harrow (in German, "*Egge*") of the disciplinary machine in the penal colony carves a message directly onto the victim's back. This mode of inscription—the tracing of the law as a wounding of the body—thus serves as a phantasmatic but quite consistent elaboration of the trope "cultivating the mind." "Every order-word," Deleuze and Guattari write, "even a father's to his son, carries a little death sentence—a Judgment, as Kafka put it."[31]

When I stipulated a *voice* as the source of emission of the *Truisms*, I made the conventional association of the deontic (ethical) mode with a personal agent. We typically register moral rules as having been spoken—*dicta, pronouncements*, etc.—and insofar as we endow them with an obligatory force, we presume an authoritative entity at their source. Further, such pronouncements, whether couched as direct injunctions or commands or, more weakly, as general rules, are in their nature directed to an addressee. Barthes says proverbs are in the "obligative" mode.[32] What does that mean? If we look at the communicative structure of proverbs—by communicative structure I refer to the coordinate elements of sender, message, receptor—it appears that one of the posts is left empty: namely that of the sender or addressor. Everybody speaks proverbs but no one stands as their author or source. And yet this in no way inhibits the transmission of moral lessons. The place of the receptor, grammatically the addressee (*you*), is occupied by a virtual subject and it is assumed by any recipient who recognizes the obligative mode of the message, that is, who places her/himself into the slot of the *you*. We need to look more closely at this kind of utterance, one that does not merely state something (constative), but encloses an impulse to realize that which is stated.

Jean-François Lyotard in *The Differend*, a philosophical treatise on the relation of language and judgment, devotes a whole section to the issue of obligation. Obligation involves the pragmatic side of ethics, thus not the issue of what values or criteria are (should) be applicable in human action but rather whether and how individuals respond to a call for action, a call based on an (often, only implicit) ethical principle.

Emanuel Levinas and Kant are invoked by Lyotard to emphasize different aspects of this problematic. For Levinas the "scandal" of obligation lies in what he terms the dispossession of the subject-addressee. Here is how Lyotard summarizes Levinas's position:

> The emphasis is on the asymmetricalness of the *I/you* relation.... An addressor appears whose addressee I am, and about whom I know nothing, except that he or she situates me upon the addressee instance.... By turning the I into its you [*toi*], the other makes him or herself master, and turns the I into his or her hostage.... Such is the universe of the

> ethical phrase: an I stripped of the illusion of being the addressor of phrases, grabbed hold of upon the addressee instance, incomprehensibly.[33]

Kant's particular contribution regarding this issue involves the gap in identifying the source of the prescriptive phrase, its authorizing power: "The Kantian argument is that prescriptive phrases, far from being regulated by principles like causality, on the same order as descriptive phrases, are themselves the cause of the acts they engender."[34]

Certainly, as Kant recognizes, obligation is not compulsion. The addressee of a prescription may respond in a variety of ways: by inquiring who is the addressor and by what right it makes a demand, by rejecting the demand itself because the addressee is not capable of fulfilling it or because it is unacceptable on other grounds. But all such responses involve a shift in the regimen of phrases (in Lyotard's terminology), that is, in the *type* of language practice involved, a shift here from an ethical phrase (prescription) to a cognitive phrase. The *I* who must submit to the message as prescription can only respond in the weaker mode of cognition, that is, of explanation, justification, excuse. But what we are inquiring into now is not whether prescription or injunction is always justifiable (clearly, it is not) or always effective (clearly, it is not), but rather the puzzle that in spite of the dissymmetry of obligation,[35] of what Levinas termed "the scandal" of obligation,[36] it still has the capacity to mark the subject, to turn any subject into an addressee who is thus compelled to take account, whether affirmatively or negatively, of the message and its addressor.

Lyotard adds: "Even if you violate it, you still recognize the law. Obedience is one thing, the feeling of obligation or respect is something else." Obligation is thus situated prior to the normative, prior to the sphere of communally sanctioned law.

> The norm is what turns a prescription into a law. *You ought to carry out such and such an action* formulates the prescription. The normative adds: *It is a norm decreed by x or y*.... [The normative] constitutes a community of addressees of the prescriptive, who qua addressees of the normative, are advised that they are, if not necessarily equal before the law, at least all subject to the law.[37]

Let me come back to the issue of interpellation. My discussion of Deleuze and Guattari's *mot d'ordre*, order language and ordering language, and then of Lyotard on obligation and prescription was designed to provide a rationale for what we may term the *force* of interpellation, its capacity to move, to transform individuals in spite of the absence, or at least the opacity, of any authoritative source. Althusser's analysis stresses the specular, the mirrorlike working, of this mechanism. There is first the well-known thesis he provides, the initial definition: "Ideology represents the imaginary relationship of individuals to their real conditions of existence."[38]

This formula already indicates a kind of twist that links awareness with illusion. The awareness on the part of individuals is "imaginary," whereas the "conditions of existence" are "real." Clearly, this formulation indicates an absolute barrier between what individuals can know ("imagine") about reality and what reality is. Thus ideology, insofar as it can be known (acknowledged, recognized) by the subject, is necessarily, as Althusser puts it, *misapprehended* (*méconnue*).[39] We already saw in the example of being hailed in the street that what the individual, insofar as he or she is a subject—that is, an individual who has already undergone subjectivation by the dominant ideology—what this individual responds to is an Other who is a function of that subjectivation.

The response to interpellation on the part of the addressee is not to a specific question, something for which a determinate answer might be framed. Nor is the response likely to be identical for all addressees who respond to this call. What is asked in the call of interpellation is that the addressee disclose what, as subject of ideology, he or she already is, though he or she normally occludes this Other that is embedded in him or her. Whether such a disclosure works for enlightenment, for betterment (*Bildung*), or otherwise as an ethical stimulus need not concern us. What is important is that we find here not ideology in a general sense, as a kind of pervasive, all-purpose *agencement*, but ideology always in the specific, determinate form of that individual as subject (of ideology).

This explanation is circular. Undoubtedly. The individual is always-already a subject of ideology, and yet when he or she is hailed (interpellated), he or she is interpellated *as/into* subjecthood (*en sujet*). This circularity is implicit in Althusser's basic formula, "*L'idéologie interpelle les individus en sujets.*"[40] The ambiguity of that *en* (as/into) cannot be disposed of.[41]

As Slavoj Žižek has argued, ideology, like metalanguage, confronts one with the problematic of positionality: if one claimed to be inside, this could be attested only from a point of observation on the outside; if one claimed to be outside, this very claim of exemption, of being in a neutral place, would be invalidated by the premise that "ideology has always-already interpellated individuals as subjects."[42] So what one is left with, Žižek continues, is the alternative of pretending to master ideology as if from the outside (to control one's place in relation to it) or to inhabit it and exhibit this in the most extravagant manner. It is the latter option that Žižek, drawing on Lacan, argues is the more effective:

> Metalanguage is not just an Imaginary entity, it is *Real* in the strict Lacanian sense—that is, it is impossible to *occupy* its position. But, Lacan adds, it is even more difficult simply to *avoid* it. One cannot *attain* it, but one also cannot *escape* it. That is why the only way to avoid the Real is to produce an utterance of pure metalanguage which, by its patent absurdity, materializes its own impossibility: that is, a paradoxical element which, in its very identity, embodies absolute otherness, the irreparable gap that makes it impossible to occupy a metalanguage position.[43]

What Žižek suggests is that it is by way of an extravagant exhibition of metalanguage, a staging of ideology as the absolute other, that ideology may be exposed.

My own argument has been that Holzer's texts address the bourgeois subject, or rather, versions of the bourgeois subject (for his number is legion) in the distorted mode of *misrecognition*. Misrecognition *is* the distortion, akin to a fantasy formation in a Freudian sense. In Althusser's model, ideology, insofar as it can be known, cognitively apprehended, will always be misapprehended, *méconnu*. Holzer's work presupposes this condition and provides a staging of the distortion, a staging that is both theater and provocation. "Manifesto," as discussed earlier, covers some of that ground. Whether such a theater of interpellation is capable of piercing the subject's resistance, his constitutive blindness, is another matter. The goal of Holzer's displays is to make palpable, by way of something like an incursion on one's sense of identity and bodily integrity, that monstrous Other, addressor and voice of interpellation.

Notes

Talk given October 17, 2001, at UC Irvine, under the sponsorship of the Critical Theory Institute. Thanks to the CTI colleagues who participated in a discussion of this talk: Mark Poster, Jim Ferguson, Liisa Malki, Chungmoo Choi, Gaby Schwab, and John Smith; to David Joselit for his valuable guidance on recent American art; and to Joshua Wilner for allowing me to revisit this topic in a talk in November 2003, at the CUNY Graduate Center.

1. Norbert Bolz, "Tele! Polis! Das Designproblem des 21. Jahrhunderts," in *Stadt am Netz. Ansichten von Telepolis*, ed. Stefan Iglehaut et al. (Bollmann Verlag: Mannheim, 1996), 143–150.

2. See Jenny Holzer, *Truisms*, spectacolor electronic sign (installation, Times Square, New York, 1982). In Diane Waldman, *Jenny Holzer* (New York: Guggenheim Museum, 1997), 49.

3. See Jenny Holzer, *Truisms* (installation, Marine Midland Bank lobby, New York, 1982). In Waldman, *Jenny Holzer*, 46.

4. See Jenny Holzer, *Writing*, ed. Noemi Smolik (Ostfildern-Ruit, Germany: Cantz Verlag, 1996), 13.

5. Ibid., 14.

6. Ibid.

7. Michael Auping, "Reading Holzer or Speaking in Tongues," in *JH. The Venice Installation* (Buffalo, N.Y.: Albright-Knox Art Gallery, 1991), 13.

8. Cf. Vincent Descombes, *Proust, Philosophy of the Novel*, trans. Catherine Chance Macksey (Stanford, Calif.: Stanford University Press, 1992), 161.

9. Holzer, *Writing*, 16.

10. Ibid., 15.

11. Ibid., 13.

12. Roland Barthes, "Leçon," cited in Hal Foster, "Subversive Signs," in *Recoding: Art, Spectacle, Cultural Politics*, ed. Hal Foster (Seattle: Bay Press, 1986), 99.

13. Jacques Derrida, "Comment ne pas parler," in *Psyche* (Paris: Galilée, 1987), 561.

14. Cited in Beatrix Ruf, "Tautological Revelations—Linguistic Monuments—Trojan Horses," in *Lustmord*, ed. Beatrix Ruf (Ostfildern-Ruit, Germany: Cantz Verlag, 1997), 107n.

15. Hal Foster, "Subversive Signs," 1.

16. Photo of matrix electronic display signboard, San Francisco, from *The Survival Series*. In Waldman, *Jenny Holzer*, 79.

17. Misty Black granite bench installation, from *Under a Rock*. In Waldman, *Jenny Holzer*, 87.

18. Rosalyn Deutsche, "Agoraphobia," in *Evictions: Art and Spatial Politics* (Cambridge, Mass.: MIT Press, 1996), 281, 288–289.

19. Krzystof Wodiczko, *Homeless Vehicle Prototype*. In Deutsche, *Evictions*, 99.

20. Ibid.

21. David Joselit, "Voices, Bodies and Spaces: The Art of Jenny Holzer," in *Jenny Holzer*, ed. David Joselit, Joan Simon, and Renata Salecl (London: Phaidon Press, 1998), 42. Details that follow regarding this show are drawn from this essay.

22. "Interview. Jenny Holzer and Diane Waldman, June 6 and July 12, 1989," in Waldman, *Jenny Holzer*, 16.

23. Janet Lyon, *Manifestoes: Provocations of the Modern*, (Ithaca, N.Y.: Cornell University Press, 1999).

24. Janet Lyon, "Transforming Manifestoes: A Second-Wave Problematic," *The Yale Journal of Criticism* 5 (1991): 118, 120. This essay is reprinted, somewhat modified, in Lyon, *Manifestoes*.

25. Jean-Luc Marion, "L'Interloqué," in *Who Comes After the Subject*, ed. Eduardo Cadava, Peter Connor, and Jean-Luc Nancy (New York: Routledge, 1991).

26. Cf. Beatrix Ruf, "Tautological Revelations," 111n22.

27. Ibid., 109.

28. Louis Althusser, *Lenin and Philosophy and Other Essays*, trans. Ben Brewster (New York: Monthly Review Press, 1971), 127–186.

29. Gilles Deleuze and Félix Guattari, *A Thousand Plateaus*, trans. Brian Massumi (Minneapolis: University of Minnesota Press, 1987), 76.

30. George Eliot, *The Mill on the Floss* (New York: W. W. Norton, 1993), 552.

31. Deleuze and Guattari, *A Thousand Plateaus*, 76.

32. Roland Barthes, *S/Z: An Essay*, trans. Richard Miller (New York: Hill and Wang, 1974), 100.

33. Jean-François Lyotard, *The Differend*, trans. Georges Van Den Abbeele (Minneapolis: University of Minnesota Press, 1988), 110–111.

34. Ibid., 119.

35. Ibid., 143.

36. Ibid., 110.

37. Ibid., 142–143.

38. Althusser, *Lenin and Philosophy*, 162.

39. "The reality in question in this mechanism, the reality which is necessarily *ignored (méconnue)* in the very forms of recognition (ideology = misrecognition/ignorance) is indeed, in the last resort, the reproduction of the relations of production and of the relations deriving from them." Althusser, *Lenin and Philosophy*, 182–183.

40. Ibid., 170.

41. Cf. Rastko Mocnik, "Ideology and Fantasy," in *The Althusserian Legacy*, ed. E. Ann Kaplan and Michael Sprinker (London: Verso, 1993), 139–156, especially 140. The problem, Mocnik argues, is how to take Althusser's "*L'idéologie interpelle les individus en sujets.*" Is the sense "as subjects," meaning that they were already subjects? But then what would the work of interpellation be? Or is the sense "into subjects"? But then they would be "trapped," locked into an ideology, incapable of saying "no" to the constitutive ideology.

42. Althusser, *Lenin and Philosophy*, 175–176.

43. Slavoj Žižek, *The Sublime Object of Ideology* (London: Verso, 1989), 156.

8 Ethnographies of the Future

Personhood, Agency, and Power in Octavia Butler's *Xenogenesis*

Gabriele Schwab

Out beyond our world there are, elsewhere, other assemblages of matter making other worlds. Ours is not the only one in air's embrace.

—Lucretius[1]

How would humanity's perception of the world change if we could learn from aliens? If the properties we assign to the natural world are expressions of the way we think ... then encounters with aliens will *change* those properties.

—Clifford Pickover[2]

Lucretius, Roman philosopher (c. 99–c. 55 B.C.E.), envisions alien worlds in terms of differing assemblages of matter. Some 2,000 years later, Clifford Pickover asserts that alien encounters affect the properties we assign to matter and the natural world.[3] Imagining alien worlds has in the human mind long been an exercise in trying to assess the properties of our earth's matter. It has also been an exercise in imagining the existence of spiritual matter and the range of immaterial things such as the soul, the self, or personhood. The piece I will present is about alien encounters or the extraterrestrial imaginary and what they can tell us about such issues as property and personhood. Ever since humans have gazed at the stars, the universe, the galaxies, they have doubted that they are "the only ones in air's embrace." Increasingly we have become concerned with learning from an alien world. The flourishing genre of science fiction envisions what we could learn about ourselves in imagined encounters with alien species.

Yet we can hardly ignore that the shadow of a human history of colonialism, wars, and genocide falls upon our futuristic visions of alien encounters. Human history does not provide us with ample ground to hope for benign encounters with other people, let alone with other species. From their very beginnings, human space explorations were steeped in a deeply xenophobic colonial imaginary. Yet some science fiction writers turn our xenophobic gaze back on us, stimulating a negative mirroring process that scrutinizes our history of violence from an alien perspective.

I will use such an imagined encounter between humans and aliens in Octavia Butler's *Xenogenesis* to approach the topic of this collection of essays. Science fiction has always been concerned with exploring alternative notions of personhood from the perspective of alien world orders and cultures. More recently, the genre also scrutinizes notions of property in alien worlds beyond the logic of late capitalism and the forces of globalization that determine living conditions on Earth. Like a seismograph, science fiction tests the boundaries of what we may conceive as the properties that define the human or the conditions under which we consider personhood. Taking liberty to use the broad connotations coagulating around "property," I expand the term beyond narrower notions of property to include the properties defining a species as well as a sense of ownership derived from an economy of belonging.

Most choices in our intellectual work bear hidden autobiographical traces. My interest in aliens goes back to a time in my childhood when my little sister Stephanie and I would spend hours in front of the radio listening to white noise. I told her that these were messages sent to us by aliens. Pretending to decipher them, I invented wild stories about imminent landings and possible abductions to a land full of mysteries and wonder. We then imagined a life on other planets with adults listening to the wisdom of children, imaginary animals carrying us in pouches, and flying houses that could take us to other stars. I recalled these fantasies during my last visits with my mother who, in her eighties, told us she did not want to die before the arrival of aliens on earth. She would search the sky for them, ready to welcome them to her home. "How will you communicate with aliens?" I asked, and she replied, "Just as I communicate with you!" The trace of a subtle reproach in her reply did not go unnoticed. In many ways, I had always been "alien" to her, but especially so after I had decided to remain as a "resident alien" in the United States. When I told my mother that the artist who did my book covers thought his paintings were channeled by aliens, she pleaded in her old age's childlike magic thinking: "Tell him to send them to me. Tell him, I'm waiting." My mother did not hold out long enough. We buried her on September 11, 2001, during the attacks on the World Trade Center. The sister for whom I invented stories of aliens died more than thirty years ago, when she was seventeen years old, of a rare form of childhood cancer. The aliens in Octavia Butler's *Xenogenesis* cure human cancers routinely, through simple genetic adjustments. I wish my sister had found an alien healer. I dedicate this piece to her memory and that of my mother because it was with them I used to share my alien visions.

Let me now turn to more philosophical reasons for focusing on the extraterrestrial imaginary. Narratives of science fiction explore the boundaries of the human as a species in relation to imagined species from other planets. They function, to borrow a term from Anne Balsamo, as "ethnographies of the future." Why are we interested in science fiction's visions of the future, and what kind of ethnographic knowledge do they convey? And why do we so persistently link "ethnographies of the future" with alien encounters? That humans prepare for the encounter with extraterrestrials has a long history in the cultural imaginary, both in Western and non-Western cultures. What distinguishes this history in our century is not only the fact that the "impossible" has become technologically feasible,[4] but also that humans for the first time have at their disposal the technological means for the destruction of their species and the planet. Environmental destruction, overpopulation, genocide, and a disproportional arsenal of weapons make the end of the human species tangible, and its imagination creates the need for survival fantasies. In their most general thrust, the latter address the dangers posed to the reproduction of the human species. Hence the politics of human reproduction has become inseparable from the danger of planetary destruction. *Xenogenesis* presupposes this irreducible intertwinement of planetary destruction and genetically engineered reproductive politics. More generally, science fiction follows two trends in figuring this linkage of planetary/human reproduction and destruction. Extraterrestrials figure either as carriers of hope for the biogenetic survival of humans and their planet, or they figure as the harbingers of planetary destruction. Fantasies of transspecies reproduction generally evolve within this larger framework. To the extent that extraterrestrials interfere in planetary reproduction by becoming sexual or merely reproductive partners of humans, they threaten the boundaries of the human species. The general ambivalence toward extraterrestrials in contemporary millennial fantasies also determines their specific status and appeal as sexual partners. Since such millennial fantasies are often but thinly disguised heirs to the colonial imaginary, they figure the aliens either as horrifying kidnappers or as supreme seducers with superhuman sexual powers. Their politics of transspecies reproduction is simply presupposed.

Anthropologist Marilyn Strathern's *Reproducing the Future: Anthropology, Kinship, and the New Reproductive Technologies* reflects a fundamental trend at the heart of futuristic thinking that bears not only upon the reproductive politics in much contemporary science fiction but upon reproductive politics more generally. Strathern's provocative title highlights the tendency to deploy an ethnographic imaginary of the future through new politics and technologies of reproduction. Octavia Butler is no exception. Her imagined communities of humans and the alien species of the Oankali in *Xenogenesis* deal with transspecies reproduction, genetic engineering, and alternative kinship arrangements. At the same time, however, Butler casts her futuristic vision as an historical allegory that reflects upon issues of colonialism, imperialism, racism, ecology, and alternative forms of economy and kinship.

Issues of kinship, genealogy, reproduction, and the boundaries of the human inevitably raise the vexed question of personhood. The latter, in turn, is intimately tied to property, if only because Western philosophies and cultures have established and in colonial contexts imposed onto non-Western cultures a long tradition of relating personhood to self-ownership. Moreover, recent developments in the reproductive technologies make it possible to think of ownership in relation to genetic material. At stake is not only the patenting of genes and genetically engineered organisms, but also the question of who exerts agency in the growing field of "assisted reproduction." Testifying to irreversible changes in the cultural and biological organization of our planet, millennial fantasies about artificial and alien or transspecies reproduction highlight the challenges posed by current biopolitics to the ethical principles of human cultures.

While science fiction deals with the kidnapping and impregnation of humans by aliens, imposed genetic manipulation, and alien-directed gene trade, the more tangible nightmares take place closer to home—as we have experienced, for example, at my home university, the University of California at Irvine, when in 1994 a scandal of major proportions erupted when whistleblowers uncovered the illegal swapping of experimentally inseminated eggs and frozen embryos without knowledge or consent of the involved patients.[5] Dr. Ricardo H. Asch, Dr. Jose P. Balmaceda, and Dr. Sergio C. Stone, three internationally reputed physicians and genetic researchers, were accused of having taken eggs and embryos from clients undergoing IVF treatments and given them to other women without consent or knowledge of the parties involved. Finally, John and Deborah Lynn Challender, a couple who had used the clinic for treatment of infertility, came forward with allegations that the doctors had removed Deborah's eggs and implanted them in a woman who bore twins. In 1995, Asch was lambasted on the Oprah Winfrey Show as the perpetrator of "high-tech baby kidnapping" and "biomedical rape."[6] This illegal transaction led to one of the biggest medical scandals in U.S. history and in the ensuing legal debates, bitter controversies were fought over issues of property and personhood. Most prominently, it raised the questions of who owned the embryo that was transplanted without consent and who owned the child that was later born to an unknown couple. We witnessed a nightmarish "gene trade," in which the notion of human agency and personhood was subjected to utter commodification. Or, as Mary Dodge and Gilbert Geis show in *Stealing Dreams: A Fertility Clinic Scandal*: "Asch, variously described as saintly and highhanded, had a laissez-faire attitude about his client's 'biological property' and was dismissive of the Challenders' and others' fierce feelings for their eggs and embryos."[7] This case is relevant because it demonstrates with utter clarity that in the politics of technologically assisted reproduction, issues of property and personhood are inseparable and intertwined.

The case also indicates the cultural anxieties about the new reproductive technologies that provide the cultural context for Butler's very different vision of her imagined alien species' politics of transspecies reproduction. Butler's aliens, the Oankali, define themselves as "gene traders" of a different kind, as space nomads who over millennia travel throughout the galaxy, temporarily settling down on a particular dying planet. There they restore and diversify its life through the trading and mixing of genetic material from their own and the indigenous alien species. The Oankali live in a harmonious ecology with both their immediate environment and the galaxy at large. They adhere to a "precapitalist" economy of ecological exchange and live in tribal kinship arrangements, moving periodically from a sedentary to a nomadic lifestyle.

In this respect, Butler's futuristic alien world functions as a historical allegory that builds on the juxtaposition between the precapitalist ecologies of indigenous cultures on the one hand and the introduction of slave economies and the imposition of race in the name of economic exploitation on the other. Within this allegory, however, Butler uses a futuristic vision of innate technologies of biogenetic engineering to unsettle the familiar binary opposition between nature and technology. Genetic information and exchange informs the Oankali's entire world. Their whole environment, including their houses and spaceships, tools, and other objects, is figured as an assemblage of sentient organisms made of the same biogenetic material as the Oankali, who relate to one another through biogenetic attunement. It is in this tension between historical allegory and futuristic vision that familiar relationships between kinship, property, and personhood become unhinged from traditional philosophical contexts. While in precontact Oankali settlements these relationships are harmoniously integrated into an all-encompassing ecology, the transspecies contact with humans disrupts this ecology by introducing conflicted relations of power and domination.

At the beginning of *Dawn*, the first volume of *Xenogenesis*, the Oankali hold a group of humans in a state of suspended animation on a gigantic spaceship. Two hundred and fifty years have passed since a nuclear holocaust has rendered the earth uninhabitable. Without Oankali intervention, the human race would have destroyed all life on their planet. After subjecting human survivors to a reeducation program that involves transspecies reproduction, the Oankali plan to restore the Earth, which is to be inhabited by the new transspecies communities. Embracing biogenetic diversity as a superior value, the Oankali attempt continually to diversify their own gene pool and thus increase the complexity and differentiation of their own species. In the opening scene of *Dawn*, Lilith Iyapo, the main character, awakes from her suspended animation, unaware that her captors are aliens.

Xenogenesis, the genesis of the alien, unfolds as a myth of origin. Borrowed from the biblical myth, Butler invokes the motif of genesis as a frame for her utopian figuration of a new, postterrestrial world. Instead of the biblical expulsion from paradise due to the original sin, humans in *Xenogenesis* are forced into exile from their planet because, due to what the aliens perceive as a fatal defect in their genetic make-up, they have destroyed its natural resources. Lilith, an African-American former anthropologist, figures as the ur-mother of a new transspecies world—albeit not as biblical Eve but as Talmudic Lilith, Adam's first wife, the nightly woman. Acculturated by the Oankali for a life in an extended family of humans and aliens, she is destined to bear their first transspecies children. The plot of *Dawn* is structured like a female *bildungsroman*, following its main character Lilith's acculturation for a life with the Oankali in an extended transspecies family, in which she will take part in raising the first generation of transspecies children. The educational trajectory during this extreme cultural encounter is marked by Lilith's gradual relinquishing of her intense xenophobia and racism toward the Oankali. However, her relationship to them remains deeply ambivalent and conflicted, even as *Dawn* ends with an imminent xenogenesis: the birth of the first hybrid of Oankali and human origin.

Adulthood Rites, the second volume, focuses on the conflicts that emerge with the new kinship arrangements between humans and Oankali. The Oankali have three sexes, male, female, and ooloi. The ooloi, a third sex that mediates sexuality and reproduction between males and females, are also the prime gene readers and specialists in genetic engineering. They are the healers of the tribal families, collectors of genetic and historical information, and agents of transspecies seduction and bonding. Humans are divided among themselves. Adapters like Lilith consent to become part of the transspecies culture, while "resister humans" experience the takeover by the Oankali as a form of extraterrestrial colonization. The Oankali have come to the conclusion that the pervasive violence that destroys human cultures is based on a genetic defect. Hence they leave humans only with the choice of either enhanced transspecies reproduction or infertility. The resisters prefer to live in isolated forest settlements and accept imposed infertility and death rather than adapting to the Oankali's "alien" value system. The mixed construct children, however, become rare commodities for the childless resister humans, who capture one of these children, Akin. After living among and bonding with humans, Akin becomes a cultural broker for the resisters, asserting their right to freedom of choice and eventually convincing the reluctant Oankali to give humans the option to resettle on Mars with restored fertility.

Imago, the last volume, focuses on hazards in transspecies reproduction. Nikanj, the first ooloi to perform the gene trade between humans and Oankali, makes a mistake in his engineering of construct children. He creates two construct oolois, a combination that the Oankali have placed under a prohibition, because they fear that human genes combined with the power of an ooloi as gene manipulator might turn into a deadly mix. The conflict arises over whether construct ooloi can be kept in the transspecies community or need to be exiled. Interestingly, Nikanj's mistake introduces unconscious affect into the actions of the otherwise supremely conscious Oankali. Nikanj has unconsciously created construct ooloi because its envy of the close bond between parents and their same-sex children momentarily distracted it, leading to its breaking the cultural prohibition placed on construct ooloi. Jodahs and Aaor, the two construct ooloi, function as transitional characters that negotiate the tensions between human and Oankali emotions. Both become so symbiotically dependent on having human mates that, without them, they lose their life energy and will to live. It is they who at the end of the trilogy plant the seed for a new town designed for the harmonious integration of the two species.

In fashioning encounters between human and alien species, the extraterrestrial imaginary cannot but import crucial preoccupations of the time. Octavia Butler responds to a pervasive millennial species-anxiety that emerges from both the increasingly threatening ecological destruction and the new reproductive technologies. Sustainable development as well as biological and cultural reproduction figure as core issues negotiated in the transspecies communities of humans and Oankali. Inevitably, human cultural encounters raise issues of colonialism, racism, and xenophobia, as well as the historical legacies of worldwide wars and genocide. Eurocentrism and colonial racism are often translated into a "speciesism," defined by Peter Singer as "the belief that we are entitled to treat members of other species in a way in which it would be wrong to treat members of our own."[8] Contrary to the human-animal speciesism, the speciesism in relation to imagined aliens operates according to a logic of radical otherness within proximity. In order even to experience racism or xenophobia in relation to another species, there needs to be an anthropomorphic imaginary, that is, a figuration that grants enough proximity both physically and culturally. The aversive reaction to a mollusk, for example, may be phobic but not xenophobic.

The extraterrestrial imaginary in popular science fiction is often but a simple extension of the colonial imaginary into a transspecies culture. Butler, however, insists on differentiation. She figures humans as racist, sexist, xenophobic, "speciesist," violent, militarist, and self-destructive, but also as "victims" of a form of extraterrestrial colonization. Initially the Oankali keep them from having a choice in restoring their biological and cultural reproduction. While most human characters perceive the Oankali as colonizers, Butler insists on the differences between human and Oankali colonization. The Oankali do not treat humans as slaves, nor do they exploit their labor or skills for proprietary purposes. Not only do they integrate humans as equal members of the new transspecies communities, they also welcome changes in their own culture and genetic material.

In human cultures, reproduction was hardly ever a matter of mere biopolitics. Rather, it was heavily implicated in power politics that also played into the organization of kinship relations. The imagined human reproduction with aliens highlights the ethical implications of reproductive biopolitics from a perspective that explores the boundaries of what different cultures define as human more generally. Butler figures the Oankali as owners of superior gene technologies whose mission consists of a double-edged task. Their goal is to diversify the gene pool of both humans and Oankali, while the humans, by contrast, perceive this engineered gene trade as an invasive mutation that heralds the end of their species. Adhering to a "genes-are-us" policy, the humans in *Dawn* question whether their transspecies offspring would still be human. As "gene traders," the Oankali, by contrast, pursue their politics of reproduction within an economy of exchange. "Trading" in this context resembles a precapitalist exchange of goods, in which genes have pure use value. They are, in other words, free from commodification and fetishization.

Butler's insistence on the pure use value of genes also bears upon the relationship between genes and personhood. If traditional philosophical discourses have figured the "soul" as the defining property of the human, the slogan "genes-are-us" indicates a new genetic determinism that defines the human within a new discourse of genes. Traditionally, discourses of the soul were intimately connected to highly politicized discourses of self-ownership. Definitions of property tended to rely on corresponding configurations of the person who owned and/or was subjected to property. In his essay on John Locke, Etienne Balibar argues that the vexed relationship between the *self* and the *own* structures not only the classical theory of "personal identity," but continues to haunt Western theories of the self and the subject, concluding that "there is nothing natural in the identification of self and own, which is really a norm rather than a necessity, and reigns by virtue of a postulate."[9]

If identity is relational, including the disturbing presence of otherness within every consciousness, we may ask how this relationality operates for the transspecies generation. What happens to identity if it is subject to a perpetual process of gene manipulation and trading? Does it still make sense to think about the ensuing changes in terms of changing identities, or is this notion inadequate to understand personhood in Oankali culture? If indeed the Oankali have no identity in this Lockean sense, would it follow that they have no self-ownership? Moreover, if personhood evolves within the relationship between the individual and the community, what are we to think about the personhood of people in slavery or other forms of oppression?

Octavia Butler establishes complex links between the gene-driven Oankali cultural ecology and human cultures under colonialism and slavery. Despotic rulers, colonizers, or slaveholders could own a person's body, but as long as they did not own the soul, they could not rob their subjects of personhood. Technologies of genetic engineering, however, come with a new threat to self-ownership, of which the patenting of genes is only the most obvious. What Donna Haraway calls the "fetishism of genes" is a more subliminal threat. Genes belong to a culture of commodity fetishism, Haraway argues, because at least discursively "genes displace not only organisms but people … as generators of liveliness."[10] For the Oankali, however, the defining property of genes is to facilitate change and diversification. Hence they have only use and exchange value and become disconnected from issues of ownership. Neither the ownership of genes nor self-ownership is ever a cultural issue for the Oankali.

If we read the Oankali's world as a historical allegory, we are of course reminded that genes as an object of commodity fetishism are part and parcel of a Western notion of genetics that is deeply implicated in the logic of late capitalism. Over and above this discourse of a genetic consumer culture, Butler places the emphasis of cultural tensions between humans and Oankali over the discourse of genes on the fact that genetics played a crucial role in the racial history of slavery and colonialism. Many of these racial tensions are also played out over issues of self-ownership. It is the humans who insist on personhood in terms of self-ownership, because in human cultures it is slavery that has most violently disrupted the connection between personhood and self-ownership. It is under slavery that humans have witnessed the ultimate conflation of personhood and property. This is why Butler's historical allegory can be read as a vision of alien contact that rejects the history of the West precisely in its intimate connection between property and personhood. The issue of self-ownership is inextricable from the violent histories that have led the planet to the brink of destruction. In indigenous preindustrial, precapitalist, and precontact communities, in which the self is predominately communal and relational, self-ownership only becomes an issue under conditions of captivity or slavery. In the wake of Western histories of colonialism and slavery, however, self-ownership becomes increasingly a social, economic, and legal value. Colonizing processes and related oppressive and exploitative economic conditions, moreover, generate concomitant psychic processes of subjugation that are often experienced as a disowning of the self. This is why Western philosophies and psychologies have tended to tie the psychic dimension of self-ownership to issues of freedom and free will, often shifting the emphasis away from the material and economic conditions that enable the latter in the first place.

In Octavia Butler's trilogy, self-ownership emerges as a psychic legacy of violent human histories. For the human characters, their material conditions of self-ownership in the transspecies communities are inseparable from their psychohistorical experience of violent human communities in which self-ownership was tantamount to freedom from bondage. Human characters therefore import issues of self-ownership into the new transspecies communities. Aaor, a transspecies character in *Imago,* speaks for the human need to claim self-ownership and freedom. "When you have Human mates ... you have to remember to let them be Human ... Sometimes they need to prove to themselves that they still own themselves."[11] For the human characters, "owning oneself" has an external cultural aspect and an internal psychic one. Self-ownership may mean freedom from Oankali domination as well as control over one's memories and inner life. In *Xenogenesis,* human self-ownership is threatened on both accounts. Not only do they feel colonized by the Oankali, they also are in contrast to the Oankali not in control of their memories, affects, or actions. They are, in other words, creatures endowed or cursed with an unconscious. "I am, but I do not have myself," is, according to anthropologist Helmuth Plessner, the fundamental psychic condition of the human.[12] Or, as Freud argues, humans are not master in their own house, but driven by unconscious memories, desires, fears, and traumatic bodily inscriptions.[13] From the perspective of the Oankali, things appear in a different light. For them, the new kinship arrangement with humans does not belong to an economy of property. Moreover, they perceive the lack of total memory recall as a mere deficiency in the human genetic make-up.

The superior access to memory and genetic information further enforces the power differential between the two species. Able to tap into their own as well as others' genetic memories, the Oankali can gather more information about humans than the humans themselves. With their access to all genetically stored memory and affect, they may even penetrate the unconscious. While this raises deep fears in humans, the construct children savor such symbiotic merging, practicing willful osmotic assimilation and taking pleasure in shaping themselves after human fantasies.[14] "Being oneself" is not bound to identity but to conditions of continual change, often osmotic in response to the needs or fantasies of others. As one of the characters says in a conversation about construct children: "I remembered being their age and having a strong awareness of the way my face and body looked, and of that look being *me*. It never had been, really."[15] Personhood, in other words, is not identitarian but relational in a radical sense.

In questions of personhood, identity, and relatedness, most humans follow a narrow identity politics, while the Oankali are radical subjects-in-process. For them, being oneself does not preclude mutations through sexual reproduction with other species. Rather than preserving biogenetic identity, the Oankali seek survival by increasing the complexity of their gene pool. Ultimately, humans and aliens in Butler's fiction clash over radical differences in their reproductive politics and concomitant anxieties about the survival of a race or a species. Reproductive politics as a site for the enactment of power and domination between species recalls once again the history of slavery and colonialism. In the process of colonial invasions, for example, forced sterilization, genocide, and deicide were often the most radical manifestation of a pervasive politics of reproduction aimed at the destruction of the other's culture, language, and means of reproduction. In a master and slave economy, the reduction of human beings to personal property granted the exploitation of their labor as well as sexual and reproductive powers. In their imagined encounters with aliens, fantasies of transspecies reproduction stage a related form of power politics.

Xenogenesis figures human survival as a drama of forced transspecies reproduction. Butler links this alien reproductive politics intertextually with the biblical myth of an exile from paradise. The biblical exile marks a transition from "nature" and natural innocence to sexual reproduction that follows the first "bachelor's birth" of Eve from Adam's rib. *Dawn* marks a new transition from "natural" sexual reproduction to genetically engineered reproduction with different species. As supreme geneticists, the Ooloi as a third sex also mediate sexual intercourse and reproduction between male and female partners. As facilitators of sex, reproduction, and genetic enhancement, the Ooloi gain an inordinate power over humans. As one of the characters says about Lilith's ooloi mate Nikanj: "It knows everything that can be learned about you from your genes. And by now, it knows your medical history and a great deal about the way you think. It has taken part in testing you."[16] For humans, Ooloi biochemical seduction is highly ambivalent because, bound to the mediation by ooloi, sexual desire and pleasure is biologically triangular. Although humans gain, as Lilith asserts, more intimacy and closeness with ooloi than they ever have in human sexual encounters,[17] they nonetheless resist the intrusion into knowledges and internal feeling states that are, in Westernized human cultures, highly private. Humans fear a "chemical bondage" to the ooloi who, after all, control not only sexual pleasure but also the access to other human mates.[18] The Oankali culture thus also challenges a long Western history of the cultural production of subjectivity based on privacy, individualism, interiority, and monogamous, heteronormative familial kinship arrangements. While humans would be able to find models of human cultures that are closer to the Oankali in preindustrialized indigenous communities, the human characters carry with them the psychic legacy of values internalized during a long history of Western colonial and imperial global culture, which ended in a nuclear apocalypse. It is this legacy of colonialism, racism, and the systematic domination and exploitation of humans by other humans that introduces power, domination, and warfare in the transspecies communities.

In spite of the bitter and seemingly irresolvable conflicts that mark the transspecies communities, Donna Haraway reads *Xenogenesis* emphatically as an ethnographic exploration of utopian personhood. As Haraway points out, Lilith's child is "the child of five progenitors, who come from two species, at least three genders, two sexes, and an indeterminate number of races."[19] From a perspective of postmodern theories, the Oankali follow a radical politics of hybridity instead of a politics of identity, adhering to a fluid economy and a practice of systematic deterritorialization at both a genetic and a planetary level. Just as they diversify their genetic material in gene trades with other species, they also disseminate it across other planets, seeking to induce the emergence of new life. Oankali politics of reproduction is thus based on emergence and mutation. Yet since total control over emergence is impossible, this politics opens the door for surprises, conflict, and mistakes, as well as power struggles. From the outset, Oankali and humans clash over reproductive politics. The human characters import their legacy of "terrestrial" racism according to which "miscegenation" is always already discursively mediated through a tropology of monstrosity. These conflicts need to be assessed from a postcolonial perspective that traces the effects of human histories of colonialism and racism into the projected future. During the pregnancy with her first child conceived by an Oankali, Lilith says: "but it won't be human.... It will be a thing. A monster."[20] As opposed to the Oankali's integrative ethics of diversification, Lilith's attribution of monstrosity to her own transspecies child presupposes that the exclusionary preservation of human genetic identity is the only value. It presupposes, in other words, a value system still wedded to colonial and racist notions of miscegenation. Butler's technique of oscillating narrative perspectives between the incompatible ethics of the two species creates a pointed ambiguity, leaving the central ethical problem—namely, the question of violence and domination—and the central epistemological problem—defining the boundaries of the human—open until the very end.

Butler uses a polyphonic variety of agonistic narrative voices from human, Oankali, and transspecies characters to address these issues. The use of genetic technologies is at the center of pronounced clashes over agency in sexuality, reproduction, and self-definition. While the Oankali perceive their interventions as the salvage and enhancement of an otherwise doomed species, the humans see the Oankali as genetic colonizers who use them, in Lilith's words, as "captive breeders." Lilith's very use of the term "captive breeders" invokes both the history of slavery and the Nazi experiments with female reproduction and genetic manipulation. But the narrative leaves no doubt that the reaction of the human figures remains bound to their pervasive terrestrial paranoia toward otherness and difference. They simply transfer the racism that generated their histories of colonialism, slavery, war, and genocide onto the Oankali. This speciesism blinds them to crucial differences in both Oankali cultural politics and psychic make-up. Within their new transspecies communities, the Oankali integrate humans as equal members of their kinship arrangements. Yet for the human characters, Oankali colonialism with a difference is a form of colonialism nonetheless.

Ultimately, Butler contrasts two forms of domination, namely the racism of humans and the biogenetic colonialism of the Oankali. Her overarching perspective, however, becomes gradually more biased toward the aliens, rejecting the racist politics of a "pure species"[21] propagated by human characters. Narrative strategies focusing on both the Oankali culture of emotions and the transitional emotional space of the transspecies generation gradually attune readers to an alien culture of feeling and relating. Initially, we see the Oankali through Lilith's aversive reactions to their radical alterity. Increasingly however, more complex transspecies language games evolve to negotiate difference. The fact that the Oankali are able to acquire human languages through accessing the totality of information stored in human cells grants them a hegemonic hold on diverse histories and cultures of human knowledge. Information, however, is not enough for meaningful attunement and communication. In many ways, the two species remain foreign to each other despite the Oankali's almost total informational access. Even the use of a common language is limited by cultural difference. While the Oankali easily master scores of human languages, language for them has an entirely different status, and remains subordinate to immediate access. They use it like a prosthetic device to compensate for what they perceive as human communicative incompetence. The most radical differences reside in a different emotional cathexis of language and speech. The Oankali tend to reduce language to a mere carrier of information, ignoring its performative dimension as well as its affective cathexis. As the Oankali's "native informant," Lilith experiences a form of "social death"[22] in response to the withdrawal of all familiar rules of sociality, communication, and emotion. Rebelling against her captivity among the Oankali, Lilith invokes the social death her own ancestors experienced under slavery.[23] Yet her impassioned rebellion clashes with the Oankali's systematic refusal of open confrontation. Faced with uncontrolled human emotions, the Oankali simply induce deep sleep as a therapy.

This strategy produces a curious effect, sustaining a pointed ambivalence within the futuristic vision. Over and again we are confronted with difficulties of emotional attunement. For better or worse, humans seem to remain fixated on familiar communicative values and affects, even when they appear deficient in light of superior technologies of communication. The two most basic human expressions of emotion are a case in point. The Oankali lack what Plessner defines as the fundamental anthropological universals, namely laughter and tears.[24] "Inhuman" in this very archaic sense, in that they neither laugh nor cry, the Oankali induce a social death that exceeds the withdrawal of rules and customs to include the primordial expressions of human emotion. If we agree with Plessner that laughter and tears emerge at the limits of language and consciousness, the Oankali do not need to laugh or cry, because for them emotion, consciousness, and the body are in complete synchrony. We soon learn, however, that the Oankali possess a vast range of emotions, including ease, joy, attachment, and love, as well as grief, mourning, and utter loneliness. They convey emotions either through direct biochemical exchange of information or through the coded body language of their sensory tentacles. Of secondary order, spoken language becomes central only in transspecies exchanges.

This bias puts alien corporeality at the center of communicative difference. The Oankali's body language generates one of the most distressing experiences of radical alterity for the human characters. Neither the biochemical exchange of information nor the Oankali body language is immediately accessible to humans. Initially it is the Oankali's corporeal difference that presents the greatest barrier for transspecies attachment and reproduction. A minimum of corporeal similarity seems to be a precondition for any meaningful imagined transspecies relationship. Philosopher Hans Blumenberg, however, argues that of all the probabilities of astronautic experience, corporeal similarity is least expectable.[25] On the other hand, a minimum of corporeal affinity or at least possibility of connection seems to be a condition of imagined cultural contact with extraterrestrials. We cannot altogether escape a certain "anthropomorphization" of extraterrestrials whenever we envision a meaningful contact with them. The "embodiments" that science fiction imagines for extraterrestrial species serves as a prime matrix for projection and transference. The naïve notions of the "little green men with huge heads" might indicate how narrowly we draw the boundaries within which we imagine unknown species. Nonanthropomorphized radical alterity of an intelligent species seems unimaginable, or at least unfit for good fiction. This tells us more about our relationship to alterity in general than we might at first assume. Butler solves this narratological challenge by endowing the alien characters themselves with techniques of "anthropomorphization." As highly superior manipulators of the genetic code, they are able to manipulate their own body and temporarily assimilate it to the shapes of human bodies. They use such manipulation within a communicative pragmatics as a mode to facilitate cultural and later sexual contact. The first Oankali appears for Lilith in the shape of a "shadowy figure of a man, thin and long-haired."[26] Only in full light she perceives the difference: "what had seemed to be a tall slender man was still humanoid, but it had no nose—no bulge, no nostrils—just flat, gray skin."[27] Instead of human sensory organs, Jdahya has long tentacles that embody his "anthropomorphized" body language and convey his focus of attention as well as his emotions. Asked whether he is male or female, Jdahya answers: "It's wrong to assume that I must be a sex you're familiar with ... but as it happens, I'm male."[28]

We must recall here that within postmodern imagination—both literature and theory—we already have a convention for exceedingly strange humanoid figures. Samuel Beckett's "Unnamable," for example, imagines himself as a constantly mutating shape and laconically asks, "Why should I have a sex, who have no longer a nose?"[29] Within theory, Deleuze and Guattari's "organless bodies" also mutate permanently, manifesting themselves in ever new shapes. But there is a crucial difference in the figuration or imagination of alternative bodies that has to do with generic conventions. A science fiction character resists our receptive disposition to translate his figuration as an alternative body-*image* or phantasm as we are so inclined to do with the figures of Beckett or Deleuze and Guattari. The corporeal figuration of an extraterrestrial requires a different "willing suspension of disbelief" precisely because within the generic conventions of science fiction we perceive the radically alien as an "imagined reality." Unlike scientific or philosophical notions of extraterrestrial life, science *fiction* is not bound to notions of a "cosmic realism,"[30] and thus unavoidably generates a kind of "literary realism" at the level of narration. This is an aesthetic paradox of sorts, since other genres may much more easily shed realist conventions precisely because they are *fictions* of an alien world. Despite the radical experimentalism of its imagined worlds, science fiction remains therefore bound to more conventional narrative techniques. While writers such as Beckett or Deleuze and Guattari invite us to imagine humans with distorted body images or philosophical concepts of a "body without organs," Butler entices us to imagine an encounter with real embodiments of alien corporeality. For Lilith, the contact with beings like Jdahya is unfathomable due to

> his alienness, his difference, his literal unearthliness ... she tried to imagine herself surrounded by beings like him and was overwhelmed by panic. As though she had suddenly developed a phobia—something she had never before experienced. But what she felt was like what she had heard others describe. A true xenophobia—and apparently she was not alone in it.[31]

Fixation on corporeal similarity in alien encounters thus produces xenophobia and racism. At a biopolitical level, the panicked reaction to the Oankali's "alien" bodies also invokes fear related to the current biogenetic reconceptualization of the human body. The unity of soma and psyche endows the

Oankali's bodies with a plasticity and fluidity that transcends the body as an identical construct. This fluidity is further enhanced by their ability to adapt osmotically to their environment. Butler thus links the radical constructivism of postmodern concepts of the body with a biogenetic concept according to which corporeality emerges from and is continually reorganized through genetic information. For the Oankali, such genetic information is not "exterior," because as gene readers they do not need any additional information technology. Human readers, however, are bound to read Butler's text from the perspective of their own embeddedness within an expansive information technology and ecology. Within an ecology based on new information technologies, the boundaries of human corporeality have become tenuous, because the exteriority of uncontrollable information that ties our bodies to new information technologies has reorganized the human organism, turning humans into sublime cyborgs. If we recall that Freud defined the ego as the projection of the body's surface, we realize how profoundly the new informational technologies affect the boundaries of subjectivity. Perhaps Rich Doyle is right when he argues that contemporary subjectivity is no longer organized according to notions of subject position and the boundaries of the body, but rather according to a continual "becoming" in the sense of Deleuze and Guattari.[32] The exteriority of information and information technologies affects the bodies of those exposed to them. The subjectivity of this "postmodern subject" has shifted from a Cartesian epistemology to an epistemology of radical exteriority.

For the Oankali, by contrast, genetic information is not "exterior," since they transmit genetically encoded knowledge with their own sense organs. In their transspecies contact, however, the Oankali must take into account human communicative incompetence. Just as they simulate a corporeal similarity to interact with humans, they also simulate human speech and communication. This simulation, however, is haunted by subliminal tensions between two radically different cultural and ethical codes. Above all, this tension concerns the use of rhetoric. To humans, the language games of the Oankali appear strange because they lack the very tools of rhetoric. Marked by a bare literality, their enunciations are free of images, metaphors, and tropes, but at the same time also free of displacement, concealment, and double meaning. They do not know lies or deceit, nor do they know an imaginary in a human sense; they lack stories, perhaps even dreams, and, as I argued, a dynamic unconscious. The Oankali's world is a world without fiction, art, and artifice, without refinement and ornamentation. To the extent that we define their language as being without depth and double meaning, we could see the Oankali as "postmodern subjects" par excellence. And yet it appears as if they are lacking something that, for humans, has always been valued as a core element of cultural life. From an Oankali perspective, this may look as if humans are not only "attached to their wounds" but also to the prosthetic devices they have designed to cope with them.

We encounter here then another deep ambivalence in Butler's juxtaposition of the ethics and value systems of humans and Oankali. In contrast to humans, who are never the sovereign agents of their own speech, the Oankali demonstrate complete agency in their discourse. While clearly superior in their technologies of information, and therefore in their self-consciousness, the Oankali's lack of cultural objects such as literature, music, or storytelling appears, from an anthropocentric perspective, as an impoverished literalism, a lack of refinement or, as we once used to say, cultural and psychic depth. The Oankali's biogenetic and kinship politics, combined with their superior technologies of genetic manipulation, seem to get rid of the racism that has led to the destruction of human communities. But in her depiction of the transspecies generation, Butler almost plays into a nostalgic vision that sees the lack of transparency that marks human personhood as what stimulates the riches of cultural and inner life. It is therefore precisely this use of artistic practices that the transspecies generation introduces into the cultural life of transspecies communities.

Yet it is easy to fall into the traps of an anthropocentric nostalgia for the arts, forgetting that while the Oankali do not use aesthetic objects, they do know aesthetics and indeed a supreme sense of harmony and beauty. Akin, a construct human, describes, for example, the pleasures of healing: "It was almost like making music—balancing endorphins, silencing pain, maintaining sobriety. He made simple music. Ooloi made great harmonies, interweaving people and sharing pleasure."[33] Eventually, the transspecies construct generation also brings human artifacts into Oankali cultural arrangements. Discovering the art of rhetoric, simulation, and acting, construct humans become storytellers and musicians and thus introduce the human use of cultural objects into transspecies culture.

The ambivalence toward art and artifice also plays itself out in relation to the Oankali's sovereign consciousness and total mnemonic recall. They do not know the dynamic interplay between conscious and unconscious life and its vicissitudes that characterizes human cultures. As beings without "interiority" and an "unconscious," the Oankali may possess full control over information, memory, knowledge, and discourse within their precontact culture. However, they lose part of this sovereignty in their new transspecies encounters. They neither possess a total grasp of the cultural values and sense of being of their transspecies partners, nor are they in complete control of their emotions and patterns of relating. Biochemical rather than rhetorical seduction, for example, comes to a limit when it encounters human resistance and resentment. With her figuration of the Oankali's superior genetic technologies, Butler confronts a pervasive fear in the cultural imaginary of our time, namely that our emotional and mental world could be reducible to biochemical and biogenetic manipulation. Such determinism would amount to an even more radical disowning of the subject than the Freudian discovery of the unconscious. The subject becomes imaginable as one that is no longer governed by unconscious drives, desires, and fears, but reduced to the pure materiality of a totally engineered body-mind-soul. In such a world, even the distinction between self and other or between one's own and another culture becomes an object of biogenesis.

Let me end by outlining three fundamental challenges *Xenogenesis* presents to our deliberations on the futures of property and personhood. (1) Butler's imagined alien world operates on the basis of a processual organic ecology in which the binaries of mind and body, nature and culture, or nature and technology, are superseded. Technology and culture are *natural* in the sense that they are organically embedded in embodied matter. Even the Oankali abodes, spaceships, and objects are sentient beings. Personhood, in this context, is always defined in relation to the environment, rather than against it. The subject and its environment are perceived as an inseparable unit operating under the assumption that every environmental intervention produces related changes in personhood. (2) The Oankali's processual ecology leads to an allopoietic ethics and practice toward otherness and difference. Hybridity, diversity, and change are privileged over identity and sameness. The diversification of the gene pool is welcomed as a technology of expansion, enrichment, and complexification. Developed in contrast to the anthropocentric and racialized ethics of Western cultures, Butler's biocentric and transplanetary ethics offers a basis for a systemically grounded critique of racism and its epistemological and political foundations. Free from the cultural paranoia and practices of Manichean splitting, which marks an exclusionary Western ethics, the inclusionary Oankali ethics is also free from what Bateson calls "destructive schismogenesis."[34] (3) Against certain trends in debates about the *posthuman*, Butler insists on reevaluating earlier, precolonial models of human communities and personhood. At the same time, she accounts for the fact that the legacies of racism and oppression left by those histories inevitably mark any encounter with a different culture or species. *Xenogenesis* is sensitive to the psychic ecologies that create conflict in cultural and transspecies encounters. The transgenerational transmission of cultural memory, trauma, psychic dispositions, and fantasies is fraught with conflict in the encounter between two species that dramatically differ in the technologies of memory and its psychic and material inscriptions. The figuration of "construct humans"—either human or alien born—serves to illustrate the ethical dilemma that inevitably ensues if cultural contact is enforced for reasons of survival.

In *How We Became Posthuman*, N. Katherine Hayles points out how strongly current cultural fantasies of the posthuman insist on values and properties of the liberal subject in the humanist tradition.[35] Octavia Butler is no exception. The staging of transcultural and transspecies conflict in *Xenogenesis* is largely organized around notions of freedom and self-ownership. Butler's science fiction, however, presents an alternative to the cultural imaginary of cyborgs and their articulation of the human in symbiotic assemblages with intelligent machines. Her extraterrestrial imaginary supersedes the cyborg imaginary in its even more radical effacement of a binary and ontologizing division between nature and technology. In the Oankali world, hyperefficient technologies of knowledge, production, and reproduction are embodied in alien beings for which gene reading and manipulation belong to the primary modes of cultural exchange, sociality, memory, and reproduction. In place of an obsolete teleological notion of progressing civilization, the Oankali's vision of the world is one of an endless—perhaps rhizomatic—differentiation and diversification of species. Instead of an individualized consciousness and autonomous will, the Oankali operate with a distributed cognition that encompasses the implicate order[36] of inner cellular and outer planetary environment. Instead of asserting mind over matter, the Oankali's mind asserts itself spontaneously as matter and materialized consciousness.

Xenogenesis organizes its vision of an alien world around the question of the boundaries of the human. The figure of the "alien" functions as an iconotrope that helps to articulate the cultural imaginary with its prominent fears and desires at the turn of the century. Along with cyborgs and posthumans, aliens are part and parcel of the metonymic chain of iconotropes that define the current *episteme*. It seems appropriate that Octavia Butler figures her aliens as gene readers. Sixty years ago, Erwin Schrödinger in his lecture "What Is Life?" predicted that the potential of the future of an organism could be read like a hieroglyph in the chromosomes of a cell.[37] German philosopher Hans Blumenberg ends his book *Die Lesbarkeit der Welt* (Reading the world), with the question of whether we humans were ever aware that with the metaphor of the "readability" of the genetic code we have become Gnostics, under the spell of a great anthropomorphic hypostasis.[38] Addressing the blasphemous and apocalyptic undercurrent of this vision, Blumenberg points out that once we are able to read the genetic code, we approach the transition from the human as reader of the world to the human as rewriter of the book of nature. The Oankali are gene readers, and yet, while they rewrite the genetic code, they do not rewrite the book of nature—at least not by their own self-understanding. Unlike humans, they refrain from committing the epistemological error of conferring a privileged ontological status onto their own species or, for that matter, onto entities instead of relationships. Personhood for them is inconceivable in terms of entities. Unlike human epistemologies that embrace deterministic thinking and a splitting of symbiotic wholes (ecosystems) or processes into supposedly independent units or "things," their epistemology is not one of biosocial imperialism. Rather, they see the biosocial imperialism of humans as a genetic defect that translates into a pervasive thinking in terms of hierarchies, immutable identities, and lineal causations of force and power.[39] The problem, Butler seems to suggest, does not lie in the "readability" or even "rewriting" of the genetic code, but in an altogether different ecology of reading and writing.

For the human species, storytelling and writing has always been a form of mourning, a work of memory and inscription to defer or defy death. We could even say that the very construction of personhood has been bound up with storytelling and writing. The Oankali are not mortal in any human sense and hence do not need storytelling and writing in order to defer or defy death. Nor do they need an attachment to personhood that is as individualized and bounded as it is for humans. But their sense of both personhood and species is linked in a very different way to what Achille Mbembe has called "the work of death."[40] Ultimately, Butler opposes the "work of death" of the human species with the Oankali's "work of life." Humans in Butler's *Xenogenesis* are driven by a pervasive work of death expressed as racism, xenophobia, homophobia, and speciesism. After all, the trilogy opens when this work of death had resulted in a nuclear holocaust on Earth. The Oankali, by contrast, are figured as life crafters of sorts, working toward the restoration and continual diversification of living material and life. They intervene in and attempt to undo the human work of death on a transplanetary scale. Ahajas, one of the Oankali mothers of construct children, says toward the end of the trilogy: "Our ancestors have seeded a great many barren worlds that way. Nothing is more tenacious than the life we are made of. A world of life from apparent death, from dissolution. That's what we believe in."[41]

The Oankali are figured here as indigenous nomads, transplanetary space travelers who, to borrow an image from *Mille Plateaux*, move through itinerant territorialities, but only to embark on a galactic line of flight, a deterritorialization that spans the universe. They use the same deterritorializing energy to operate at the molecular level, continually to transform their own temporary embodiments as well as those of their environment. Inviting—indeed, celebrating—the continual mutation of their genes, they embrace otherness, difference, and heterogeneity, infusing the galaxies with a monumental state of eternal becoming that humans would once have called miscegenation.

As Donna Haraway has argued, *Xenogenesis* is survival fiction, but at stake is not a mere survival of an identitarian species. Butler's vision is projected into a distant future after human struggles for identitarian cultures have succumbed to global nuclear devastation. The Oankali, however, continue to struggle for the survival of knowledges. This struggle puts a new spin on the transcoding of colonial and extraterrestrial discourses. While the humans often construct their fantasies of aliens after their fantasies about indigenous people, Butler's text suggests that the humans need extraterrestrial or indigenous knowledges in order to survive by undoing their work of death. The trilogy ends with an allegory of new life. Jodahs, the first construct ooloi, performs the "seeding" of a new genetically engineered town,[42] based on an ecological vision of a thoroughly sentient environment that is as genetically and emotionally attuned to its inhabitants as they are to it. This ending highlights the diametrical opposition between Butler's fantasy of the Oankali's culture of gene readers and engineers of genetic diversification and the proprietary logics of the Human Genome Diversity Project. Genes, for the Oankali, cannot be owned, commercialized, monopolized, or patented by individuals or corporations. Genes cannot become fetishized objects of value in a consumer culture. Life, for the Oankali, is a common property that cannot be owned and needs to be protected from pillage and destruction. This is the ethics on the basis of which the Oankali life crafters oppose their "work of life" to what they perceive as the human's "work of death." It is an ethics that resembles the ethics of the first people on this earth, which included the integration and protection of other species and the galaxy in their cosmologies. Through the detour of an extraterrestrial imaginary, Butler draws on indigenous knowledges that have survived repression and marginalization. The Oankali's use of their own indigenous knowledge to undo the work of death prepares, Butler seems to suggest, a new ground for working through the devastating legacy of colonialism and genocide. In this sense, *Xenogenesis* indeed bears traces of a utopian ethnography of the future.

Notes

I gratefully acknowledge the challenging and stimulating feedback I received from Lindon Barrett, David Goldberg, Gregg Lambert, Clara McLean, James McMichael, Simon Ortiz, Manuel Schwab, and Martin Schwab.

1. Quoted in Clifford Pickover, *The Science of Aliens* (New York: Basic Books, 1998), 61.

2. Ibid., 60.

3. Clifford Pickover is researcher of the IBM Thomas J. Watson Research Center.

4. See Hans Blumenberg, *Die Vollzähligkeit der Sterne* (Frankfurt: Suhrkamp Verlag, 1997), 351.

5. See http://today.uci.edu/news/release_detail.asp?key=73. See also http://64.233.161.104/u/isearch?q=cache:icnxeIxAiVoJ:www.uci.edu/fc/press_releases/1995/0516.html+asch+balmaceda+stone&hl=en&ie=UTF-8.

6. Gina Maranto, "Test-Tube Treachery," *Los Angeles Times Book Review*, February 1, 2004.

7. Ibid.

8. Quoted in Roderick Nash, *The Rights of Nature: A History of Environmental Ethics* (Madison: University of Wisconsin Press, 1989), 138.

9. The concluding sentence of Balibar's essay (chapter 1 in this volume).

10. Haraway, Donna, *Modest_Witness@Second_Millenium.FemaleMan©_Meets_OncoMouse™: Feminism and Technoscience* (New York: Routledge, 1997), 135.

11. Octavia Butler, *Imago* (New York: Warner, 1989), 172.

12. Helmuth Plessner, "Die anthropologische Dimension der Geschichtlichkeit," in *Sozialer Wandel: Zivilisation und Fortschritt als Kategorien der soziologischen Theorie*, ed. Hans Peter Dreitzel (Berlin: Neuwied, 1972), 160.

13. Freud makes such statements in various places. See, for example, Sigmund Freud, "The Ego and the Id," in *The Freud Reader*, ed. Peter Gay (New York: Norton, 1995), 656.

14. Butler, *Imago*, 89.

15. Ibid., 90.

16. Octavia Butler, *Dawn* (New York: Warner, 1987), 20.

17. Butler, *Imago*, 147.

18. In this vein, the "tasting" of humans with tongues and tentacles serves both to create intimacy and to collect genetic information. Genetic research as a kind of intimate "fieldwork" is "natural" for the Oankali because they know neither a separation of body and mind nor one of nature and culture. Emphasizing the ethnographic implications of *Xenogenesis*, Donna Haraway concludes: "Anthropologists of possible selves, we are technicians of realizable futures. Science is culture" (Haraway, *Modest_Witness*, 230). But what kind of anthropology, culture, and especially "realizable future" are at stake here? Octavia Butler's "imagined community" of humans and aliens unfolds as a drama of forced reproduction.

19. Haraway, *Modest_Witness*, 227.

20. Butler, *Dawn*, 246.

21. See Butler, *Dawn*, 245.

22. For a definition of the concept of "social death," see Maya Nadig and Mario Erdheim, "Ethnopsychoanalyse," in *Psychoanalyse: Ein Handbuch in Schlüsselbegriffen*, ed. W. Mertens (Munich: Fink, 1983).

23. See Orlando Patterson, *Slavery and Social Death: A Comparative Study* (Cambridge, Mass.: Harvard University Press, 1982).

24. See Plessner, "Die anthropologische Dimension."

25. Hans Blumenberg, *Die Vollzähligkeit der Sterne* (Frankfurt: Suhrkamp, 1997), 353. "Denn spezifische Leibgleichheit ist etwas, was unter allen Wahrscheinlichkeiten astronautischer Erfahrung am wenigsten zuverlässig erwartet werden darf."

26. Butler, *Dawn*, 9.

27. Ibid., 11.

28. Ibid.

29. Samuel Beckett, *The Unnamable* (New York: Grove Press, 1958), 23.

30. Blumenberg, *Die Vollzähligkeit der Sterne*, 537.

31. Butler, *Dawn*, 22.

32. See Rich Doyle, *On Beyond Living: Rhetorical Transformations of the Life Sciences* (Stanford, Calif.: Stanford University Press, 1997), specifically chapter 1, "The Sublime Object of Biology," 1–24.

33. Octavia Butler, *Adulthood Rites* (New York: Warner, 1988), 272.

34. See Gregory Bateson, *Steps to an Ecology of Mind* (1972; repr., Chicago: University of Chicago Press, 2000), specifically "Culture Contact and Schismogenesis," 61–72.

35. N. Katherine Hayles, *How We Became Posthuman: Virtual Bodies in Cybernetics, Literature, and Informatics* (Chicago: University of Chicago Press, 1999), 283–291.

36. See David Bohm, *Wholeness and the Implicate Order* (London: Routledge, 1980), 140–213.

37. Erwin Schrödinger, *What Is Life? The Physical Aspect of the Living Cell* (Cambridge: Cambridge University Press, 1944).

38. Hans Blumenberg, *Die Lesbarkeit der Welt* (Frankfurt: Suhrkamp, 1981), 383.

39. See also Anthony Wilden, *System and Structure: Essays in Communication and Exchange* (New York: Tavistock Publications, 1972), 210.

40. See Achille Mbembe, *On the Postcolony* (Berkeley and Los Angeles: University of California Press, 2001), 173–211. See also Achille Mbembe, "Necropolitics," *Public Culture* 15, no. 1 (Winter 2003): 11–40.

41. Butler, *Imago*, 138.

42. "I sorted through the vast genetic memory that Nikanj had given me. There was a single cell within that great store—a cell that could be awakened from its stasis within yashi and stimulated to divide and grow into a kind of seed. This seed could become a town or a shuttle or a great ship.... I took the remaining mass—the seed—still within my body to the place the Humans and the visiting families had agreed was good for people and towns.... Here the town could grow and always have the companionship of some of us. It would need that companionship as much

as we did during our metamorphoses.... 'This could be a good place to live,' one of our elders commented.... I chose a spot near the river. There I prepared the seed to go into the ground.... I planted it deep in the rich soil of the riverbank. Seconds after I had expelled it, I felt it begin the tiny positioning movements of independent life" (Butler, *Imago*, 219–220).

9 (Un)masking the Agent

Distributed Cognition and Stanislaw Lem's "The Mask"

N. Katherine Hayles

What makes someone—or something—count as a person? While the holocaust and other atrocities provide horrifying examples of humans not counting as persons, increasingly intelligent software packages offer the spectacle of bots being mistaken for human interlocutors. In light of these confusions, let me advance a proposition: to count as a person, an entity must be able to exercise agency. Agency enables the subject to make choices, exercise free will, express intentions, and perform actions. To be a person is to have agency, and to have agency is to invite interpretation of the actor as a person, whatever the substrate that composes him, her, or it.[1] Not so long ago, the neuter pronoun could have been safely omitted in discussions of agency, but the last two decades have been marked by dramatic advances in artificial life, and these in turn have shaken ideas about agency. Because agency is so deeply enmeshed with personhood, a shift in its plate tectonics has the potential to initiate wide-ranging changes in the codes that govern subjectivity. The result is a retrofitted person who looks very different from her pre-earthquake brothers and sisters, embodying different stabilizing structures, enacting new kinds of dynamics, and producing and being produced by new stories about persons human and nonhuman.

In this reconfiguration, three sites of cultural and technological exchange are especially important. First is the traffic between conscious and nonconscious entities. Nonconscious entities become capable of contesting for the meaning of personhood when they are conceived as agents. Whether situated within or without the body, formed by evolution or designed by humans, embodied in carbon or fabricated from silicon, they act, but do not know they do so. When we recognize them as agents, they provoke us to ask how their actions relate to consciousness, sparking a debate about whether consciousness is necessary for fully achieved agency. The second site of exchange is the traffic between language and artifact. Human agency has been reformulated by theorists who liken us to artificial life forms, and artificial life forms have been conceptualized as agents by comparing them to humans. In the feedback loops that circulate between metaphor and artifact, human and artificial life mutually define each other. The third site of exchange concerns the level at which agency should be located. Crucial to current rethinking of agency are theories envisioning it as a function located not only in the conscious mind but distributed throughout the body and environment. Conscious/nonconscious, human/artificial, localized/distributed—these are the border crossings that have reconfigured the landscape of agency and, with it, contemporary ideas of personhood.

Whenever wide-ranging changes take place, inevitably there are retrogressive moves that pull back from radical implications toward more comfortable and familiar ideas. Already the fissures that have torn apart conventional ideas about the human are being back-filled to create the impression of unifying coherence that poses no threat to human agency. But underneath, a plane of tension still exists, reminding us that further movements can erupt at any time. My concern here is twofold. On the one hand, I want to examine critically the cross-traffic between language and artifacts, especially when this traffic is used to erase the complexities of embodiment; on the other hand, I want to challenge premature closures that would too easily recuperate agency back to the conscious mind conceived as the ultimate arbiter of action. After analyzing arguments and artifacts crucial to reconceptualizing agency, I will turn to a literary text that enacts these issues in particularly powerful ways: Stanislaw Lem's 1976 novella "The Mask."[2] Hovering between the human and nonhuman person and between consciousness as the seat of identity and nonconscious program as the cause of action, "The Mask" reveals with subtle potency why the link between agency and personhood is so crucial.

Embodying Consciousness and Situating Agency

One of the boldest and at the same time veiled attacks on human agency came with Richard Dawkins's *The Selfish Gene*.[3] Dawkins's argument displaces agency from conscious humans into the genes, who are described as possessing desires, intentions, and strategies. Agency is thus detached from its original site—the conscious human subject—and reattached elsewhere. In the process, humans are described as "lumbering robots," machines under remote control with no choice but to execute their programs. In this imagined encounter, humans seem to lose consciousness while the genes appear to gain it. In an important sense, however, agency continues exactly as before, for the genes are envisioned as embodying within themselves characteristics of the human subject as it is constituted through capitalism, displaying the earmark traits of selfishness and competitiveness.

Throughout, Dawkins insists this reinscription is only a matter of speaking, a vivid shorthand for more cumbersome technical language. When he is about to script the individual into the gene's evolutionary stable strategies, a crucial transition in his argument, we read this disclaimer: "Remember that we are picturing the animal as a robot survival machine with a pre-programmed computer controlling the muscles. To write the strategy out as a set of simple instructions in English is just a convenient way to think about it."[4] When he wishes to explain altruism, a sticky but essential point for his argument, we encounter the following: "If we allow ourselves the license of talking about genes as if they had conscious aims, always reassuring ourselves that we could translate our sloppy language back into respectable terms if we wanted to, we can ask the question, what is the single selfish gene trying to do?"[5] These disclaimers are disingenuous, for without constructing the genes as actors, the story could not be told. Dawkins's contribution, which he calls a shift in perspective so dramatic as to amount to a new paradigm, is to identify an internal actor distinct from the individual. If the gene is not in control of the program—if the selfish gene were only a metaphor that could be discarded at will—the motive force driving Dawkins's narrative would collapse. Without this narrative, there are only shifts in populations that can be statistically measured but not causally explained. The entire argument, then, depends on a narrative in which the selfish gene, far from being a rhetorical flourish, is the constitutive actor.

Moreover, through these disclaimers Dawkins constitutes his analogies as linguistic actors. He insists the analogies are inhabited by a "respectable" discourse that stands ready to relate a real scientific narrative. This "real" narrative does not of course exist in Dawkins's text, except insofar as it is called into a kind of virtual presence by the analogies. Thus a reflexive structure emerges in which the story of mobile, long-lived genes who inhabit lumbering robots is told through analogies presenting themselves as deft, nimble robots inhabited by a long-lived, lumbering language. Through the symmetries and asymmetries of the genes as *fabula* and analogies as *szujet*, agility and inertia are differentially parceled out. The analogies attributing agency to the genes are mobile, like the genes themselves, as they leap easily from body to body, but the underlying "real" language has enormous inertia, with the result that agency can be reassigned but not re-signed—that is, not fundamentally reconstituted.

Deleuze and Guattari share with Dawkins a performative language that enacts what could not otherwise be achieved. They differ, of course, in that they achieve the radical reconceptualization of agency that eludes Dawkins. Like Dawkins, they give evidence that intelligent artifacts played a seminal role in their thinking about agency. Early in *A Thousand Plateaus* they celebrate a simple form of artificial life called cellular automata (CA), contrasting them with the centered systems they deplore.[6] Governed by a simple set of rules, cellular automata are composed of cells, each of which calculates its state depending on the state of its immediate neighbors. Once all the cells have done this calculation, they then recalculate their states, taking the new states of their neighbors into account, and so on through successive generations. On today's computers, cellular automata proceed through generations very rapidly and can be programmed to give the impression of dynamic motion. Because of their dynamism, CA arrays have impressed more than one observer as being a simulation of life itself. Deleuze and Guattari describe cellular automata somewhat inaccurately as "finite networks of automata in which communication runs from any neighbor to any other."[7] In fact, each cell samples only the cells immediately adjacent. By claiming for cellular automata a less rule-bound dynamic than they in fact possess, Deleuze and Guattari imply that any configuration whatever is possible, an idea they push to the extreme in deterritorialization and reterritorialization. Cellular automata fit their purpose because they are completely mechanistic, computational, and nonconscious, but nevertheless display complex patterns which appear to evolve, grow, invade new territories, or decay and die out. In the pattern called the "Glider," for example, a gliderlike shape appears at one edge of the screen and moves toward the other edge, as if enacting what Deleuze and Guattari call a "line of flight." Cellular automata also appear later in their description of schizoanalysis, which "treats the unconscious as an acentered system, in other words, as a machinic network of finite automata (a rhizome), and thus arrives at an entirely different state of the unconscious."[8] The implication is that the unconscious, like cellular automata, is both mechanistic and decentered.

Whatever the case with the unconscious, these ideas have obvious limitations when applied to the human organism. Unlike the freeform patterns of cellular automata, humans have biological requirements that make the skin an organ vital to survival. Yet Deleuze and Guattari leap over this objection with a powerful performative rhetoric that makes it seem as if the body could deterritorialize and reterritorialize as easily as cellular automata, which in themselves have limitations Deleuze and Guattari do not accurately represent. As a result of these reinscriptions, the body becomes the Body Without Organs, an assemblage rather than an organism, which does away with the consciousness as the seat of coherent subjectivity. Reconceptualized as entities following flows of intensities and planes of consistency, humans become mutating assemblages that can absorb a variety of entities in their environments, including machines as well as organic matter. Instead of conscious thought, the Body Without Organs is driven by desire. So central is desire that Mark Hansen argues that it assumes a fetishized quality in *A Thousand Plateaus*, flaming with incandescent intensity that alone has the motive force to drive assemblages into new configurations.[9] Indeed, since consciousness is fragmented, the organism dispersed, and signification thrown out, desire is virtually the only agent left on the playing field. "Make consciousness an experimentation in life," Deleuze and Guattari urge, "and passion a field of continuous intensities, an emission of particle-signs.... Desubjectify consciousness and passion."[10] The net effect of this rhetorical transmutation is to construct the Body Without Organs as cellular automata whose computational rules are re-encoded as desire.

At the same time that humans take on attributes of computational media in Deleuze and Guattari, machines acquire biological traits. Adopting the terminology of biological evolution, they write, "we may speak of a *machinic phylum*, or technological lineage, wherever we find a *constellation of singularities, prolongable by certain operations, which converge, and make the operations converge upon one or several assignable traits of expression*."[11] Endorsing Leroi-Gourhan's ideas about "technological vitalism" that takes "biological evolution in general as the model for technical evolution," they assert "there is indeed a machinic phylum in variation that creates the technical assemblages, whereas the assemblages invent the various phyla. A technological lineage changes significantly according to whether one draws it upon the phylum or inscribes it in the assemblages; but the two are inseparable."[12] By making the phylum depend on the assemblages and the assemblages on the phylum, Deleuze and Guattari suggest that technological evolution produces distinct genetic forms that emerge from a daisy-chain of interconnection that eludes linear causal explanation. (In another context, Francisco Varela calls such dynamics "co-dependent arising" to emphasize the mutual interdependence of each component on the others.)[13] Although Deleuze and Guattari speak of the machinic phylum as "matter in movement, in flux, in variation, matter as a conveyor of singularities and traits of expression,"[14] it is not clear what drives these mutations, since the desire that played such a large part in disaggregating the human organism does not receive equal emphasis with machines. We are left to suppose that humans are assemblages driven by the blind force of desire, while machinic phyla are assemblages driven by the blind force of evolution.

In "Machinic Heterogenesis," Guattari addresses this point by interpolating the human and mechanical into one another, arguing that the "mecanosphere ... superimposes itself on the biosphere."[15] Seeking to open Maturana and Varela's self-enclosing concept of autopoiesis to alterity, Guattari argues that even a mechanism as simple as a lock and key has a repertoire of structural forms through which it can move. This deterritorializing "smoothing" opens the discrete machine to transformation and, by a nonrational leap of inference, to desire: "all machinic orderings contain within them, even if only in an embryonic state, enunciative nuclei [*foyers*] that are so many protomachines of desire."[16] Thus machines are made like humans because they are driven by desire, even as humans are made like machines because they can be disassembled and reassembled. "It is thus impossible to refuse human thought its part in the essence of machinism."[17] In this view, "human" connotes no essential quality but rather marks the historical starting point of a certain line of inquiry. For if the human has been mechanical all along, any language that represents it as "contaminated" by the mechanical mistakes its own process of discovery for the hybridization that was always already there.

Clearly the performative force of language plays a crucial role here, as it does in *A Thousand Plateaus*: much is asserted, almost nothing is demonstrated. If language thus possesses a kind of agency, the next step would be to suppose that language itself is a machine and hence subject to the same processes of deterritorialization and reterritorialization that characterizes "desiring machines." Guattari edges toward this realization when he asks: "But how long can we continue to characterize the thought put to work here as human? Doesn't technicoscientific thought emerge from a certain type of mental and semiotic machinism?"[18] He takes structural semiotics to task because it fails to capture "figures of expression that work as diagrammatic machines in direct contact with technical-experimental configurations."[19] Whereas semiotic systems posit "distinctive oppositions of a phonemic or scriptural order that transcribe enunciations [*énoncés*] into expressive materials that signify," machines operate differently, using a signifying process that "does not derive from repetition or from mimesis of significations."[20] Although obscurely expressed, the point here seems to be that semiotics has falsified the workings of language by interpreting it through structuralist oppositions that covertly smuggle in anthropomorphic thinking characteristic of the conscious mind. The model for language should rather be machinic operations that do not need structural oppositions, because they have available to them a more materialistic level of signification in which representation is enfolded together with material processes (an idea to which we will return). "Existence is not dialectic," Guattari exclaims. "It is not representable. It is hardly even liveable!"[21]

Guattari's "lack of reverence toward the Lacanian conception of the signifier" now becomes explicit. Semiotics is flawed because it "does not get us out of structure, and prohibits us from entering the real world of the machine. The structuralist signifier is always synonymous with linear discursivity," whereas heterogeneous machines refuse to be "orchestrated by a universal temporalization."[22] The difference here between the "heterogeneous machine" of Guattari and the "linear discursivity" of semiotics may be a case of what Freud called the narcissism of minor differences, the tendency of closely related ideologies to exaggerate their differences precisely because they are so close to one another. For surely the crucial point is that both Guattari and Lacan conceive of language as a machine. Thus the very linguistic processes that reconceptualize human agency by recoding it as an intelligent machine are themselves reconceptualized as essentially mechanistic in their operations.

John Johnston, in his important analysis of Lacan's development of a theory of the unconscious, shows that automata theory was crucial to Lacan's thought.[23] The key idea Lacan lifted from automata theory is the notion that symbol manipulation has inherent in it certain structural relationships that can be used to program a Turing machine, an abstract machine composed of only two parts: a head that reads and writes binary symbols forwards and backwards on a tape, and the tape itself, posited to be infinitely long. Turing proved that from this simple machine, it would in principle be possible to make any calculating machine whatever, including the Turing machine itself.[24] Working by analogy (although not always explicitly stated as such), Lacan transposed these ideas onto the unconscious, conceiving of it as a machine operating upon language without needing anything like anthropomorphic awareness to perform its operations. Thus Guattari is correct in asserting that linearity is essential to the Lacanian conception of the signifier, but he underestimates the flexibility with which the Turing machine can operate. By enfolding the abstract operations of calculation into the material operation of the tape, Turing simplified the computational load and achieved an economy of operation that made his Universal Machine so powerful an idea it is routinely regarded as providing the theoretical basis for modern computers.

Lacan's conception of the unconscious as a kind of Turing machine enabled him to transform profoundly Freud's view of the unconscious (notwithstanding his claim that he merely made explicit what was implicit in Freud). When Freud posited the death drive, he thought of it as an unconscious tendency to move toward the inanimate, a return to prebiological origins. There is a sense in which this view of the unconscious is deeply anthropomorphic, for it identifies the present state of the (conscious) subject with life, from which point the unconscious moves *back* toward the inanimate. By contrast, as John Johnston clearly shows, Lacan envisions language as *beginning* in the mechanistic operations of the unconscious, from which emerge the higher order processes of conscious thought.[25] The direction of the vector changes from back to up; that is, from regression to emergence. Equally important, mechanistic operations are conceived as providing the basis for consciousness rather than representing a return to the preanimate. Thus the important distinction shifts from living/nonliving to mechanistic intelligence/conscious awareness. Indeed, given the claims that artificial life is indeed a form of life, the divide between the animate and nonanimate has become increasingly problematic. Like Lacan, theorists of artificial life focus on the intelligences that can emerge from mechanistic operations in both protein- and silicon-based life forms. The difference between Lacan's linear model and Guattari's "heterogeneous machine" pales in comparison to the looming fact that both theorists envision human cognition as always already interpenetrated by machinic processes, what John Johnston calls the "in-mixing" of human psychology with cybernetics.

The net result of these feedback loops between artificial life forms and biological organisms has been to create a crisis of agency. If humans are like machines, whether figured as robots, cellular automata, or Turing machines, then agency cannot be securely located in the conscious mind. If machines are like biological organisms, then they must possess the effects of agency even though they are not conscious. If genes have agency and act like tiny machines carrying out programs, then agency itself needs to be rethought, a conclusion Dawkins evades in *The Selfish Gene* but confronts later in *The Blind Watchmaker*.[26] If desire acts like a free-floating agent, then perhaps it too should be anchored in mechanistic operations, a suggestion Guattari makes in "Machinic Heterogenesis." If language emerges from the operations of the unconscious figured as a Turing machine, then linguistic expressions of desire are always already interpenetrated by the mechanistic. If desire and the agency springing from it is at bottom nothing more than the performance of binary code, then computers could have agency fully as authentic as humans. In significantly different ways, Dawkins, Deleuze,

Guattari, and Lacan all use automata to challenge human agency, and in the process, create agents of automata.

These theorists have another commonality as well: they are alike in not resting their cases on empirical research. Rather, they strive to change perceptions through linguistic redescriptions in which artificial life forms play crucial roles.[27] The artifacts they enroll in their redescriptions—the robot, cellular automata, the Turing machine—are used primarily as tropes, partaking more of the cultural Imaginary than the research laboratory. We are ready now for the curtain to go up on the next act, which will examine traffic flowing in the opposite direction, that is to say, redescriptions that begin with artifacts created in the laboratory and circulating through the human. This empirical research reinforces and extends linguistic redescription because it provides working examples of artificial life forms that can exercise agency, even though they lack conscious awareness. Redescription should not in any sense be seen as *separate* from the manufacture of artifacts. Rather, the artifacts are intended precisely to facilitate redescriptions of biological life, especially human life. Redescription goes on inside the laboratory as well as outside, just as the cultural Imaginary is produced through artifacts as well as language.

Subsuming and Extending Minds

Compelling examples of how minds can operate robustly in an environment with little or no consciousness have been built by Rodney Brooks, a roboticist at the MIT Artificial Intelligence Laboratory. One of his first attempts was Herbert, a mobile robot designed to collect soda cans from around the laboratory and deposit them at a central location. To build Herbert, he used what he calls "subsumption architecture," consisting of layers of distinct activity-producing systems that have minimal communication with one another.[28] For example, one layer includes ultrasonic sonar sensors that cause the robot to halt when it is near an object. When this layer is inactive, another layer generates random course headings, causing the robot to wander. Yet another layer includes an edge detector, causing the robot to stop and change direction when it is near stairs. Sometimes emergent behaviors appear, and when they have adaptive value, Brooks calls them "cheap tricks," unexpected bonuses arising from the interaction of relatively simple sensing and computation systems. Such emergent behaviors are crucial to the success of Attila, a mobile insectlike robot that uses independent systems to guide each of its six legs.[29] Rather than have a central unit compute the robot's gait—a fearsomely complex computational problem—each controller operates according to a program that tells it to keep the leg upright in the context of its environment, which includes what the other legs are doing. The gait is thus not a predetermined program but an emergent property that arises from the six legs interacting with one another. Each time Attila is turned on, it learns to walk anew. Typically, it staggers around until after a few seconds a smooth gait emerges.

Attila illustrates an important point about subsumption architecture. In contrast to symbol-based artificial intelligence, these robots have no central unit that constructs a representation of the environment. "The world is its own best model," Brooks is fond of saying.[30] At most there is a small control module which adjudicates conflicts between different systems. Thus the systems have no consciousness, although Brooks claims that they have an insect level of intelligence. Lest we sneer too quickly at this accomplishment, Brooks reminds us that on an evolutionary time scale dating from the beginning of life, insects emerged at a point that was about 90 percent of the time required to evolve humans. The hard problem, he asserts, is learning to move robustly in a three-dimensional environment. Once this problem is solved, the rest is relatively easy. To make good his claim, Brooks has recently been developing Cog, a robot consisting of a moveable torso, hands, and head that has eye motions and other cognitive features modeled on human neurology.[31] The point is not to program behaviors into the robot but rather let behaviors develop through training and interaction with the environment. At present Cog has learned to visually track objects in the environment and play catch with a human partner. Brooks makes no secret of his belief that humans evolved in ways similar to his robots, building higher-level capabilities on distributed cognitive systems performing relatively simple tasks. Consciousness itself, he believes, is a "cheap trick," an emergent behavior that arose relatively late in human evolution. It will eventually be possible, he thinks, to evolve human-level intelligence from the likes of Cog.

Maja Mataric's robotic rat, also developed in MIT's Artificial Intelligence Laboratory, provides a clever illustration of how computation can be simplified by taking the world as its own best model. Equipped with sonar sensors and a compass, the robot rat has three "layers of competence."[32] One layer initiates a behavior of boundary following, a second proprioceptive system detects landmarks by combining the rat's motion and its sensory input, and the third uses the information to construct a map of the environment. The map, created by combining motor and sensor readings, is constructed using a series of landmarks. All the nodes on the map process information in parallel, and they communicate using spreading activation. Once the rat has learned the landmarks, the researcher specifies a goal, and from that node, activation spreads throughout the map, providing a direction vector for the rat to follow. "As the activation wave is propagated through the network," Mataric explains, "it accumulates the length values of the landmarks it passes. Consequently, at each landmark, the shortest path towards the goal corresponds to the direction with the shortest accumulated length."[33] The rat need only follow the shortest length from node to node to achieve the shortest overall path. Thus the computation to find the goal is carried out *on the map itself*. In effect, the map itself acts as the controller, and the nodes on the map act as the information sources used to construct a plan. This enfolding together of map and controller eliminates the need to create a higher-level representation that would construct from the map a plan to reach the goal, thus greatly simplifying the computational load and allowing the rat to operate robustly in its environment with real-time efficiency. Extrapolated to humans, the robot rat shows how action to reach a goal can be efficiently achieved without the need for any central module that would correspond to consciousness.

The leap to humans has been made by Jerome H. Barkow, Leda Cosmides, and John Tooby in *The Adapted Mind: Evolutionary Psychology and the Generation of Culture*. They argue that such modular construction is exactly how human neural structures have evolved. Through eons of interacting with complex environments, humans have evolved modules that are "functionally specialized to produce behaviors effective in solving particular adaptive problems."[34] These modules are richly structured in a content-specific way and generate at least some of the cultural content of human societies, including "certain behaviors, artifacts, and linguistically transmitted representations."[35] Although the authors caution readers not to expect humans seen as "organic functional machines"[36] to have the same clean, parsimonious designs as artificial machines designed with a particular purpose in mind, they nevertheless insist that programmed modules provide a robust account of how humans are hardwired with proclivities that are dynamically played out in conjunction with variable and complex environments. *The Adapted Mind* follows in the path of E. O. Wilson's sociobiology, but with a richer, more flexible, and more computationally oriented interpretation of human behavior. For example, they note that the human tendency to impute desires and beliefs to other humans appears everywhere in human cultures. They point out that such a "belief in beliefs and desires cannot be justified by observation alone," since other hypotheses could also explain the behaviors. Thus they postulate "developmental programs or cognitive architectures" that "must impose this way of interpreting the world of other humans on us."[37] The desire that Deleuze and Guattari see as the motive force for mutating assemblages becomes in their account a computational program developed through eons of evolutionary adaptation. Although their rationalistic argumentation sounds very different than the passionate rhetoric of Deleuze and Guattari, they share the strategy of explaining desire by modular computational processes that encompass desire itself.

Similarly, in explaining the human tendency to acquire language, they postulate a "language acquisition device" that pre-programs humans to learn language. These proclivities take shape in the context of a local language environment that has the effect of initializing the module to specific phonemes, pronunciations, and so on. The situation can be likened to PROMs, programmable read-only memory chips. PROMs work by allowing input that determines their programming, but once this initialization has taken place, further input does not change its fundamental structure. As they put it: "The human language acquisition device is an open behavior program whose constructed product, adult competency in the local language, varies depending on the language community in which the individual is raised."[38] By emphasizing the extent to which human neural structures are pre-programmed, and using a computational model to explain human behavior, *The Adapted Mind* provides further evidence that many complex behaviors can take place with minimal or no input from the conscious mind. So successful have these arguments been that George Lakoff and Mark Johnson in *Philosophy in the Flesh* proclaim as one of their premises that most thought is not conscious.[39] Although they are not necessarily committed to a computational model, I doubt this claim could have been made without the cross-traffic between artificial minds and biological organisms that locates agency in semiautonomous modules operating below consciousness.

There are many additional sources for this story, but rather than pursue the argument through a sea of examples, I want now to turn to a complementary narrative that, instead of dispersing agency below consciousness, extends it beyond consciousness into the external world. Andy Clark, who calls this the "extended mind model," writes: "Mind is a leaky organ, forever escaping its 'natural' confines and mingling shamelessly with body and with world."[40] That cognition takes place not only in the neocortex but elsewhere in the brain as well as in the central and peripheral nervous systems has been experimentally documented by neurophysiologists, including Antonio R. Damasio, in *Descartes' Error: Emotion, Reason, and the Human Brain*.[41] More controversial is the notion that mind extends out into the world, not only metaphorically but literally, as it enrolls a variety of artifacts into its cognitive system.

The proposition has been beautifully illustrated by Edwin Hutchins in *Cognition in the Wild*, in his account of a crisis aboard an oceangoing naval vessel when it suddenly loses steam power as it is entering a harbor, thus rendering its navigational system useless.[42] As the men scramble to navigate by hand, they begin to function as a self-organizing system without any agent in the system consciously deciding how the system should be arranged. When one man shoves a calculator across to another, saying "Here, you do this," he is responding only to the fact that he cannot keep up with the flow of information. Through such responses, change propagates across the system as if it were a moving wave traveling through human and nonhuman agents, rearranging the system so it can operate more efficiently. The calculator's position, the results it displays, and the lines drawn on the harbor map merge seamlessly with human action and cognition. Thus Hutchins argues that it is not only a metaphor to say that drawing a line on a map is remembering and erasing it is forgetting. Cognition "in the wild," that is, as it occurs in real-life situations rather than the laboratory, is not confined to mind alone but extends outward into the environment in flexible arrangements that bear more than passing resemblance to Deleuze and Guattari's assemblages.

In calling this active enlistment of external objects into the human cognitive system "extended mind," Andy Clark emphasizes that artifacts function as more than external memory storage. Rather, they enable transformations of thought that would not otherwise occur. Caes van Leeuwen, Ilse Verstijnen, and Paul Hekkert, for example, have studied how artists work with sketches.[43] As the artist draws, a dynamic interactive process takes place in which the form emerges in active conjunction with her ideas, lines drawn and erased, and even the quality of the paper and charcoal. Any division which would locate cognition solely in the artist's mind is highly artificial, for every part of the system contributes to the final result. Without paper to sketch on, the artist's ideas would not take the same shape or perhaps would not take definite shape at all, remaining a swirling, inchoate impression. As a writer, I can testify to the importance of material objects in conceptual processes. When I sit down to draft an essay such as this one, I usually have some ideas in mind, but it is only when I write an outline that they take shape as coherent argument. As I scribble down thoughts, drawing arrows from one line to another, crossing lines out, adding others, my manipulation of the writing materials functions as an integral part of my composition. Like the artist's sketch, my writing emerges out of this active interplay between my preexisting thoughts and the external objects I enroll into my cognitive system.

There are many other everyday examples that show cognition as a distributed function. For example, Hutchins recounts the operations he performs when he opens the combination lock on the storage shed in his yard. As he twirls the dial, he begins to rehearse in his mind the sequence of numbers necessary to open the lock. Then as he performs the manual operations of dialing the numbers, he also says the numbers aloud, creating a redundancy that makes his performance more robust. All these components—the shape of the dial, his mental rehearsal, and his verbal articulation—work together to create the cognitive act. The extended mind was brought home to me when I recently tried to place a call from my elderly aunt's antique rotary phone. I discovered that I had forgotten my card number; all I remembered were the motions evoked as I interacted with a touch-tone keypad. Faced with an artifact that presented the numbers in a different spatial configuration, I was as helpless as Thomas Edison before a Palm Pilot. I finally solved the problem by drawing the touch pad on a sheet of paper, using the numbers on the rotary phone as a prompt to remember how the symbols are configured. Then I manually touched the numbers, writing them down as I did so. The incident made clear to me the extent to which I had enrolled the touch keypad into my cognitive system. Without it, I could not successfully complete the simple task of dialing a number that I knew very well—but knew through my body and extended cognitive system rather than my neocortex.

The ability of material objects to extend the human cognitive system is amplified when the cognitive field is represented by what Hutchins, following Mark Turner, calls "conceptual blends."[44] For example, in the memory palaces popular in the Renaissance, each object in an imagined room represented something to be remembered, and the memoirist simply walked in his imagination around the room to recall the topoi for his speech. Suppose now that overlaid onto this imagined topography is a three-dimensional component, in which the height of each object correlates with the details to be developed with each topic. Now there are two signifying schemes, one correlating material objects in two-dimensional space with the order of topics and a second correlating height with subtopics. Many more complex examples were discussed by Hutchins in a recent presentation at UCLA, including tables that enabled one to calculate the time of high tide by overlaying a compass rose onto a graph of a twenty-eight-day lunar calendar.[45] When material objects are enrolled as "anchors" and linked to recall or calculation, cognition is simplified, because part of the computational load is carried by objects in the environment. As with Mataric's robotic rat, calculations can be carried out directly on the physical environment, without needing to go to more abstract internalized levels of representation.

Without a doubt, the most powerful object in the extended mind of contemporary humans is the computer. An extensive literature—including my own recent book *How We Became Posthuman*—explores the ways in which computers interact with humans to extend their cognitive, sensory, and bodily reach.[46] Oddly, this scholarship remains distinct from the literature on extended mind, which tends to focus on simpler objects that are often not computational. Of course, it is important to recognize that noncomputational objects are part of our cognitive systems. Still, the computer remains conspicuous by its absence. Andy Clark's fine book *Being There: Putting Brain, Body, and World Together Again* is a case in point. Although Clark discusses the work of Rodney Brooks, Maja Mataric, and other roboticists, he instances them as parallel cases of distributed cognition rather than as objects enrolled in human cognitive systems. Moreover, he does not discuss at all such obvious candidates as virtual reality, graphic user interfaces, or keyboard designs. Perhaps researchers making a case for the extended mind think that including the computer would be like shooting fish in a barrel—the point is so obvious that making it would not be much fun. Yet this silence elides an important difference between the computer and, say, a sketchpad. While the sketchpad embodies information in its form and function (for example, the glued binding placed at the top so the full page can be easily accessed), this is simply not of the same order of magnitude as an image-processing program like Illustrator. Illustrator is not merely an extension of the human cognitive system; it is a powerful cognizer in its own right, performing cognitively sophisticated acts of which the human user remains oblivious. Indeed, almost all users are ignorant to a greater or lesser extent (usually greater) of the computer's actions, from the programming language down to the compiler language and further still to the assembly code. The computer performs many acts that are not directly controlled by the user and that not infrequently conflict with the user's desires. Examples are legion, from the corrections Microsoft Word makes in capitalizing a word I do not want capitalized to the annoying animated office assistant that constantly appears on the screen to tell me information I do not wish to know.

The computer's capacity to exercise independent agency, which grows more powerful and pervasive every day, makes enrolling it into our cognitive system a dicey proposition. If an agent this smart and powerful is part of us, who really is in control? With this question, the crisis in agency springs fully into view. We become the "lumbering robots" Dawkins envisioned, run now not by tiny genes but the powerful coding machines we call computers. We experience the dissolution of subjectivity urged by Deleuze and Guattari and mutate into machines running cellular automata programs. We operate in culture using the modular programming units postulated by Barkow, Cosmides, and Tooby, functioning as biological computing devices whose hardwiring determines many of our actions. We perform like the robots that Rodney Brooks builds, possessing an epiphenomenal consciousness that remains oblivious to the true nature of our cognitive processes. And when our mind extends into the environment, it encounters other powerful computational cognizers who are as likely to annex us into their cognitive systems as we are to enroll them into ours. The selfish gene and subsumption architecture, deterritorialization and evolutionary adaptive psychology, the Lacanian unconscious and extended mind work together to alter fundamentally our vision of what it means to be human. Although we can still exercise conscious agency, it works in conjunction with pre-programmed routines within and without, which also control the outcome, sometimes decisively.

No sooner does the crisis in agency become explicit, however, than efforts appear to restore control to conscious mind. An example is the approach Daniel C. Dennett takes in *Kinds of Minds: Toward an Understanding of Consciousness*. The problem he addresses in this sequel to *Consciousness Explained* is how to explain the human as a distributed cognitive system in which cognition happens at every level, from the macromolecules of DNA and RNA on up. Echoing Dawkins, whom he acknowledges as a source for this book, he critically rewrites the selfish gene. "These gigantic molecules are tiny machines—*macro*molecular *nano*technology. They are, in effect, natural robots."[47] Note that it is the *genes* that now become the robots rather than the humans. As "natural robots," the genes possess agency, although of a different kind than ours. Enacting a rhetoric very different than Dawkins, Dennett denies motives, intentions, and desires to genes, restoring these attributes to conscious humans:

> Their agency is not fully fledged agency like ours. They know not what they do. We, in contrast, often know full well what we do. At our best—and at our worst—we human agents can perform *intentional* actions, after having deliberated consciously about the reasons for and against. Macromolecular agency is different; there are reasons for what macromolecules do, but the macromolecules are unaware of those reasons. Their sort of agency is nevertheless the only possible grounds from which the seeds of our agency could grow.[48]

This passage performs a crucial redescription of agency, for it re-presents the problem not as an actual redistribution of agency but rather as a problem of understanding how agency can flow upward, culminating in consciousness that remains fully in control ("we," as conscious subjects, "know full well what *we* do").

The answer Dennett proposes, interesting in its own right, is perhaps less important than his construction of the problem. Theorists have debated the relation of mind to brain for a very long time. What Dennett is after differs in a subtle but important way from these debates. Mind/body debates center on how the materiality of the brain relates to cognition, particularly conscious thought. Often the rest of the body is not taken into account at all. By contrast, Dennett begins by conceding that even macromolecules are minds that think and possess some degree of agency. The problem then focuses not on how material structures relate to thinking, but rather on how different levels of thinking agents correlate with one another and particularly with the conscious mind. Dennett's references make clear that his reconceptualization depends heavily on the intellectual context I sketched earlier. Without this work in autonomous agents, cellular automata, robotics, and extended mind, it would not be possible to assume "minds that think" include a wide variety of nonconscious entities.

Dennett's answer to "how minds think" relocates control back in the conscious mind, thus resolving the crisis that made distributed cognition seem so threatening and out of control—that is to say, out of *our* control. He proposes to make sense of distributed cognition by adopting the "intentional stance." "The intentional stance is the strategy of interpreting the behavior of an entity (person, animal, artifact, whatever) by treating it *as if* it were a rational agent who governed its 'choice' of 'action' by a 'consideration' of its 'beliefs' and 'desires' "[49] The scare-quotes make clear that the intentional stance is an attitude consciousness takes toward distributed agents, rather than attributes that agents possess in themselves. To make the point even clearer, Dennett provides a helpful discussion that distinguishes between three different kinds of agency: conscious intentionality, an intentionality that comes from what he calls "aboutness," and the intensionality (spelled with an "s") that philosophers distinguish from extensionality. While full-blown intentionality occurs only in conscious entities, intentionality as "aboutness" occurs in nonconscious entities such as artifacts. A pair of scissors, to use an example used both by Dennett and Clark, has an "aboutness" that causes us to understand how it should be used—the finger-sized open loops, placed to accommodate the forefinger and opposing thumb, make obvious its intended purpose. The scissors can thus be said to have a kind of intentionality that inheres in its design and function. Intensionality refers to a distinction between the extensional part of an utterance, which concerns the thing referred to, and the language used to reference it, the intensional part. The implication is that language possesses a kind of agency that manifests itself in linguistic formulations that carry meaning in themselves, apart from the content (a proposition, as we have seen, that is central to Lacan's conception of the unconscious).

By subordinating "aboutness" and intensionality to the full awareness of conscious intention, Dennett creates a conceptual structure in which agency exercised by nonconscious entities is folded smoothly into—and more to the point, *under*—the agency exercised by conscious mind. Here the elision of the computer becomes especially significant, for it possesses not only "aboutness" but also the kind of intentionality Dennett reserves for consciousness, which hinges on the ability to make representations of the representations created by lower nonconscious entities. For example, when Crick and Watson make a three-dimensional model of the double helix, they create a representation of the nonconscious agency that a DNA strand employs when it uses lock-and-key topology to make a duplicate of itself. Like Mataric's robotic rat, DNA uses itself as a map to guide the process of topographic mirroring, thus simplifying the computational load so no conscious action is required. In Dennett's account, consciousness reverses this process, exfolding representations out of representations out of representations. In this respect, consciousness functions like a computer, which also builds up representations out of material enfoldings. At the bottom level of the computer are processes that enfold together the electronic polarities with symbolic representation as the bit stream is created. From this level, equivalent to DNA using itself as a map, the coding levels become progressively abstract, piling representation on representation. While I would not want to claim that computers have consciousness (at least not in their present state), recognizing this parallel would force Dennett to make a finer distinction between consciousness as a representation-creating engine and computers that operate similarly. Moreover, recognizing the parallel would also bring into question consciousness as the necessary end point for this process, since computers can create high-level representations without consciousness. Finally, the extended mind model would also suggest that the enfolding together of symbolic representations with material objects is also a strategy that consciousness uses to reduce the computational load, thus further eroding the distinction between consciousness as a representation engine and DNA as a nonconscious mapmaker.

As it is, the "intentional stance" locates the granting of intentionality to nonconscious entities in the conscious mind, as if it were *noblesse oblige* bestowed by human consciousness on the rest of the agents in the world. Such a construction pulls the teeth of the problem by making the other agents seem all too innocuous. This is especially so in view of the increasing sophistication and autonomy of artificial lifeforms, which in many instances already exercise agency that supersedes human agency, for example in the intelligent software that flies the X-29, a fighter plane so aerodynamically unstable no human pilot can safely keep it aloft.[50] The crisis in agency cannot then be resolved simply by folding other kinds of agency under the conscious mind. The "intentional stance" may be a helpful characterization of the imputations that the conscious mind makes to other artifacts and persons, but it does not and cannot solve the deeper question of whether nonconscious agents act apart from or in conflict with the perceptions of conscious awareness.

For a deep exploration of these issues, I turn to Stanislaw Lem's powerful story "The Mask." At the heart of this disturbing tale is a conflict between a conscious mind that can think and an underlying program that determines action. To make the conflict more intense, Lem arranges matters so the conscious mind has no direct access to this program, much as we have no direct access to our genes or the computational modules that, in the view of Barkow, Cosmides, and Tooby, determine our behavior. In the conflict between representations the conscious mind makes to itself and the representations narrated as actions performed, the crisis of agency is bodied forth as an inescapable and tragic condition of thinking mind(s).

Consciousness Agonistes

"The Mask" begins with a threshold. On one side is a consciousness who names "the it that was I."[51] This narrator recounts an experience that is at once a physical movement, a birth, and an erotic encounter, but an encounter in which the narrator plays a passive role, an object of unknown gazing eyes, "snoutlike flattened heads" that touch, "pincer hands," and "flat mouths in a rim of sparks" that give a final "quivering kiss" that "tautened the me" and cause the narrator to "crawl into a round opening without light."[52] On the other side of the threshold is a beautiful woman who knows herself to be such. At the moment the narrator crosses the threshold (which is both spatial and linguistic), consciousness undergoes a dramatic change, feeling "the rush of gender so violent, that her head spun and I shut my eyes. And as I stood thus, with eyes closed, words came to me from every side, for along with gender she had received language."[53] At this liminal moment, the narrator moves from an "it" already receding from awareness into a linguistically enculturated "she" whose movement over the palace threshold (for that is where she now perceives herself to be) plunges her into the Symbolic. As her perception snaps into cultural focus, the objects that an instant before *it* had described as a "colored confusion of vertical trunks" with "globes" containing "tiny buttons bright with water" become the lords and ladies attending a court ball, whose eyes are turning to follow the woman the narrator has become. Thus from the beginning we have reason to doubt that the narrator's consciousness is the seat of identity, for it emerges into full articulation as if it were as epiphenomenal as the insect robot Attila's gait, springing into existence only after another kind of awareness, an awareness that inhabits an "it" and not "she," has moved the narrator through the birth channel and out into the world, negotiating the intervening spaces in a fashion that consciousness does not remember.

These abrupt transitions between physical spaces are characteristic of the consciousness as long as the narrator remains a woman, suggesting that consciousness here operates as if it were a machine being turned on and off. Precisely because the sphere of consciousness is limited, its operation within that staging area is all the more frenetic, as it seeks to establish its conditions of possibility. As the woman progresses into the ball, her consciousness speeds along in a hyperrational mode that Jo Alyson Parker, in her fine Lacanian analysis of "The Mask," finds impossible to accept as female.[54] Indeed, consciousness suspects its own hyperrationality. As the narrator tries to make sense of her situation, she realizes that "this self-determined thinking of mine seemed in its correctness just a bit too cold, unduly calm, for fear remained beyond it—like a thing transcendent, omnipresent, yet separate—therefore my own thoughts too I held in suspicion."[55] Knowing that she should be afraid but unable to feel the hormonal surges that make fear an experience inhabiting the self, she comes close to being the subject we call Cartesian, doubting everything, including her own thoughts.

Why should she feel fear? Because she becomes aware that although she can think whatever she pleases, she is only partially able to control her actions. She quickly determines that she is intended for Arrhodes, a brilliant thinker who has dared to question the authority of the King. This "aboutness" is knowledge that comes to consciousness but does not originate there, appearing to the narrator as a predetermined fact. When she drops her fan before Arrhodes in a clichéd gesture of seduction, she feels a blush appear, but like fear, this blush does not inhabit her, appearing to the consciousness as if it were a foreign intrusion. "The blush did not belong to me, it spread on my cheeks, claimed my face, pinkened my ear lobes, which I could feel perfectly, yet I was not embarrassed, nor excited.... I'll say more: I had nothing whatever to do with that blush, it came from the same source as the knowledge that had entered me at the threshold of the hall."[56] This separation between consciousness and the bodily actions consciousness observes reveals a fatal gap between thought and agency. Though consciousness feels it comprises an identity in itself, as if it is, as the narrator says, "one," it must face the fact that another kind of agency also inhabits the body, and moreover it is an agency to which consciousness has no direct access and must strive to apprehend through inferences and observations. "Everyone knows it is impossible to turn the eyeball around," she thinks, "such that the pupil can peer inside the skull."[57]

In her dance of seduction with Arrhodes, the narrator displays a brilliance and satirical edge that both fascinates Arrhodes and makes him afraid, for he senses immediately this is no ordinary woman, bluntly demanding "Who are you?" Asking this question of herself, the narrator flashes onto the pasts of three entirely different women, Mignonne from the north, Angelita from the south, and Tlenix, each accompanied by intense though fragmentary sensory memories. She also senses that her choice will determine the "truth," that "each one could take on substance if I acknowledged it," and that "the images unmentioned would be blown away."[58] Consciousness here senses its position as a PROM, an intelligence that can be programmed by the initial choice of input but that, once the choice has been made, will lose this flexibility as input merges with software and software rigidifies into hardware. Significantly, she chooses not to answer Arrhodes, thereby preserving an indeterminacy that she seeks to fill instead with her own option, imagining herself as that quintessentially marginalized female figure, the madwoman tenderly cared for by patronizing relatives.

This identity cannot take, for it has not been included among the possible inputs. Yet the narrator's response is significant, for it shows that consciousness is determined to assert its own agency over and against the other agency inhabiting the body. Conversing with Arrhodes, the narrator tests the limits to which she can go. She tries to say something stupid, knowing that will be an effective turn-off for Arrhodes, but she finds herself unable to be anything but brilliant. When she tries to warn him outright, telling him in response to his request for an assignation, "Better to say: never and nowhere," she can utter the warning only in the clichéd language of a lover who feigns reluctance to spur on desire. She realizes this too late, desperately adding, "I do not toy with you, my fine philosopher, look within and you will see that I advised you well," another articulation that goes awry because when Arrhodes looks within, he sees only the desire that is real enough to him but that she knows to be a fatal trap set by his deadly adversary, the King. "What I wished to add," consciousness thinks, "I could not utter. I was able to think anything, strange as it may seem, yet in no way find my voice, I could not reach those words. A catch in my throat, a muteness, like a key turned in a lock, as if a bolt had clicked shut between us."[59] As the narrator will come to realize more fully later, the most insidious threat to her agency is not a direct prohibition on her actions. Scary as that is, more frightening is a co-optation that turns whatever she tries to do to the purposes of the other agency inhabiting the body.

The seductive dance continues when the narrator meets Arrhodes the next day in a garden—another abrupt transition preceded by a period of unknowingness. For when she left the ball, she entered a carriage that was more like a coffin, imprisoning her within a space too small for her to stand fully upright. As she lies in the darkness, she thinks again of her three prearranged pasts and compares them to her dim memories when she experienced herself as neuter. Becoming increasingly aware not only of the alien agency within her body but also of the exterior agents who arranged for it to be there, she muses on the fact that she can remember the time before. "I think it had to be that way, that it would have been impossible to arrange things otherwise," she speculates.[60] Desperately seeking for a way to make her own will count, she tries to put together an identity not predetermined by the other's agency: "Out of discrepant elements I could construct nothing of my own, unless I were to find in the design already existing some lopsidedness, chinks I might penetrate, thereby to rend open the structure and get to the core of it."[61] And so she returns to her memories as a neuter, ironically thinking that "certainly they should at least have wiped out that sequence on my back, the animation of my nakedness, inert and mute, by the sparking kisses, but that too had taken place and now was with me."[62] The memory functions as what evolutionary biologists call a spandrel, a ride-along effect not selected for but that emerges because it comes along with attributes that are selected for. Out of this spandrel, this unplanned excess, she hopes to find the chink that will let her assert agency.

Her desire for an agency she can call her own becomes the driving force of the narrative—or rather, it drives a narrative of self-determination within the larger narrative scripted by the alien agency that also inhabits the body. Thus desire is multiple, living both in consciousness and program. While consciousness knows its desire from the inside, it knows the desire of program from the outside, as if seen from a distance by an observer.

> I had love, but elsewhere—I know how that sounds. Oh it was a passionate love, tender and altogether ordinary. I wanted to give myself to him body and soul, though not in reality, only in the manner of the fashion, according to custom, the etiquette of the court.... My love was very great, it caused me to tremble, it quickened my pulse, I saw that

> his glance made me happy. And my love was very small, being limited in me, subject to the style, like a carefully composed sentence expressing the painful joy of tête-a-tête.[63]

Her love is great within the scripted confines of the program that has written it to be so. But for consciousness, love is an alien utterance performed without touching the pulse of the thinking mind, which sees but does not experience it. "And so beyond the bounds of those feelings I had no particular interest in saving him from myself or another, for when I reached with my mind outside my love, he was nothing to me."[64]

Remembering how she rebelled in the carriage as she realized the limits of her agency, she also recalls the exuded snake head that gave her an injection that turned the consciousness off. For the consciousness, Arrhodes is important not as a lover but as a potential ally against foreign agents, who themselves have formed an alliance across her body's boundaries. "Yet I needed an ally in my struggle against whatever had pricked me that night with venomous metal.... Therefore I could not reveal the entire truth to him: that my love and the venomous prick were from one and the same source."[65] Love is a program, passing time is an injection, and both come from agency outside the thinking mind. Ironically, Arrhodes too is following a cultural program that dictates his actions. The consciousness intuits that he "would surely be conventional in his love" and so "would not accept in me the kind of liberation I desired, the freedom that would cast him off. Therefore I could only act deceitfully, giving freedom the false name of love."[66] One kind of agency comes from program and dictates love; another comes from consciousness, which can exercise agency in this cultural context only by calling it love, although its object is not Arrhodes but the articulation of will independent of program. Arrhodes is not so much a love object to the consciousness as he is a tool it hopes to use to assert its own subjectivity.

The dance of seduction ends with another birth and, with it, a subtle transformation of agency. Ordering Arrhodes to leave her alone in her chateau, the narrator stands before a full-length mirror and, following an inexplicable impulse, cuts herself open from sternum to crotch. When she parts the layers of skin, she sees nestled within her flesh the metallic body of an insectile robot and realizes "it was not *it*, a foreign thing, different and other, it was again myself." At this moment, Arrhodes comes in and sees her exposed: "it was I, still I, I was repeating to myself when he entered." Gaping in response to her gaping open, he turns and flees. As the narrator works to free herself from her human mask, "Tlenix, Duenna, Mignonne first sank to her knees, then tumbled face-down to the side and I crawled out of her," whereupon the discarded human skin lies "like a naked thing, her legs thrown apart immodestly" in a seductive pose of which the narrator no longer has need.[67]

Carol Wald in "The Female Machine: From von Neumann to Richard Powers" has written brilliantly about "The Mask" as part of a tradition of powerful men using female automata as tools against other men.[68] With the narrator's transformation, the King's plot to assassinate Arrhodes stands fully revealed. But female agency also asserts itself in this design, for we learn that the King "had sworn to his dying mother that if harm befell that wise man it would be of his own choosing."[69] Hence the seduction plot. To keep his word to his mother, the King must arrange matters so that Arrhodes *chooses* the narrator and initializes the robot's program, whereupon she metamorphoses into an insectile assassin who will pursue him to the ends of the earth. Male power has the ability to act, but only within the constraints imposed by female influence, a formation enacted in a different configuration within the narrator, where male power manifests itself in action and female agency in thought.

After the narrator's transformation, consciousness undergoes a subtle but important change as well. Gone is the hyperrational quality of detached thinking, as if the mind were an engine racing at high RPM while disengaged from the drive train. The consciousness still thinks, but now feels more at one with the body, yielding to the "shining metal [that] had written into it movements which I began to execute."[70] Moreover, the consciousness also finds itself permeated by the exquisite distinctions of smell that the body's superb olfactory equipment makes possible. Despite this transformation, the consciousness continues to desire its own agency, although what that agency might mean becomes more complicated as the sharp division between mind and body eases. For example, the robot wonders why she pauses for three days after Arrhodes flees before taking up his pursuit. She suspects this may be her program operating to make sure Arrhodes has time to realize the full terror of his situation. But she also thinks of it as a challenge to her skill as a hunting machine, an opportunity to demonstrate an expertise with which she identifies. Agency here is neither folded back under consciousness nor separated from it; rather, agency of mind and program have blended together to form an uneasy heterogeneous amalgam. Thinking from within this state, the consciousness suspects that her agency has been from the start infected with the will of another. Recalling the moment when she split herself open, consciousness realizes "that act of self-evisceration had not been altogether my rebellion ... it represented a foreseen part of the plan, designed for just such an eventuality, in order that my rebellion turn out to be, in the end, my total submission."[71] She suspects that precisely the desire authenticating her as an autonomous subjectivity—her intense desire to act as a free agent—has always already been co-opted by the program, a thought so scary she can think it only after her metamorphosis, when she accepts the program not merely as an exterior function but also an interpenetration of herself. "Thus the hope of freedom could have been just an illusion, nor even my own illusion, but introduced in me in order that I move with more alacrity, urged on precisely by the application of that perfidious spur."[72]

Behind this realization lurks an even more unnerving question. Why does consciousness, obviously necessary for the seduction of the intellectual Arrhodes, need to persist after the narrator's transformation into an insectile robot? The narrative supplies an ad hoc explanation in the monk's suggestion that humans know how to disguise themselves so as to defeat the computations of an algorithmic program; thus the robot's artificial intelligence has been constructed so it can put "questions to the quarry, questions devised by the foremost experts on the individual characteristics of the human psyche."[73] This explanation scarcely suffices to explain the consciousness's active thoughts while on the chase, however, or her realization that "I was not (after all) a lifeless mechanism equipped with a pair of hunting lungs, I was a being that had a mind and used it."[74] She may have been given a mind for purposes other than her own, but having it, she intends to use it for herself. Still, her mind in its insectile state struggles with other cognitions remote from consciousness. As she continues in the hunt for months, consciousness displays a disconcerting tendency to hibernate:

> By now I had forgotten the appearance of this man, and my mind, as if lacking the endurance of the body, particularly during the night runs, drew into itself till I did not know whom I was tracking, nor even if I was tracking anyone; I knew only that my will was to rush on, in order that the spoor of airborne motes singled out for me from the welling diversity of the world persist and intensify.[75]

Here agency emerges not from subjectivity but from a nonconscious cognition that operates much like the spreading activation of Matatric's robot rat, achieving its goal simply by following the path of intensifying activation.

The ambiguity of agency becomes fully apparent when the narrator, having lost the scent, appeals to a wayside monk for help. Woven together in her appeal is falsehood and truth, programmed fate and her own will, prescripted determination to kill Arrhodes and her hope that she can spare him. The monk reveals that Arrhodes had sought sanctuary but had been abducted by kidnappers who intend to exploit his fine mind as their tool. The narrator at once suggests she can kill the abductors, but the monk is also aware of her nature as a programmed assassin. After refusing to give the robot confession because he believes she lacks free will and therefore does not count as a person, the monk asks if she wants the monastery's physician (conveniently a former roboticist) to see if he can defeat the program. Reasoning that he can give her wrong directions to Arrhodes as well as right, she consents to the examination. The physician finds that her sting cannot be removed without killing her. But in addition, he also sees:

> A mechanism which none of your predecessors possessed, a multiple memory of things superfluous to a hunting machine, for these are recorded feminine histories, filled with names and turns of phrase that lure the mind, and a conductor runs from them down into the fatal core. Therefore you are a machine perfected in a way unknown to me, and perhaps even an ultimate machine.[76]

Her female gender is thus revealed as somehow essential to her nature even after the seduction plot has ended, linking it to her earlier search for "chinks" in the program that would enable her to "get to the core of it."

Reinforcing this revelation is imagery that figures Arrhodes as her mate as well as her prey. Driven simultaneously by desire and program, her thoughts display a complex ambivalence. When the physician, in one of the anachronistic touches characteristic of Lem's humor, offers to sprinkle iron filings on her core in a move he says will slightly increase her free will, she agrees because she notices them "both look at me," implying this is a ruse to gain their trust.[77] But when she later addresses the reader directly, acknowledging "no doubt you would like to know what my true intentions were in that final run," her thoughts reveal a deep confusion about her goal.[78] She says she would like to kill Arrhodes on her own accord, because she knows he cannot possibly love her now that she is no longer a woman, a remark suggesting that she still desires him. She also thinks he owes her his death, for otherwise she would be "big with death, having no one to whom to bear it," a bizarre image that positions him as father to the death her stinger contains, and therefore responsible for supporting it. Yet again, she wonders whether, if she kills his abductors and saves him, she might force him "to exchange the disgust and fear he felt towards me for helpless admiration," thus allowing her possibly to "regain—if not him, then at least myself,"[79] an idea that links her agency with his admiration.

Why does Lem explicitly include the assertion that gender is connected to her "fatal core," a connection apparently superfluous to the plot now that the robot has shed her human mask? An interview with Lem by Zoran Živkovi in 1976 throws fascinating light on this question. Connecting his use of a female persona in "The Mask" with the female character of Rheya in *Solaris*, Lem suggests that the two stories represent a significant departure from his usual choice of male protagonists. The passage is so revealing that it deserves to be quoted at length.

> Of that which still remains a mystery to me, and there's quite a good deal of it, I would isolate the problem of the being—a being rationally created, evolving from an empirical method, created so to speak just as a house is built. That being, or rather the heroine Hary [Rheya], becomes a person and in that sense acquires a dominant position in relation to her creator. This problem obsessed and occupied me for so long that I returned to it last year, writing a story entitled *The Mask*. This piece no longer deals with an artificial human in the third person and he is not described externally; now it is the heroine herself who speaks in the first person, she is conscious of her origin and status, she gradually finds out the truth about herself. Here too, we have the classical problem of the freedom and non-freedom of the programmed mind. Why was this problem so interesting that I had to treat it on two occasions? I'm not entirely sure. I'm also not sure why I was interested in precisely a woman, and not in a man or some neutral gender—which is a much more frequent occurrence in my writings. Not only can I not explain this to others but I am unable to explain it to myself.[80]

In *Solaris*, Rheya appears as a creation of the sentient ocean, culled from the deep memories of Kelvin's mind.[81] Visually identical to the wife whom Kelvin lost when she committed suicide, Rheya begins to individuate as a person separate from his perceptions. She has a profoundly different physical structure than humans, and she slowly becomes aware that Kelvin is lying to her about her true nature. Racked by guilt at his wife's suicide, Kelvin tries to get rid of the memories the Rheya simulacrum embodies by ejecting her into space, but the simulated Rheya simply reappears, having been reconstituted by the ocean. She finally asserts her autonomy in the only way she believes possible—by committing suicide—and her suicide note is the only communication the reader has from her that is not mediated by Kelvin's perceptions. In "The Mask," the narrator also physically differs from humans, but the split between a male narrator who speaks and a nonhuman female who acts is now differently arranged so that the female has the power of articulation and the male-conceived program has the power of action. In both stories female agency is thrown into question, and in both a female character struggles to assert her independence in her relation with a human male who is at once her lover and antagonist. Whatever the reasons for this formation, it seems clear that gender is central to the power it exercises over Lem's Imaginary. Without attempting to psychoanalyze Lem (which would be doubly presumptuous in view of his comment that he himself does not know why these female characters fascinate him), I conclude that there are deep connections between the female's struggle for autonomy within the story and her relation to her creator, understood here as a consciousness beyond the reach of the character's introspections, whether a sentient ocean working in collaboration with Kelvin's unconscious, an all-powerful King, or Lem himself. The female's alien nature thus enacts not only her difference from humankind but also her gender-specific difference from her male creator. In these stories, the female is at once the intimate mate and the terrifyingly alien other, bearing within herself the imprint of her creator's will as well as her own ambiguous agency. It is as if the female, to succeed as a character, has to assert an agency independent of the male mind that conjured her into being. The more she tears herself away, the more she achieves reality as an autonomous subjectivity; but the more she achieves autonomy, the more she resists her creator's agency and thereby threatens to defeat her putative purpose for being. Given these complexities, is it any wonder she is compounded of life and death, love and agony?

These complex interrelations reach explicit articulation within "The Mask" when the monk demands to know what the narrator will do, now that she has received the treatment to widen slightly her margin of action. When she answers that she does not know—which, given the confused motives described above, is probably accurate—the monk responds, "You are my sister." Stunned, the narrator asks him what he means. "Exactly as I say it," he answers, "and it means I neither raise myself above you nor humble myself before you, for however much we may differ, your ignorance, which you have confessed to me and which I believe, makes us equal in the face of Providence."[82] Harboring an irreducible ambiguity, the monk's response reinscribes within the story Lem's own inability to understand his creative choices. The robot can be understood as like him because she does not know if the program will completely determine her actions, which implies that she believes she has free will, however slim the margin. In this sense, she is his sister because she counts as a human person. She may also be like him because he operates according to biocultural programs that dictate his actions, making his consciousness unsure how he will act. In this reading, she is his sister because he counts as a robot. The entangling of meanings here is like the entangling of the female character's agency together with her creator's will, so that the story can be understood to be *simultaneously* about human agency and robotic programming, male authorship and female self-birthing.

When she was given birth by the assembly line, the narrator lay passively on her back for most of the journey,[83] as she did when the monks operated on her.[84] In this position she cannot wield her stinger; for that, she needs to be standing upright, so it can emerge from its "ventral shaft" and thrust forward. When she thinks back on the monk's words acknowledging her as his sister, she remarks, "I still could not understand them, but when I bent over them something warm spread through my being and transformed me, it was as if I had lost a heavy fetus, with which I had been pregnant."[85] The image recalls her thinking of the death she carries as Arrhodes's unborn child. Here too the most likely reference for the "heavy fetus" is death, but this time it is the death of herself as a programmed robot, after which she could possibly be born again as an autonomous person. But the ambiguity lingers, for she also imagines herself *bending over* the monk's utterance, the position from which she can enact the King's command through her phallic stinger. Thus in the same thought she figuratively gives birth to herself as an autonomous agent by losing the King-impregnated fetus of death and adopts the posture that makes her a vehicle for the King's will.

This upright stance reappears when she finally tracks Arrhodes to the castle where he has been taken by his abductors, only to discover that a mortal struggle has taken place and he lies unconscious and bleeding on the stairs. "Had he opened his eyes and been conscious, and—in an inverted view—taken me in entirely, exactly as I stood over him, stood now powerlessly carrying death, in a gesture of supplication, pregnant but not from him, would that have been a wedding—or its unmercifully arranged parody?"[86] Both "bride and butcher," the narrator exercises her agency in the only way she can, by delaying her fatal sting while she waits to see if Arrhodes will recover. If he does, she is clear that her programming will enact his death, and so enmeshed is her consciousness with it that she does not know "if I truly desired him to wake."[87]

Only when he "groaned once more and ceased to breathe" does she alter her posture. Feeling "my mind at rest," she lies down beside him and wraps "him tightly in my arms, and I lay thus in the light and in the darkness through two days of snowstorm, which covered our bed with a sheet that did not melt. And on the third day the sun came up."[88] The three days continue a pattern that has marked her life from the beginning: her courtship lasted three days, she lingered for three days before beginning the hunt, and she experienced three births, first on the assembly line, then in her entry into language and gender, and finally in her metamorphosis into the insectile robot. Does the faint promise of resurrection hint that she can experience a fourth birth, breaking the pattern and becoming at last her own person now that she has fulfilled her programming? Earlier she had thought about what she would become if she were to abandon her goal and strike out on her own. The King would order robotic dogs to hunt her down as mercilessly as she pursued Arrhodes, and even if she were by some miracle to survive, all human society would find her abhorrent. Significantly, this information comes in the middle of the tale, so that it lingers in the reader's mind as fading memory rather than active narration as the story reaches its end. Granted this slight margin of forgetfulness, we can edge toward asking the question forbidden by the closure of the plot: what kind of life could she be born into? Certainly not into the coherent subjectivity of an independent human who has never had reason to question whether she has free will. But perhaps in these posthuman days, when the crisis of agency remains far from resolved despite attempts to smooth it over, she might count as a person, albeit a nonhuman one. If so, then we can say to her with all the rich ambiguities that attended the monk's utterance, "You are our sister."

Notes

1. For a discussion of how agency implies personhood in artificial-life creatures, see N. Katherine Hayles, "Simulated Narratives: What Virtual Creatures Can Teach Us," *Critical Inquiry* 26, no. 1 (Autumn 1999): 1–26.

2. Stanislaw Lem, "The Mask," in *Mortal Engines*, trans. Michael Kandel (San Diego: Harcourt Brace Jovanovich, 1992), 181–239. The first English edition was published in 1977; the first Polish edition was published in 1976.

3. Richard Dawkins, *The Selfish Gene*, rev. ed. (Oxford: Oxford University Press, 1989). Originally published in 1976.

4. Ibid., 69.

5. Ibid., 88.

6. Gilles Deleuze and Félix Guattari, *A Thousand Plateaus: Capitalism and Schizophrenia*, trans. Brian Massumi (Minneapolis: University of Minnesota Press, 1987).

7. Ibid., 17.

8. Ibid., 18.

9. Mark Hansen, *Embodying Technesis: Technology Beyond Writing* (Ann Arbor: University of Michigan Press, 2000).

10. Deleuze and Guattari, *A Thousand Plateaus*, 134.

11. Ibid., 406.

12. Ibid., 407.

13. Francisco J. Varela, Evan Thompson, and Eleanor Rosch, *The Embodied Mind: Cognitive Science and Human Experience* (Cambridge, Mass.: MIT Press, 1991).

14. Deleuze and Guattari, *A Thousand Plateaus*, 409.

15. Félix Guattari, "Machinic Heterogenesis," in *Rethinking Technologies*, ed. Verena A. Conley (Minneapolis: University of Minnesota Press, 1993), 13–27, especially 17.

16. Ibid., 25.

17. Ibid., 15.

18. Ibid.

19. Ibid.

20. Ibid.

21. Ibid., 25.

22. Ibid., 23.

23. John Johnston, "The In-Mixing of Machines: Psychoanalysis and Cybernetics," unpublished manuscript. I am grateful to him for sharing with me this essay prior to its publication.

24. A. M. Turing, "On Computable Numbers, with an Application to the Entscheidungsproblem," *Proceedings of the London Mathematical Society*, 2nd ser., 42 (1936): 230–265.

25. Jacques Lacan, *The Seminars of Jacques Lacan: Book II, the Ego in Freud's Theory and in the Technique of Psychoanalysis 1954–55*, trans. Sylvana Tomaselli (New York: Norton, 1988).

26. Richard Dawkins, *The Blind Watchmaker: Why the Evidence of Evolution Reveals a Universe Without Design* (New York: W.W. Norton, 1987).

27. Dawkins is a partial exception, for he references a great deal of empirical research. But his argument about the selfishness of genes and the subordination of human agency to a survival machine working at the behest of the genes is a rhetorical point, not an experimental one.

28. See Rodney A. Brooks, "New Approaches to Robotics," *Science* 253 (September 13, 1991): 1227–1232.

29. Rodney A. Brooks and Anita Flynn, "Fast, Cheap, and Out of Control: A Robot Invasion of the Solar System," *Journal of the British Interplanetary Society* 42 (1989): 478–485.

30. Rodney A. Brooks, "Intelligence without Representations," *Artificial Intelligence* 47 (1991): 139–159. See also Luc Steels and Rodney A. Brooks, eds., *The Artificial Life Route to Artificial Intelligence: Building Embodied, Situated Agents* (Hillsdale, N.J.: L. Erlbaum Associates, 1995).

31. Rodney A. Brooks, Cynthis Breazeal, Matthew Marjanović, Brian Scassellati, and Matthew M. Williamson, "The Cog Project: Building a Humanoid Robot," *Lecture Notes in Computer Science* (Springer-Verlag, forthcoming). See also Rodney A. Brooks, Cynthia Breazeal (Ferrell), Robert Irie, Charles C. Kemp, Matthew Marjanović, Brian Scassellati, and Matthew M Williamson, "Alternative Essences of Intelligence," *American Association for Artificial Intelligence* (www.aaai.org, 1998). Cynthia Breazel has taken the Cog head and embedded it in a facially expressive robot she calls Kismet, also adding "drives" and "emotions." Her idea is to create an embodied form that will encourage humans to interact with it and, in the process, teach it. "What we are doing," she remarks, "is putting humanity into the humanoid." Quoted in Cynthia Breazel, "The Robot That Loves People," *Discover* (October 1999): 67–73, especially 72.

32. Maja Mataric, "Navigating with a Rat Brain: A Neurobiologically-Inspired Model for Robot Spatial Representation," in *From Animals to Animats: Proceedings of the First International Conference on Simulation of Adaptive Behavior*, ed. Jean-Arcady Meter and Stewart W. Wilson (Cambridge, Mass.: MIT Press, 1991), 171.

33. Ibid., 172.

34. Jerome H. Barkow, Leda Cosmides, and John Tooby, *The Adapted Mind: Evolutionary Psychology and the Generation of Culture* (Oxford: Oxford University Press, 1992), 24.

35. Ibid.

36. Ibid., 61.

37. Ibid., 90.

38. Ibid., 46.

39. George Lakoff and Mark Johnson, *Philosophy in the Flesh: The Embodied Mind and Its Challenge to Western Thought* (New York: Basic Books, 1999).

40. Andy Clark, *Being There: Putting Brain, Body, and World Together Again* (Cambridge, Mass.: MIT Press, 1999), 53.

41. Antonio R. Damasio, *Descartes' Error: Emotion, Reason, and the Human Brain* (New York: Avon, 1995).

42. Edwin Hutchins, *Cognition in the Wild* (Cambridge, Mass.: MIT Press, 1996).

43. Cees van Leeuwen, Ilse Verstijnen, and Paul Hekkert, "Common Unconscious Dynamics Underlie Uncommon Conscious Effects: A Case Study in the Iterative Nature of Perception and Creation," in *Modeling Consciousness Across the Discipline*, ed. J. Scott Jordan (Lanham, Md.: University Press of America, 1999).

44. For a discussion of "blended spaces," see Mark Turner, *The Literary Mind* (Oxford: Oxford University Press, 1996).

45. Edwin Hutchins, "Material Anchors for Conceptual Blends," Lecture, University of California at Los Angeles, April 24, 2000.

46. N. Katherine Hayles, *How We Became Posthuman: Virtual Bodies in Cybernetics, Literature, and Informatics* (Chicago: University of Chicago Press, 1999).

47. Daniel C. Dennett, *Kinds of Minds: Toward an Understanding of Consciousness* (New York: Basic Books, 1996), 20.

48. Ibid., 20–21.

49. Ibid., 27.

50. For information about the X-29, see the Web site of the NASA Dryden Flight Research Center, at http://www.dfrc.nasa.gov/gallery/photo/X-29.

51. Lem, "The Mask," 181.

52. Ibid., 181–182.

53. Ibid., 182.

54. Jo Alyson Parker, "Gendering the Robot: Stanislaw Lem's 'The Mask,'" *Science-Fiction Studies* 19 (1992): 178–191.

55. Lem, "The Mask," 199.

56. Ibid., 190.

57. Ibid., 194.

58. Ibid., 192.

59. Ibid., 194–195.

60. Ibid., 196.

61. Ibid., 202.

62. Ibid.

63. Ibid., 208.

64. Ibid., 208–209.

65. Ibid., 209.

66. Ibid.

67. Ibid., 213–215.

68. Carol Wald, "The Female Machine: From von Neumann to Richard Powers," unpublished manuscript. I am grateful to her for making the essay available to me before publication, and also for calling my attention to "The Mask."

69. Lem, "The Mask," 193.

70. Ibid., 215.

71. Ibid.

72. Ibid., 231.

73. Ibid., 229.

74. Ibid., 221.

75. Ibid., 218.

76. Ibid., 227.

77. Ibid., 221.

78. Ibid., 231.

79. Ibid., 232.

80. Zoran Živkovi, "The Future Without a Future: An Interview with Stanislaw Lem," *Pacific Quarterly (Moana): An International Review of Arts and Ideas* 4, no. 3 (July 1979): 258.

81. Stanislaw Lem, *Solaris*, trans. Joanna Kilmartin and Steve Cox (New York: Berkley Publishing, 1971). The first Polish edition was published in 1961.

82. Lem, "The Mask," 226–227.
83. Ibid., 202.
84. Ibid., 229.
85. Ibid., 230.
86. Ibid., 238–239.
87. Ibid., 238.
88. Ibid., 239.

Contributors

ETIENNE BALIBAR is professor of French, English, and comparative literature at the University of California, Irvine.

LINDON W. BARRETT is professor of comparative literature and director, African American studies, at the University of California, Irvine.

PHENG CHEAH is associate professor of rhetoric at the University of California, Berkeley.

JAMES G. FERGUSON is professor of cultural and social anthropology at Stanford University.

ALEXANDER GELLEY is professor of comparative literature at the University of California, Irvine.

N. KATHERINE HAYLES is professor of English at the University of California, Los Angeles.

AKIRA MIZUTA LIPPIT is professor of cinema, comparative literature, and Japanese culture at the University of Southern California.

BILL MAURER is associate professor of anthropology at the University of California, Irvine.

GABRIELE SCHWAB is Chancellor's Professor of English and Comparative Literature and faculty associate in anthropology at the University of California, Irvine.

MARILYN STRATHERN DBE is Mistress of the Girton College and William Wyse Professor of Social Anthropology at Cambridge University.

Index